SMASH

Using Market Shaping to Design
New Strategies for Innovation,
Value Creation, and Growth

SMASH

Using Market Shaping to Design New Strategies for Innovation, Value Creation, and Growth

BY

Suvi Nenonen
Kaj Storbacka
University of Auckland Business School,
New Zealand

emerald
PUBLISHING

United Kingdom – North America – Japan – India – Malaysia – China

Emerald Publishing Limited
Howard House, Wagon Lane, Bingley BD16 1WA, UK

First edition 2018

British Library Cataloguing in Publication Data
A catalogue record for this book is available from the British Library

ISBN: 978-1-78743-798-2 (Print)
ISBN: 978-1-78743-797-5 (Online)
ISBN: 978-1-78743-839-2 (Epub)

Printed and bound by CPI Group (UK) Ltd, Croydon, CR0 4YY

ISOQAR certified
Management System,
awarded to Emerald
for adherence to
Environmental
standard
ISO 14001:2004.

Certificate Number 1985
ISO 14001

INVESTOR IN PEOPLE

CONTENTS

Acknowledgments   ix

Preface   xiii

1. **Your Strategy Playbook Has Expired**   1
   Nokia: From Hero to Zero by Doing Everything by the Book   1
      Hero — Best Products and Most Efficient Supply Chain   2
      Zero — Expiry of Nokia's Strategy Playbook   4
      Nokia's Expired Playbook May Be Your Book!   7
   Uber: Transforming Transport by Intuitive Market Shaping   9
   Poor Market View Makes for Poor Strategy   14
      Markets Are Not Industries!   15
      Don't Think Product Markets, Either!   17
      The Poor View Impoverishes Strategy from Every Angle   20
   Embrace the Rich Reality of Market Systems   24
      Markets Are Complex Adaptive Systems   25
      What the System View Tells Us about Markets:
      Emergence, Design, and More   27
      The *Function* of a Market System Is Exchange,
      for the *Purpose* of Value Creation   29
      Markets Are Socially Constructed, so You Can
      Reconstruct Them, too   30
      Putting It All on the Table: Rich and Poor Views,
      Side by Side   31
   The Pay-off: Strategies for Market Shaping   32
      What Is Market Shaping Anyway?   32
      FAQs about Market Shaping   36
      The Strategic Baby and the Bathwater   38
   Making the Rich View Actionable: Introducing the
   "Market Fan"   39
      The Rest of the Book   44

2. **Frame Your Market**   49
   UPS: Thinking Outside the Boxes   49
   "So, What Do You Do?": Define Your Business   51
      Your Business Definition Frames Your Market   52
      Your Frame Filters and Interprets Intel   53
      Beware! The Product View Worms Its Way in through
      Restrictive Business Definitions   55
      Cast Out the Worm! Polish Your Frame for Clarity,
      Point It for Choice   56
      Brainstorm New Business Definitions by Zooming Out
      and Zooming In   57
   Zoom Out: Leave Product Myopia Behind   58
      Focus on Firm Resources and Capabilities   61
      Focus on Network Resources and Capabilities   62
      Focus on Customer Processes and Situations   66
      Focus on Other Beneficiaries' Processes and Situations   69
      Zooming Out Too Far: Beware Reckless Diversification   72
   Zoom In: Find Growth Pockets and Adjacencies   73
      Zooming In as Turbocharged Market Segmentation   74
      The Tool for Zooming In Is the Business Arena Generator   75
      Three Broad Applications of the Business
      Arena Generator   76
      Customize Your Own Arena Generator   78
      Starbucks: A Zooming In Success Story   85
   Decouple Market Shaping and Business Redefinition   86

3. **Shape Your Market**   91
   Stora Enso: Many-Layered Market Shaping   91
   Exchange: What Is Sold, How It Is Priced, and
   How Buyers and Sellers Find Each Other   94
      Sales Item: What Is Being Exchanged, Exactly?   95
      Pricing: How Much Is It Worth?   99
      Matching Methods: How Do Sellers and Buyers
      Find Each Other?   103
   Network: Right Partners, Right Know-How,
   Right Infrastructure   106
      Actors: Do We Have the Right Actors in
      Our Network?   107

Roles and Know-How: Is Work Division Optimal;
Does Everyone Know What They Need to Know?   112
Infrastructure: What Do Customers Need to Use
Our Products and Services?   115
Representations: Harnessing Language, Information, and
Symbols   118
Your Language: Naming, Describing, Familiarizing   119
Information: Helping Others to Make Sense of the
Market   123
New Symbols to Legitimize Markets: Events,
Awards, and Associations   126
Rules of the Game: Influencing Standards, Regulations, and
Social Norms   129
Standards: Without Them, Nothing Fits Together   130
Regulations: Defining What Is Legal   134
Social Norms: Making Things Acceptable
and Desirable   138

4. Learn Shaping Principles and Plays   145
Les Mills International: Working Out with
Winning Timing   145
Timing Is Everything   149
Understanding When Your Market Is Shapeable:
Striking While the Iron Is Hot   149
Shapeable Market: First Mover or Fast Follower?   153
Non-Shapeable Market: The Art of Active Waiting   156
Make Your Strategy Win-Win-Win   158
Ensuring Win-Win-Win within the Minimum Viable
System   158
Quantifying the Win-Win-Win to
Get Others on Board   163
Collaborate to Shape, Compete to Share   166
Use Generic Plays   169
Relocate the Exchange Interface   170
Directly Deliver Step-Change in Use Value   176
Use Market-Widening Pricing   179
Widening Customer Catchment Area   184
Breaking Supply and Efficiency Bottlenecks   189

5. **Leadership for Market Shapers**   199
    KONE: Lifted Up by a New Type of Leadership   199
    Redefining Leadership   203
        Inform Yourself about Resource Potentiality   204
        Perform the New Market   205
    Explore — Not Look Ahead, but Look Around   206
        Explore the Potentiality and Density of Resources   207
        Sense Value by Triangulation and Peripheral Vision 208
        Cultivate Diverse Perspectives on Your Own Firm   212
    Experiment — Not Plan and Control, but Probe
    and Respond   215
        Experiment at the Boundaries   216
        Invest in Experiments according to Affordable
        Loss and Simple Rules   218
        Create a Safe-to-Fail Environment   221
        Foster and Exploit Emergence   223
    Express — Not Read the Map, but Draw the Map   225
        Put the "Art" into "Cartography": Market Expressions
        as Art   226
        Choose Language that Moves Market Actors   228
        Claim Markets with Labeling and Symbolic Actions 232
    Engage — Not Take the Lead, but Share the Lead   235
        Build Credibility for the Market-shaping Initiative 237
        Orchestrate to Activate   241
        Pivot Yourself to Greatness — Repeatedly   243

Notes   249

References   281

About the Authors   301

Index   303

ACKNOWLEDGMENTS

Kaj insists on cultivating an image of book-writing à la Swedish film director and author Ingmar Bergman's writing process – months of toil on a far-flung Scandinavian island with the company only of our interior muses. But while we write from homes on offshore islands both in New Zealand and in our native Finland, the process of realizing the volume in your hands has been anything but a solitary endeavor.

We are firm believers in what we call theorizing *with* managers, rather than merely about them. As social scientists, we see little point in detaching managers from knowledge creation; we would much rather make and shape our new ideas and frameworks in partnership with them. Therefore, our first and most fundamental thanks belong to those 37 companies who welcomed us in and shared their experiences through the four "SMASH – Strategies for MArket SHaping" consortia projects in Finland, New Zealand, Singapore, and Sweden. From A to Z, the 37 companies are: Affecto, Aktia, Beca, Blunt Umbrellas, Comptel, Designer Textiles, Fletcher Building, Fonterra, Griffin's, Heartland Bank, Huhtamäki, IAG, Icehouse, Inspecta, K. Hartwall, Kiwibank, Lemminkäinen, Lobster Exporters New Zealand, MetService, New Zealand Trade & Enterprise, Normet, NZ Post, OP Group, Outotec, ReGen, Relacom, Spring Sheep Dairy, Tamro, Texus Fibre, Tru-Test, Turners & Growers, Uponor, Villa Maria, Vodafone, Wärtsilä, YLE, and Zespri.

The four consortia projects would never have taken shape and held together, though, without the robust and responsive organizational backbone of the institutions we work in. Our deepest thank-yous are therefore also extended to Talent Vectia Ltd, The University of Auckland Business School, and Hanken & SSE Executive Education Ltd.

The foundational research for this book has been financially supported by the Royal Society of New Zealand and their Marsden Fund grant (grant number UOA1333). During this research project, we had the privilege of studying in detail 21 successful market shaping firms in the four economies through a series of 82 interviews. Those companies and their executives are the unnamed heroes of this book. And to the extent we had muses, these were they: the insights from the research project have inspired many of the ideas we present in this book. Here is also the place to thank our wonderful research project team for their stellar and unstinting work: Dr. Charlotta Windahl, Dr. Catherine Frethey-Bentham, Mattie Wall, Joel Allen, and John Lim, we owe you more than you can imagine.

Academic work always stands on the shoulders of giants, past and present. Looming particularly large for us is the late Professor Robert F. Lusch, who was a continuous inspiration for us and directly influenced the last chapter of our book. Our collaborations and conversations with several individuals have been vital to the evolution of our own thinking over the last 10 years: Dr. Melissa Akaka, Professor Luis Araujo, Professor Roderick J. Brodie, Professor Pennie Frow, Professor Hans Kjellberg, Professor Cristina Mele, Professor Kristian Möller, Professor Adrian Payne, Professor Jaqueline Pels and Professor Stephen L. Vargo.

Research and writing also require safe and stimulating intellectual homes. We are deeply grateful to the former Dean, Professor Greg Whittred, and former Associate Dean, Professor Jilnaught Wong, for welcoming us to New Zealand and The University of Auckland Business School. Thank you for trusting us and opening so many metaphorical doors for us. In Finland, two people in particular have provided us platforms to test and develop our

frameworks. Tom Lindholm, CEO of Talent Vectia, and Kaj
Åkerberg, Business Development Manager at Hanken & SSE
Executive Education: thank you for believing in us, year after
year.

On the writing side, we want to thank our brilliant and devoted
freelance editor, David J. Thompson. David is not only masterly
at the micro tasks of turning our "Finglish" into proper sentences,
but he is also our most trusted macro critic of logic, structure, and
flow ... or lack thereof! All the flair and wit in the following pages
have also flowed from David's pen. We may have done the heavy
lifting of figuring out what we wanted to say, but David's magic
made it both lucid and, we hope, enjoyable.

Finally, no amount of research or writing would have sufficed
without connection to a publisher! One of the legends of marketing, Professor Jagdish N. Sheth introduced us to Jeanne Glasser
Levine, President of Pub Zone Consulting, who was instrumental
in making that connection. And as the final link between us
and the reader, Charlotte Maiorana, Senior Editor and Nick
Wolterman, Assistant Editor at Emerald Publishing deserve the
last word of thanks.

Lest that list forgets anyone: we are deeply grateful for *all* the
support we have received. And in case we share the love too
widely: while we owe most of the insights that follow to others,
any errors, of course, are completely our own.

Suvi Nenonen and Kaj Storbacka
Krokö and Waiheke Island
August 2017

PREFACE

Time and again, in one company and one country after another, our consultancy and research experience hammers home one point: What makes or breaks strategy is whether managers "get" something so overarching it mostly escapes attention: the very nature of markets.

For, whilst markets are the core concept of economics and commerce, they have so far been overwhelmingly glossed over or misunderstood by orthodox strategy. But in 2018, business has crossed a threshold of complexity where a correspondingly complex market view becomes indispensable.

FOUNDATION: MARKET VIEWS MAKE OR BREAK STRATEGY

Today, only by getting the nature of markets as *complex adaptive systems*, can firms hope to read and respond to their environment? More enticingly, only by learning to operate, and co-operate, in complexity, can they take part in proactively adapting that environment to themselves — instead of reactively adapting themselves to the environment? And therein lies the strategy's new prize, which turns established strategy paradigms on their head. Mastering the collaborative dynamics of complex market systems enables Strategies for MArket SHaping — SMASH. Market shaping unleashes value gains from greater market size, efficiency, and profitability which dwarf the zero-sum wins eked out in market-share increments by traditional competitive strategy.

The importance of market views — in other words, why readers should even care — crystallizes from our opening pair of case histories: the puzzling fall of Nokia Mobile Phone and the dazzling rise of Uber. Infamously, Nokia plummeted from sure market leader to a fire sale of its mobile phone business line in a few short years. Yet, conventional explanations for the demise of Nokia Mobile Phone miss the forest for the trees. Those explanations overlook the secret lurking in plain sight by seeking answers at the firm level: failures of Nokia's leadership, or failures in product-related competitive advantage against industry rivals, causing loss of product market share.

Ironically, Nokia CEO Stephen Elop raised his eyes to the market level and glimpsed the true explanation in the leaked Burning Platform memo from 2011. He concluded: "Our competitors aren't taking our market share with devices; they are taking our market share with an entire ecosystem. This means we're going to have to decide how we either build, catalyze, or join an ecosystem." Elop's ecosystem epiphany, of course, was too little, too late. But he can hardly be faulted for that. What really stands out is that Nokia went *from hero to zero because it did everything by the book* — a strategy playbook complete with an implicit view of markets that had passed its use-by date.

If Nokia was the model student following all the rules of the doomed old school, Uber Technologies Inc. doesn't just represent the new school; it's unschool. The online ride-sharing company, with its game-changing app that lets riders hail, track, and pay for a cab online, and its alleged non-workforce of mere partner drivers, is shaking up market institutions and flouting the rules of the old taxi-scape. Uber understands that markets are shapeable, makeable systems. It's a born market-shaper — and one of the most radical.

ORTHODOX STRATEGY STATES NO VIEW OF MARKETS, BUT IMPLIES A POOR VIEW

The case histories generalize. Nokia represents the received view of markets and strategy, while Uber gestures toward an intuited, but as yet unarticulated, alternative. For decades, the received wisdom of management strategy has largely skipped over articulating any theory, or view, of markets. However, by working backwards we can deduce the views it implied. Our text dubs these as the poor views.

The standard playbooks still weighing down managers' bookshelves have taught a single meta-formula of strategic success. Broadly, the formula goes: Analyze your market to identify opportunities, find your unique position, and create a master plan to outwit your competition.

Working backwards, this strategic posture makes assumptions, assertions, and approximations about markets, which imply that markets are either very simple, like a supply and demand graph, or utterly incomprehensible.

Variously:

- The market is externally given: from whence it came, we cannot know. The exception is that occasionally a heroic outlier launching a breakthrough technology manages to conjure into being an entire new market.

- Market opportunities are precursors to strategy. The non-heroic majority of firms are stuck with the market they've chosen, and must adapt their firm to the opportunities that they find.

- Market dynamics are deterministic. They can be analyzed, predicted, and operated on using the everyday mechanical logic of cause and effect.

- Markets are synonyms for the aggregate demand for products — hence phrases like "the mobile phone market." What this view leaves out is the value created when customers use the product.

- Markets are industries. Consequently, we create institutions that limit our ability to look beyond the boundaries of the industry: statistics that measure the growth of the industry, and trade associations that stabilize the market.

None of these premises is true, and many are incompatible.

Poor Market Views Impoverish Your Strategy Playbook

To strategize on this basis is to build strategy on sand. In most cases, the operating environment is so inherently unpredictable that market analyses aren't worth the pixels they're written in. The poor views impoverish strategy from every angle:

- They make strategy reactive and defeatist because markets are supposedly given.

- They doom firms to compete for market share in a zero-sum competitive game.

- Their very dominance kills the hallmark of good strategy: originality.

- Finally, they miss the main chance: to unleash value that is orders of magnitude greater than market-share increments. In other words, they miss *market shaping*, achieved by adapting markets to the firm, not vice versa.

If these poor market views and the strategy built on them are so deficient, why do they still prevail? We argue they have persisted partly because of sheer incumbency; partly through self-reinforcing definitions in the data on markets and industries; and partly for the lack of an articulated alternative. But the day of reckoning has come in one field after another as markets have crossed a threshold of complexity. Globalization, digitalization, and network effects render the old models of markets and strategy obsolete.

A RICH MARKET VIEW REQUIRES SYSTEMS THEORY

Drawing on the transdisciplinary science of systems theory, and combining insights from biology, psychology, and sociology as well as economics and management, we offer the rich reality of markets as complex adaptive systems. That's "complex" like an ecosystem or a society, rather than merely "complicated" like the flight deck of a Dreamliner. Indeed, as frequent fliers, we're delighted that airplanes still obey mechanical cause and effect. But complex systems don't. They can be neither controlled nor safely predicted. Markets as systems constantly evolve; partly by random "emergence," partly by the deliberate market shaping efforts of the likes of Uber and its smart entrepreneurial cousins. Consequently, the firm is part of the market, rather than the market being external to the firm.

Markets are complex systems of exchange for the purpose of co-creating value. More precisely they create what classical-era economics called "use value" to the customer. Use value is as opposed to our standard neoclassical metric: exchange value, which is really price. Yet boosting use value — which is limitless — can ultimately boost exchange value, markets, and profits.

The complex systems' view of markets has always been true but only recently become essential. Recognizing markets as complex systems spells strategic implications. Notably, just as markets are socially constructed, so they can be reconstructed by social methods. And while they cannot be predicted or controlled, they can be *influenced* by market players.

THE BOOK REBUILDS STRATEGY ON THE RICH VIEW OF MARKETS

Rooted in the richness of market systems, the book therefore traces the three main resulting shifts in strategic thinking: (1) from firm focus to context focus, where the relevant context is our definition of the market; (2) from competing and winning to value creation and cooperation; and (3) from analysis, prediction, and planning to non-predictive strategizing and experimentation.

The book weaves these three strands together into a cohesive strategic framework – market shaping. Market-shaping strategies acknowledge that much of firm performance, both turnover growth and profitability, is explained by the markets where a firm operates. Crucially though, strategic choices go beyond market selection, entry and exit; markets are malleable and therefore firms can – and should – actively seek to shape them in their favor by value-creating coalitions.

KEY CONTRIBUTION: AN EASY, ACTIONABLE FRAMEWORK FOR MARKET SHAPING

Market shaping is not entirely new. Research by Boston Consulting Group and McKinsey suggests that 9% of firms already engage in market shaping. However, most of them do so intuitively. Therefore, their methods are hard to replicate. What is new – and the book's key contribution – is systematizing and articulating a universal, teachable, and actionable framework for understanding and shaping markets. Whereas traditional strategy skipped glibly over the subject, SMASH recognizes markets as strategy's necessary foundation and then rebuilds.

Crucially too, our framework is one that any firm can grasp and practice. It does not take traditional market power and resources, or intuitive genius, to understand markets as complex systems and to shape them to your own benefit. As a master metaphor and structural device, we use the colorful, reader-friendly diagram of a market Fan, comprising four layers plus a core. The Fan groups and orders the 13 elements of markets we've identified that savvy market shapers of any size can influence, in closely explained and topically illustrated ways, to reshape the whole.

1

YOUR STRATEGY PLAYBOOK
HAS EXPIRED

What is market shaping? And what, exactly, is "the market" anyway?

Stunningly, strategy has never adequately defined one of its central institution, the market. Old playbooks got away with a hodgepodge of assertions, assumptions and approximations. But the undeniable complexity of modern markets confronts us with the truth. Markets are elaborate, evolving ecosystems – think biology, not machinery. Today, strategy must embrace complexity or die.

Market shaping is the first strategy to embrace and exploit the truth about markets. It elegantly distils their complexity. And it shows how any firm can then turn strategy on its head – by adapting the market to the firm instead of the firm to the market, opening up untapped value in the process. The value market shaping unlocks defines strategy's new "main chance."

NOKIA: FROM HERO TO ZERO BY DOING EVERYTHING BY THE BOOK

In 2007, Finnish multinational Nokia was the darling of the global mobile phone market. CEO Olli-Pekka Kallasvuo smiled from the cover of *Forbes* magazine, and felt secure enough to dismiss Apple's new offering, the iPhone, as a "niche product" which wouldn't "in any way necessitate us changing our thinking".[1] Few would have questioned him.[2]

Nokia kept notching up successes for several years, but remarks such as this came back to haunt it when everything seemed to go wrong at once and the company nosedived. In September 2013, the once-mighty brand sold its mobile phone business to Microsoft for 5.4 billion euros. A paltry sum, when only six years earlier Nokia's annual operating income from the same business was over 5 billion euros. What reduced the uncontested market leader to a fire sale of its main business line?

The demise of Nokia, or more precisely Nokia Mobile Phone, is an epic saga, with many twists and turns over two decades before the final reversal. To grasp it properly, we need to analyze both its rise and its fall — both the "hero" and the "zero" chapters.[3]

Hero — Best Products and Most Efficient Supply Chain

Let us begin at the beginning. Nokia stepped onto the world stage as a key player in influencing the development of the Global System for Mobile Communications Standard. You'll know it by its more household abbreviation: GSM. GSM paved the way to the second generation of digital mobile telephony — called 2G.

The first GSM phone call was made in 1991 on a network built by Telenokia and Siemens with a phone built by — you guessed it — Nokia. In 1993, Nokia became the only mobile phone manufacturer whose entire GSM phone range supported Short Message Service, or SMS. (SMS refers of course to "txts," the add-on that became a killer app of mobile telephony and rewrote our language like a bad, vowel-less Scrabble hand in the process.) This, just a year after the first SMS message was sent. And as early as 1996, Nokia provided a smart phone with Internet connectivity: the Nokia 9000 Communicator.

The late 1990s and early 2000s were the golden years for the mobile phone manufacturers. Double-digit growth was spurred by the rivalry between the main players: Nokia, Sweden's Ericsson, and Motorola from Illinois. By the mid-2000s, Nokia was on top. Success stemmed largely from its super-efficient supply chain, affordable and reliable phones, the fastest ramp-up process for the new mobiles (hugely important in a business with 18-month product lifecycles), and the widest range from which operators worldwide could select models for their local consumers.

In 2000, the market entered a transition stage. Over the next few years, 2G would gradually be phased out and 3G phased in. Put simply, whereas 2G brought mobile telephony from analog to digital, 3G deserves credit for bringing voice and data fully under the same standard. The growth rates of mobile phone users and Internet users, and a convergence of digital technologies, sent telco operators into a bidding frenzy, especially the Europeans. Operators spent over 125 billion USD on 3G licenses.

Nokia understood that 3G was the next big thing in mobile telephony and threw itself into this third generation hoping history would repeat. Certainly, the early days showed promise. In 2002, Nokia became the first mobile phone manufacturer to launch a 3G handset. The same year saw the first Nokia smart phone to sport a built-in camera: the 7650. The company followed this up in 2003 with its mobile game deck N-Gage, which combined a portable game console with a mobile phone. And Nokia's first music phone hit the market in 2005.

Anecdotally, it also seems that Nokia's engineers had showcased a touch-screen phone in-house as early as 2000,[4] but the company halted development because its market research predicted consumers would prefer keyboards to touch screens. And you would trust your company's consumer insight when it had researchers on the ground in every continent not inhabited primarily by penguins.

Yet, the 3G market was proving an unpredictable beast. In 2000, Nokia erred wildly with a forecast of over 300 million mobile phones connecting to the mobile Internet within two years. The true figure came in at just 1% of that. Sure, the 3G handsets were more expensive than their 2G predecessors, but this hardly explained the slow adoption. Something else was at play, and it was weighing down Nokia's ascendancy.

What hid the downturn in Nokia's fortunes due to 3G was that, during the transition, 2G of course continued to run alongside it. Luckily, Nokia's 2G handsets were still selling like hot cakes. That was perhaps why Kallasvuo could make his airy dismissal of the iPhone in January 2007, for that year was the zenith of Nokia's fortunes thanks to the continuing, albeit waning, success in its 2G market. Consolidated turnover of 51 billion euros, operating profit of almost 8 billion euros, cash reserve of nearly 7 billion euros, market share of 37.8%[5] of the global mobile phone market, hefty investments in R&D (11% of turnover) and the most efficient supply chain in the industry.

Zero – Expiry of Nokia's Strategy Playbook

How, then, to explain the nosedive and that humiliating sale to Microsoft six short years later? You've probably heard some of the conventional accounts. It was Icarus syndrome: Management grew arrogant, flew too high, crashed, and burned.[6] It was consumer preferences: underestimating the importance of aesthetics and a smooth user experience à la Apple. It was sluggishness in updating the operating system: hanging on to the old-fashioned Symbian for too long, and failing to develop MeeGo fast enough. It was hesitation introducing the touch screen. And so on.[7]

None of these explanations withstands scrutiny. For starters, Nokia's management stayed substantially unchanged, and always took cutting-edge advice from top-drawer recruits and world-class management consultants. More's the pity, but Nokia itself didn't much change.

Consumer preferences weren't to blame either. Until 2011 Nokia was still the clear market leader in mobile phones, with 23.8% market share.[8] And the rival who eventually overtook it was Samsung, not Apple. Finally, if you disaggregate, the company's decline started well before the iPhone débuted.

We believe conventional explanations for the demise of Nokia Mobile Phones miss the forest for the trees. They look for answers at the firm level: in failures of Nokia's leadership, or failures in product-related competitive advantage against industry rivals, causing loss of product market share.

If you stand back, a bigger picture emerges — one defined by what we'll expound as complex markets. Recast thus as a tale of two markets, Case Nokia Mobile Phones reveals a firm with essentially constant strategy tracking a rise during the 2G market boom, then a slowdown after 3G arrived, and eventually a fall as 2G phased out and 3G took over. Could there have been something radically different about the 3G operating environment that stopped Nokia from successfully replaying its winning strategies from the 2G environment? Was there something about the 3G market for which the company and its strategy were fundamentally unprepared?

Stephen Elop was recruited from Microsoft to succeed Kallasvuo as CEO. In the notorious "burning platform" memo of 2011,[9] Elop confided what he thought had gone wrong. The memo was never meant for public consumption, but leaked to the press. To our mind, the core of the memo is a completely new definition of the market — both Nokia's own market and markets in general: "The battle of devices has now become a war of ecosystems, where ecosystems include not only the hardware and software of the device, but developers, applications, ecommerce, advertising, search, social applications, location-based services, unified communications and many other things. Our competitors aren't taking our market share with devices; they are taking our market share with an entire ecosystem. This means we're going to have to decide how we either build, catalyze or join an ecosystem."

Elop saw past product markets and viewed markets as ecosystems of interdependent actors. He saw that these systems go beyond mere products or "devices"; that their dynamics dwarf uncoordinated, unilateral company strategies such as Nokia was following; and that such systems can be deliberately shaped – or in Elop's words "built" or "catalyzed" – as well as just joined in a me-too fashion.

Nokia had contributed to the emergence of the 2G market by actively engaging – together with competitors – in the creation of the GSM standard. However, the 2G market was less complex than 3G. It required relatively few actors to create value to the end users: the handset manufacturers, the producers of the telecommunication networks and the companies operating those networks. The GSM standard used for 2G meshed these neatly together: The consumer could rely on getting her calls and SMS messages regardless of the brand of her mobile phone, her and her friends' telco operators, and the manufacturers of their networks.

But the 3G standard introduced data into the picture and made the market ecosystem inherently more complex. What kind of content and data-based services should be made available to 3G phones? Who would create that content? How would the IP rights to this content be enforced? How could existing content, such as television shows, be rendered compatible with mobile phones and their small screens? How should operators charge their customers for data? How would operators even measure data usage?

Nokia tried to apply the old, 2G market rules (such as first mover advantage and focus on the quality and numbers of devices) to the new 3G market game. However, the more complex, volatile new market had taken the old market playbook past the point where it could function at all, even as an approximation; it revealed the limits of the old book and its old view of markets.

What really stands out in all this is that Nokia did far more right by the traditional[10] strategy playbook than it ever did wrong. The failure of Nokia was nothing less than the failure of the playbook itself. *Nokia went from hero to zero precisely because it did everything by the book – a book that had passed its use-by date.*

Nokia's Expired Playbook May Be Your Book!

Why should that concern you? Because we're talking here about essentially the same playbook that is still, today, repeated as variations on a theme between the covers of the myriad strategy, management and marketing titles on your bookcase and ours. Roughly, that book says: Position your firm to the best market, hopefully a growing one, then plan and execute a long-term strategy to adapt the firm to that market by cultivating a competitive advantage, and so compete for the holy grail of market share.

Now, the traditional playbook is a useful volume as far as it goes, with some genuine insights, but it is flawed and becoming less workable by the month. In particular, it is increasingly compromised by its inherited picture of markets. For the traditional book is based on a theory about markets that is fatalistic, incomplete, often circular, and at times plain contradictory. That theory was always flawed at a deep level in the ways just listed, just as the systemic theory that we're going to replace it with was always more correct. We've said that in the mobile telephony context, 3G took the old playbook past the limits where it could function. But exactly how did the old view continue to pass as viable for so long, and how does it continue to do so today?

We see several explanations for the persistence. First, particularly in simple and stable contexts, it contained just enough truths to be of some use. Second, its weaknesses were not stress-tested often or severely enough to throw the whole theory into question – market-shaping exceptions like Apple under Steve Jobs could be put down to freaks of nature. This situation lasted while the majority of markets remained fairly static and their workings approximated mechanistic laws of cause and effect. By contrast, 3G and other 21st-century markets with their exponential network effects have assumed a positively ecological level of complexity and global connectedness: Think biology or sociology, not machinery. Third, no really well-developed and validated alternative theory was circulating in the mainstream. Fourth, the now-emerging theory of markets as complex systems is just that: more complex. It should be no surprise, then, that managerial applications wishfully cleaved to the simpler *status quo*. We all secretly wish for easy solutions to wicked problems, don't we? Nowadays, as the markets of the 21st century increasingly resemble 3G more than 2G in complexity, unpredictability, and malleability, the old theory and the playbook based on it will serve you less and less well and leave you more and more exposed to the increasing number of companies that have intuited ecosystems thinking, the way Nokia was exposed to Apple. And in the book you're holding, of course, we seek to supply the missing alternative theory and step-by-step advice on how to put it into practice. We're aiming to make the intuition systematic and learnable. Like so often in life, the first step in learning the right way to do things is to unlearn the wrong way – the old playbook. But before we weed out and unlearn the bad theories and practice one by one, let's sneak a peek inside that – so far exclusive, intuitive – club of the market shapers and makers. These are the outlier firms. The exceptions that prove the rule. The few which have somehow managed to build their strategies on rock, not sand. Unsurprisingly, most club members are either helmed by the founding entrepreneurs or at least deeply entrepreneurial in their culture. They're also more likely to be found in disrupted industries. Often they are the disruptors themselves. More specifically, market shapers and market makers draw on a cohesive set of characteristics and strategic plays of 14 designable market "elements" which we're going to hang our academic and consulting hats on and which you in the field can apply. At the heart of that set, of course, is market-level thinking. It's the level of strategizing beyond company, competition and product which Nokia CEO Stephen Elop glimpsed too late: "building, joining, or catalyzing" entire "ecosystems"; adapting the market, not *to* the market.

Now, you'll already have spotted an obvious candidate for such a positive case story: that "freak of nature," Apple. We'll take Apple's story as read. But to mix things up a bit let's sample another sector. This sector lies beyond pure digital wizardry, where the rubber literally hits the road: urban transport and the brilliant, brazen bad boy on the block, Uber.

UBER: TRANSFORMING TRANSPORT BY INTUITIVE MARKET SHAPING

If Nokia was the model student following all the rules of the doomed old school, Uber Technologies Inc. doesn't just represent the new school; it's unschool. The online ride-sharing company, with its game-changing app that lets riders hail, track, and pay for a cab online, and its alleged nonworkforce of mere "partner" drivers, is shaking up market institutions and flouting the rules of the old taxi-scape. The very word Uber, slang drawn from the German for super, breathes unbridled ambition. It's a born market shaper — and one of the most radical.

Co-founding entrepreneurs Travis Kalanick from California and Canadian Garrett Camp dreamt up the concept one snowy winter's night in Paris in 2008. The pair were frustrated trying to hail a cab during some down time from a LeWeb conference, but their minds were on the taxi problem back in their city of residence, tech hub San Francisco. They kicked around ideas like splitting the costs of a Mercedes S-class and a driver between themselves before cottoning on that they could tap existing private car owners. UberCab (as originally christened) was founded in 2009. It went into beta launch in 2010, road tested in New York and later that year débuted in San Francisco. Swatting down fines and cease and desist notices for operating like an unlicensed taxi company, Uber (with newly streamlined name) and its budget option UberX soon spread through the United States, Europe, and Asia. The funding snowballed with the popularity. It now operates in over 60 countries.

Characteristically for market shapers, Uber's founding entrepreneurs are still at or close to the helm, with Kalanick and Camp as CEO and chair, respectively. And it's hard to imagine a more entrepreneurial motto than Kalanick's "Always be hustling." Uber's disruptive, too, from tip to toe. But the company made it to the magic 50-billion-dollar valuation faster than Apple or even Facebook. How did they pull it off?

Back in Paris, Camp had muttered that you ought to be able to hail a ride at the tap of a button. Now, the button-tapping was clearly going to involve an app, and Uber's app is crucial. It's a whole new way of bringing together passengers and drivers. Yet the definitive market-shaping innovation was the structural shake-up which the tech leveraged: reconfiguring constituent parts of the old taxi and private car systems into a new market shape. For notably, the other constituents of the new market already existed: cars, drivers, passengers, smartphones. Only, their functions were about to change. Private car owners would begin moonlighting as chauffeurs. Their vehicles would morph from household convenience to revenue-earning asset. Unlike taxi drivers, these drivers would be — very pointedly, for the regulators' attention — partners setting their own hours rather than employees. Meanwhile, would-be passengers could now track their rides' arrival in real time almost like taxi dispatchers, and with a wonderful sense of control, through the latest addition to their smartphones' bank of apps. All of which revolutionized the value to Uber's users compared with traditional taxi services.

To signal the enhanced experience, the users would be nicknamed "riders." Echoing "drivers" on the other side, this appellation differentiated Uber users from traditional clients or passengers of a taxi company. It added a soupcon of the cooperative camaraderie of carpooling which befitted the democratized sharing economy model. The company's marketing still plays up such peer-to-peer virtues. For one, it promotes its nonprofessional drivers as "people just like you" − presumably as opposed to uniform-clad taxi company drones whose main interest is that you not muss up the upholstery. The company went beyond true peer-to-peer, though, by interposing their brokerage and organization. Yet Uber were still turning owners of private cars into paid providers much the way that Airbnb was simultaneously turning couch owners into landlords. After several iterations Uber had re-envisioned the urban transport space and, to borrow Elop's words, catalyzed the ecosystem of riding cars.

Meanwhile, digitalizing and centralizing the financial transaction out of the hands of the drivers and customers and into the app and the credit card companies have enabled Uber's (in)famous "surge pricing." When the demand for rides surges above driver availability due, say, to sudden inclement weather, a sporting event or even simply a public holiday, Uber ups its fares in that area to a new market-clearing price. The premium pumps up supply, as drivers already on the road nearby and others who were resting flock to the happy hunting ground. Simultaneously, the premium dampens demand as lower-price users pay drop out. The risk, of course, is to passenger goodwill. For riders, surge pricing is price gouging by another name. At time of writing, Uber was apparently trialing upfront price quotes and ditching the lightning icon and fare multiplication notice from its screen to at least paper over the organized opportunism.[11]

For the most part, the company has actively courted goodwill and trust from both riders and drivers. Besides the financial incentives to the two groups of cheaper (nonsurge) rides and a second income, respectively, Uber touts the safety that comes with transparency. Vulnerable riders like tourists are less likely to get taken for a figurative ride financially, or worse, since in theory at least passengers' ratings of their drivers will report and effectively constrain dodgy operators. Conversely, drivers can guard against bad apples in the back seat by checking their colleagues' rating of the next intended passenger.

Like other members of the market-shaping club, Uber has advertised its new vision for the market as delivering wins all round. We'll take the win to Uber itself as given. The other obvious beneficiaries are drivers and riders. Society and the economy are also cited as gaining — from better access to transport, more mutually beneficial driver—rider exchanges and even from fewer drunk drivers. And indeed Uber has propelled both overall market growth and efficiency. Cars are earning more often, and less often either sitting idle or taking up lane space under-occupied.[12] Uber itself has also grown considerably. In 2015, the company's revenue was estimated at around $2 billion.[13] Such lightning growth has come with a price, though. It is widely believed that Uber is losing money. This may or may not be a good thing, and draws frequent comparisons to Amazon's early years.[14] Nevertheless, investors appear to be keeping faith in Uber and its strategy. In 2016, the valuation of the company weighed in at a whopping $68 billion.

So far, this Uber fairytale has omitted one group loudly crying foul. That is the old incumbents: licensed taxi drivers, taxi companies, and their industry associations. Like that bad boy at school, Uber has eaten their lunch. They accuse it of piracy. On their side, often, the incumbents have their jurisdiction's law and the government. And to them, Uber has not merely sailed close to the wind or danced a jig on the head of a legal pin with its redefinition of what look remarkably like taxi services. Rather, it has ploughed a corporate juggernaut through the law. Indeed, among intuitive market shapers we've analyzed, Uber has taken the most radical, brazen approach to molding its market's rules of engagement. Where other firms might have courted lawmakers and industry associations, Uber has tried to harness sheer market forces and public popularity to pressure for regulatory acceptance. Apparently it's counting on its hefty war chest for legal fees.[15]

Now, unlike Nokia, Uber didn't need to bridge an old and a new reality — a (2G) world where the old playbook could get by and a (3G) world where only a new one would suffice. Uber was moving into an essentially empty space. What's more, it struck when the iron was hot. The Great Recession was biting. Many future riders and drivers were on their beam ends. And the jurisdictions where Uber was trialing were consciously looking for new economic ways of being.

But like fellow intuitive shapers, Uber knows markets will continue to change. Rather than let the grass grow under its feet, the corporate is actively probing to find the next big disruptions in transportation. Setting aside for the moment more exotic ventures into pizza delivery and helicopter rides, Uber is therefore especially targeting electric cars, driverless cars, and the twilight of our car-owning culture itself. Thus, riders can already insist on an electric car in some locations, and the 2016 UberGREEN pilot project collaborated with electric car providers BMW and Nissan. In 2015, Kalanick tweeted that the entire Uber fleet would be driverless by 2030[16] — and safer for it.[17] And car-owning riders might gladly surrender their second-biggest asset as more of a liability once Uber or similar operators can free them of parking hassles, paperwork, mechanics' and insurance bills and the need to dedicate a fraction of their home to a roller-doored concrete shrine to the automobile.

None of this is to claim that Uber will become the General Electric of the 21st century. Nor is it to endorse what may be seen as borderline-bullying tactics. You will have caught wind of the company's string of PR disasters, from surge pricing during Hurricane Sandy and a hostage-taking in Sydney, Australia, to allegations of a sexist culture and even rape, plus questions over the security of users' data.[18] Then there's the ill will and sometimes highly disruptive strikes[19] of taxi and minicab competitors, in certain instances vindicated by their governments. In August 2016, our made-in-America star also announced that it would merge Uber China with the local rival Didi Chuxing, effectively throwing in the towel on its Chinese operations. Perhaps most ominously, disaffected drivers have started asking: Is Uber working for us or are we working for Uber?[20] And of course the only thing the media love to talk up more than a meteoric success story is a fall from grace.

Yet, after Uber, the transport market will never be the same — other players have already started following the trend of "Uberification" — and its membership of the club of intuitive market shapers is assured. We can do one better than observe club members, though, nose-pressed to the glass. With a few more pages' unpicking of where the traditional strategy playbooks went wrong and the intuitive minority went right, you'll be able to start practicing market shaping for yourselves.

POOR MARKET VIEW MAKES FOR POOR STRATEGY

Time and again, our study of business success and failure hammers home one point: Bad, old theories or views about markets are the biggest limit on strategy today. Not "getting" markets is why Nokia Mobile Phones failed and why conventional accounts for its demise flop in a similar fashion. It's also why innovators such as Uber are able to shape their markets right around the globe.

Pretty much all the traditional strategy playbooks are founded on poor theories of markets. In fact, they barely reveal a coherent theory worthy of the name, or even a definition. What they offer is a hodgepodge of assertions, assumptions, and approximations. Management strategy isn't the only offender. Most mainstream commerce and economics as taught and practiced for the last 30 years share the same weakness. As Nobel economics laureate Douglass North observes:[21] "It is a peculiar fact that the literature on economics contains so little discussion of the central institution that underlies neoclassical economics – the market."

Ironically, even marketing, which you could be forgiven for thinking would distill some wisdom on the subject, lacks a robust, realistic, useful definition, and theory of markets.[22]

Successive generations of strategy playbook repeat bad or incomplete theories – myths and half-truths – about markets like articles of faith, or supply only partial corrections. The persisting mistakes are so built into our language, our mindsets, our definitions, and even our data that we hardly notice them. But again, *you need to know where you're going wrong before you can go right*. So, if you'll forgive us for dwelling on the negative, we've identified the cardinal errors about markets which are alive and well and misleading business strategy today.

Markets Are Not Industries!

Both managers and media often reduce the context in which they operate from a "market" to an "industry," as though the two were interchangeable. We call this reduction the industry view of markets. Whatever managers mean by, say, "the steel market" (and more on the flaws of such phrasing in a moment), they feel equally happy to refer to as "the steel industry." And in market reports we hear that the "construction industry" is taking a hammering, as it were, or "the airline industry" is taking off.

Latching onto industries as the relevant concept of the firm's context, and a powerful explanatory factor, is not without justification. For a century, economics and its sub-field industrial organization have said that industry structure explains much of a firm's performance, especially firm growth. Recent, more managerial studies back that up. In 2007, McKinsey & Company looked at turnover growth among some 200 large companies around the world in various sectors from 1999 to 2005.[23] The companies' annual topline growth averaged 8.6%. Of that, fully 5.5% came from industry growth, with 3% from mergers and acquisitions activity — which is likewise industry level — and a bare 0.1% from growth in market share. So industry-level effects massively dominated market share effects. Industry growth and mergers and acquisitions activity explained nearly 80% of the growth differences in this cohort, versus just 20% from market share changes up or down.

Moreover, in 2013, a much bigger McKinsey study of 2,888 companies looked beyond growth effects and investigated industry influence on economic profitability. Now, standard theory assumes economic profit is the product of firms' own actions. Yet, industry again accounted for a handsome 40% of the effect. So the context where the firm operates seems to explain its performance — both topline and bottom line — to a large extent.

The problem with the industry view is that industries — implicitly defined above as a group of firms providing similar products or services — make for a woefully incomplete conceptualization of markets. The industry view tells us something about production and competition but nothing about customers, let alone any wider ecosystem such as Nokia's Stephen Elop glimpsed too late and Uber's Travis Kalanick and Garrett Camp grasped all along. Yet, without customers, the slickest industry's production is worth nothing! Additionally, the industry perspective leaves little room to influence a firm's fortunes: You may streamline your production processes and devise shrewd competitive strategies, but the industry determines your fate — and it lies outside your sphere of influence.

Don't Think Product Markets, Either!

The commonest (mis)conception of markets, however, is what we call the product market view. We all implicitly espouse this when we toss off phrases like "the mobile phone market." Folk often tack on a place, as in "the mobile phone market *in China*," so we'll also sometimes refer to this as the product-geography view, but it's essentially the same beast. Likewise, formulae that incorporate the who-to, like "the mobile phone market among young consumers," are really only the same beast in drag. So often does the beast in its three forms (product; product + geography; and product + customer segment) rear its head in strategy discourse that we'll often abbreviate the whole lot to "the product view." Oh, and coming back to mobile phones again, "products" are what Nokia CEO Stephen Elop meant by "devices" when he said: "Our competitors aren't taking our market share with devices; they are taking our market share with an entire ecosystem."

In its defense, the product view is not one-eyed like the industry view. It acknowledges, or at least waves at, the supply side, before focusing on demand. But demand, despite being the product view's primary focus, features only in the form of customers. This still critically over-simplifies the picture. Specifically, as you'll recall from ECON: 101, the product market view is fond of reducing the mysteries of markets to a two-dimensional supply-and-demand graph. This model abstracts from all the complexity to leave only buyers, sellers, product, and price. Yet, in one of a howling host of internal contradictions, the product view then seems to forget it's just an abstraction and acts as if this graph were a reliable proxy for the market. Suddenly, the market is reduced to a meager price-setting mechanism. Making a breathtaking leap of faith, that mechanism holds other things equal and considers all the outside factors it can model are sufficiently unusual to merit the name "shocks." The trouble is — and trust us on this one – other things are never equal, and "external" factors are routine, not shocking.

There's a more insidious problem with the product view. Its over-simplification tips us into a flawed metric of demand and a very incomplete concept of value. The balance between supply (producers) and demand (customers) determines both the price of the product and how many products are being exchanged. When you multiply the quantity of product being exchanged by the price, you get something that the classical economists (the 19th-century forebears of today's neoclassicals) would have called *exchange value*. But if you think exchange value adequately measures the size of the market, think again.

To paraphrase Oscar Wilde: The product market view turns us into cynics who know "the price of everything and the value of nothing."[24] Exchange value based on price is just one measure of value (or of market size). An equally important concept for strategists is its forgotten classical counterpart, *use value*.[25] Use value is the value experienced by the customer; the utility of the product or service; its power to satisfy needs and wants. Use value is created – surprise, surprise – when a customer uses a product. Customers engage in value-creating processes in order to achieve their own goals, and they use their own resources and capabilities in these processes. To increase this value creation, customers interact with suppliers in a market in order to access suppliers' resources, typically packaged in the form of products. Hence, according to the use-value perspective, the goal of a supplier is not so much to produce valuable things to be exchanged as it is to help customers to create value for themselves.

Far from splitting hairs, we believe the classical distinction between exchange and use value remains key. As the distinction got lost, we all ended up equating value with exchange value. This was another dangerous simplification, and again a supply-centric one. With it we not only come back full circle to the idea that market just means aggregate demand for a product plus a wave at supply; we literally reduce markets — the central concept of all economics and the economics-based disciplines, including strategic management — to sales figures. Suddenly markets are just yesterday's sales figures spat out by a black box.

Yet, firms forget use value at their peril, for exchange value is merely a reflection of use value, as no one will pay more than a product is worth to them. And while exchange value is an abstract figure outside the average, price-taking firm's reach, use value can be innovated and boosted by the firm in countless, lucrative ways. Imagine if Uber had treated the value in its market as purely the fixed number of dollars a passenger would exchange for a conventional taxi ride. By adding the convenience and sense of control from its app, the company could entice far more people to ride with it thanks to their extra use value, and during peak periods customers were even prepared to pay the surge premium and thus exceed ordinary taxi exchange value.

Circularity: Available Data Bias Us Toward the Product Market View

Market views and data related to these get distinctly circular. Just as the dominance of data about *markets as industry* biases us into equating a firm's context with industry, so a dominance of data about *product markets* biases us into equating markets with the exchange value of products. Measuring markets in terms of product sales is so institutionalized that other measures are seldom to be seen. Starting from industrial classification and national statistics, the dominant paradigm is to use products or product categories as the organizing idea.

It turns out industries are the only context-level classification for which detailed, comprehensive empirical data are readily available. By contrast, there are just no data to measure the size of markets according, say, to the use value they generate. How, for example, would Uber have measured the extra use value created by its uber-convenient, empowering app — other than by running this as a real-world experiment and watching?

Granted, a hole in the data can't make our case. But it is certainly conceivable that the correlation between industry growth and firm growth could be picking up demand-side causes. Hence, perhaps the growing and profitable industries are just serving growing and profitable markets.

Another institution reinforcing the product-based market views is stock market analysis (the analysts all work to neoclassical economist precepts). Strikingly, studies show that analysts fail to put a value on uniqueness in strategies or market definitions.[26] As a result, capital markets systematically discount uniqueness in their choice of companies to invest in. This, in turn, puts pressure on companies to stick to myopic choices when it comes to markets and strategies, as the analysts' models do not comprehend more creative ones. As it would seem obvious that uniqueness drives economic rents and company value, it is clear that capital markets are in need of new thinking tools as well.

The Poor View Impoverishes Strategy from Every Angle

Little do the industry and product views of markets tell us about where markets come from or how they evolve. Instead they serve up a gruel of deterministic models such as the product life-cycle model. This blandly holds that you launch a new product to the market and it goes through a series of stages: introduction, growth, maturity and decline. Tough luck if you are in a declining market. And too bad, also, if such models don't withstand empirical scrutiny.[27]

All this is classic *black box* thinking. It says the market is an incredibly important device whose workings firms can never fathom. Indeed, the thinking is almost mystical. And if markets are mystical or unfathomable, firms cannot predict them or influence them. That makes them *given*: exogenous or external to the firm.

Whatever is given or external, strategists won't waste energy trying to influence. So, the flawed industry and product market views lead strategists to try nothing proactive regarding this incredibly important thing, the market. Let's look in more detail at how such poor market views impoverish strategies from every angle — the ways in which they build strategies on sand.

Market opportunities as precursors to strategy. The traditional competitive strategy playbook starts with plays to scan the external and given market for opportunities for business development, or to "do industry analysis," if you prefer that term. These opportunities form the input to the company's strategy process, whose whole point becomes planning how to realize them. In essence, the identified market opportunities are precursors of strategy. This thinking forms the flaky backbone of the many management practices grouped under the term "market orientation." Market orientation shakily prescribes that companies should acquire, share, and utilize knowledge about customers and market conditions. The utilization means that the company should adapt to changes in the market, by improving products and customer service.

Adapting to the market is defeatist and reactive. That buzzword "adapt" — and the same would apply to "agile" — is putting it too favorably, though. We reckon any theory saying markets are black boxes which hugely influence the firm but which can't be influenced or even properly understood by the firm is, if nothing else, *defeatist*. It should not be a boast to be market driven. As Professor Robert Burgelman[28] of Stanford describes such a *reactive* mode, "Being market driven is for wimps! Firms with ambitious strategies drive the market." Apple, Uber, and the other intuitive market shapers have understood this.

Adapting to the market through market orientation only ekes out small gains. Market orientation[29] says firms should learn about customers and market conditions to improve their products and customer service. But the benefits of that are circumscribed by the narrow definition of markets: "How many mobile phones can be sold per year [in China, to the youth market, and so on], and what kind of mobile phones do consumers prefer?" What's more, the McKinsey studies we discussed above show that market share gains are a very inefficient way to raise topline growth – and many executives know painfully well that those last extra market share percentage points are likely to destroy your bottom line.

Competing for market share when everyone defines their market by product is zero-sum. By definition a theory that tells you to compete for market share reduces your strategy to a zero-sum game. That limitation is built into not only the words "share" and "compete" but also the poor market view itself. Whole markets/industries get defined around products, so you have the insurance market, the petroleum market and so on. But since every company in the market uses the same market defini-tion, they automatically start to view each other as competitors. And because you're defining the market in terms of the current product (rather than, say, customers and their value creation), there are scant opportunities to grow the market. *Ergo*, you end up with a self-fulfilling prophecy that competitive strategies are inevitable.

Any narrow view that everyone subscribes to dooms your strat-egy to be unoriginal. There's another point to do with the ubiquity of the received industry and product views of markets. If everyone subscribes to the same view, and that view is narrow, then your strategy ends up being "me too," unoriginal – and plain boring. Yet, is originality not the hallmark of good strategy?

The obsession with industries and products ignores the real competition. Meanwhile, as psychologist and Nobel prize–winning behavioral economist Daniel Kahneman would remind us, we are always prone to WYSIATI thinking: What You See Is All There Is.[30] Dwelling on industries, your own products and rivals who supply similar ones biases you toward overrating the importance of these factors. Often your customers could satisfy their needs without your product at all. For example, the real competition for a movie theater doesn't come from other movie theaters but from alternative ways of spending a couple of hours of free time: meeting a friend for coffee, reading a book, going to a cooking class. In this kind of reality, how effective are traditional competitive strategies that consider the industry boundaries sacred?

The obsession with exchange value misses the opportunities of growing use value. The exchange value focus overlooks the goldmine of business opportunities that resides precisely in use value — over on the demand side of the market which the industry view omits and the product view misunderstands. Because use value always sets the maximum exchange value (again, who would pay more than the value they gained?), you can increase the size of your market by creating more use value. In theory, there are unlimited opportunities for use-value creation. You can improve your current product or introduce new ones to generate more gains for your customer or "reduce his pains."

Bottom line: the standard view misses the main chance — market-level changes and market shaping. The bottom line is that traditional strategy practice based on poor market views misses the main chance for strategy: changes at the market level, and in particular deliberate market shaping. Standard strategy thinks small; market-shaping thinks big. As Nokia saw, changes at the market level swamp unilateral changes at the firm level. The assumption of standard competitive strategy is that you have to adapt your firm to the market and then compete for a slice of the market pie. As we'll continue to say, the insight of market shaping is that, with the right knowledge and timing, you can often adapt the market to your firm, bake a much bigger pie in the process, and carve yourself a much more ample and mouth-watering portion.

Grains of Truth in the Poor Market View

As we said when first describing the demise of Nokia as the demise of the traditional business strategy playbook, the received wisdom is by no means totally wrong. It's just incomplete and therefore likely to lead to Nokia-type failure as soon as market conditions get highly complex or volatile, as they did in the 3G mobile telephony market and increasingly do elsewhere. Despite these shortcomings, the restricted market view based on industries or the exchange value of products contains several grains of truth.

First, the standard view does hold that it is easiest to grow in a growing market. This is true. Second, it is also true that firms can to some extent choose which markets they operate in (short of shaping the market) and that in rare circumstances a breakthrough product or technology will allow the innovating firm to create a whole new market. However, it is far from the whole truth.

For the whole truth, we need a comprehensive theory of markets and a comprehensive practical repertoire of strategy, so that we are no longer seeing markets through one eye and making strategy with one hand tied behind our back.

EMBRACE THE RICH REALITY OF MARKET SYSTEMS

Let's pause to take stock. The previous sections marked where Nokia Mobile Phones and almost everyone else have been stuck: the traditional strategy playbook with its generic, deeply flawed views of markets. We explored those views and how they lead to all sorts of poor strategic practice. Now for the good news. As we saw from the Uber example, it is possible to approach markets and strategy in another way. This section sets out in glorious technicolor the rich reality of markets as systems for value creation.

And the next section shows how this market view leads to the new practice of market shaping.

To fill the gaps left by the incompleteness and inadequacy of those poor market views, we've gone back to basics. And we've drawn on many disciplines: not only management, economics, and marketing, but also sociology and psychology. This takes us well beyond the narrow neoclassical economics or 1950s industrial organization view of markets. We wanted a market view that would hold for all markets at all times; not only, say, Nokia's 2G market but also its 3G market. So it had to be a general model. Of course it had to be the best fit for the evidence of how markets actually work, so as to explain and predict as much as possible. We also required it to be learnable and useable so that strategy could exploit its insights.

We reckon our market view below delivers on all those things. We call it the rich reality because it captures real markets and is rich in both description and strategic possibilities. And although we and others have articulated many parts of this view in isolation, we believe that no one has articulated all the main parts, let alone put them together as a unified vision with actionable managerial tools.

Markets Are Complex Adaptive Systems

Markets are a classic case of a complex adaptive system (CAS). Mathematicians developed CASs as a distinct category between systems that are ordered but very complicated, like the flight deck of a modern airliner, and outright chaotic systems, like weather, which is subject to the famous "butterfly effect." Other CASs include the brain, your family, any biological ecosystem, and the economy. The "adaptive" bit means the system is constantly evolving and adapting, not that you have to adapt to it.

We boldly call this theory the rich reality. It has always been true, and was already more complete than the old industry and product views even while they remained serviceable. Ever since markets started racing up the exponential curve of complexity, the way mobile phones crossed that threshold of complexity from 2G to 3G, the system view is *the only map of markets that will work.*

You'll recall Nokia CEO Stephen Elop's burning platform memo and his epiphanous but belated glimpse of "ecosystems." The latter word captures a lot about the rich reality of markets. To be picky though, it might still sound as if you and your firm have to adapt to the ecosystem, because natural evolution is all about adapting to the ecosystem and then competing in it. Trouble is, that's the whole idea we're leaving behind. The notion of natural evolution might in turn leave little room for design, whereas market shaping refers to a kind of interplay between design and spontaneous evolution. Finally, our theory of adapting the market is win-win. So whereas evolution sounds "dog-eat-dog," you could say almost our theory is in this respect just the reverse! The term we prefer is CASs. We turn to those now.

A CAS is an entity comprising many diverse parts, both living agents and nonliving things. ("Adaptive" means the system is constantly evolving and adapting, not that you have to adapt to it.) The parts depend on each other through dense interconnections. Together they behave as a unified whole. However, the whole is more than the sum of the parts, and you can't predict its behavior or properties from theirs. Unlike rigid or mechanistic systems, even very complicated ones, CASs *don't obey simple laws of cause and effect.* They have no center, let alone a central control mechanism; no master *control* at all. However, they are subject to *influence* and a *degree* of prediction. The shape of a CAS continually evolves from a combination of deliberate design influence and random "emergence." Positive and negative feedbacks, respectively, amplify or dampen the effect of stimuli on the system.

Markets in a Nutshell

Markets are CASs of exchange for the creation of value, which includes use value to consumers. Markets subsume industries and add multiple layers of designable elements. Rather than obeying ordinary laws of cause and effect, markets constantly evolve from both emergence and deliberate design: deliberate shaping.

What the System View Tells Us about Markets: Emergence, Design, and More

Because CASs don't obey ordinary laws of cause and effect, we have to throw out the simplistic view of markets as supply-and-demand curves. Also heading for the trash can is the old, linear view of strategy as a detailed master plan drawn up in phase one and executed in phase two.

On the other hand, CASs are no longer a total mystery, or a black box. They're not impenetrable, just complex! And you and I successfully navigate complex social systems every day, by using our social intuitions. At some level, we intuit the workings of social groups like the family, the neighborhood, or workplace politics.

The firm is one of the agents or actors, *inside* the market system. Although CASs don't follow ordinary cause and effect in a way that even an expert consultant can predict, they are amenable to a degree of influence by their parts, and those include the firm. Figure 1.1 illustrates the difference between the poor and rich view of markets. The left-hand side of the diagram represents the old view. Markets 1 and 2 are "out there," outside the firm's sphere of influence and containing a given demand. All that the firm can do is choose which one to enter. On the right-hand side we see the new, subtler, and richer view. The firm is part of its

Figure 1.1. From Poor Market View to Rich Reality of Markets.

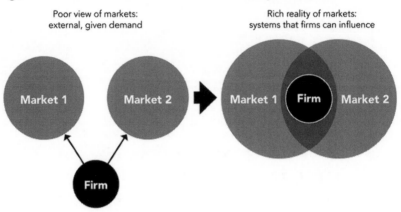

market and exerts some influence over it. These market systems are partially overlapping, and sometimes a firm may choose to be part of — and influence — several systems at the same time.

As we'll shortly elaborate, in our theory markets coalesce from a growing and increasingly sophisticated network of buyers, sellers, competitors, distributors, other actors, and material and immaterial infrastructure, plus much more. Had you spotted that this theory also accounts for market formation and change, which the old, fixed views couldn't? CAS tells us that markets will continually evolve — and that we'll have to deal with it! So, markets have complex but comprehensible histories (origin stories, if you like) and futures. They do not pre-exist as eternal givens. Neither do they pop magically into and out of existence, nor are they fixed while they're around. The statistics and other data traditionally used as portrayals of the market are merely a snapshot, like a still from a movie, which also only captures certain dimensions and is disappointingly black and white. Sure, the numbers from yesterday represent yesterday's market, but do they represent today's? Timing will become everything.

The *Function* of a Market System Is Exchange, for the *Purpose* of Value Creation

Specifically, markets are CASs *of exchange, for the creation of value*. And we do need to be very specific about that. Common definitions which include exchange but omit use-value and the value creation aspect sound curiously zero-sum, as though the same resource is simply being shuffled around the system in a grand version of the children's birthday game pass-the-parcel. Even saying, as people often do, that exchange in markets occurs to create value, glosses over the fact that value comes in two main flavors, and that creation really means co-creation. Just as markets divide into supply and demand, *so does value divide into exchange value to the supplier and use value to the customer/user.* In a firm-focused, production-centric view such as the traditional business strategy approach, value too easily comes to mean what is really only exchange value – the value to the producer or seller – or, worse still, the price.

Since we are writing strategy for firms not customers, we are of course *ultimately interested in the exchange value the producer can achieve*, and price is how it is denominated. You'll recall from our dissection of the product market view and later comments that *what dictates exchange value is use value: the value to the customer*, or (better put) the user. A user will willingly pay a higher price if she can get more use value out of the product. So use value should be integral to the firm's market view, and any way to increase use value offers potential gains in exchange value right back. This is where co-creation comes in. The firm's product is only one component in the customer's use value. Consider cars for instance. Greenhouse gases and traffic jams aside, the car is a magnificent invention. But without other components of the customer's value creation – roads, fuel, fuel stations, traffic rules, driving instruction, and so on – it actually has no value.

Markets Are Socially Constructed, so You Can Reconstruct Them, too

Markets are social systems.[31] As far as we know, there are no markets without humans. Man is the trading animal, and a market is a microcosm of society. The parts that make up market systems are human agents and human creations.

The original meaning of market as the bustling town marketplace of yore — "Ye Olde Markete," if you will — made the human side clear. Picture that marketplace and you picture the beating heart of a community where people came together to exchange things in order to get value they couldn't get by themselves. Think: colorful and very human bazaar, not: drab, automated stock exchange.

Today, the parts of a market system are still human agents and their creations. It's just easy to forget this in all the abstract talk about price mechanisms, mathematical models and supposedly natural, rather than human-made, laws of supply-and-demand and market forces. These are all highly depersonalized, as though they were "given" scientific truths and humans' only involvement was in discovering them. But we've seen these supposed truths are incomplete and flawed. That's hardly surprising, since they're trying to pin down messy human behavior. Plus, they're human postulates themselves. Even these abstract concepts are created by us humans. (The same goes for our CAS theory — only, ours doesn't contradict itself and is a far better fit with reality!) Similarly, human made are the other aspects of market systems: the networks of people, the physical marketplace, and its rules and conventions and language, to name but a few.

The key point for us is that, being socially constructed, markets *can be consciously reconstructed*. Because humans can be persuaded, incentivized or, where laws or sheer market power are involved, coerced by other humans, the firm has a means of influencing the human agents and their creations. This is how you can turn social reconstruction to your advantage.

Fundamentally, viewing markets as shapeable systems suggests that *opportunities are not precursors* of strategy; rather they *are outcomes of deliberate efforts to shape markets*. As companies engage in market shaping activities, opportunities occur and companies need to be nimble at capturing the value from these. This indicates that finding a sustainable competitive advantage may not be that important.[32] What is important, however, is that companies have a contingency plan to deal with the upcoming prospects for an expansion of available resources or possible constraints created by other actors in the market.

Additionally, this line of reasoning recommends a change in the unit of analysis: We should not make strategy for a company — we should make strategy for the system. Furthermore, strategy ought not to be viewed as winning a zero-sum game; nor ought the focus to be on competing.[33] On the contrary, it should clarify how the company can engage in collaborative activities with market actors (suppliers, customers, and partners) in order to improve the creation of the use value. Companies that can promise improved value creation for several actors simultaneously are the ones most likely to be successful in shaping their respective markets. The job of the market leader is not to increase own market share at the expense of others, but rather about creating a positive sum game where many market actors grow the market together.

Putting It All on the Table: Rich and Poor Views, Side by Side

As discussed in the previous sections, there are some fundamental difference in the poor view(s) of markets and the rich, systemic view. These differences also translate to serious differences in firms' strategies, measures of success, and types of innovations pursued by these firms. Figure 1.2 summarizes these differences.

THE PAY-OFF: STRATEGIES FOR MARKET SHAPING

The pay-off to all the theory above is that it enables you to become a market shaper. In an age of acronyms, we've dubbed our strategies for market shaping "SMASH" for a couple of reasons. First, they're iconoclastic: These strategies smash the icons of old market views and old strategic wisdom. They flip the adaptation process on its head, by saying Adapt the market to your firm, not vice versa. And second, they offer enormous, largely untapped potential for growing entire markets and their profitability to the benefit of many market actors. To use a quaint phrase, we think this makes them pretty smashing; and hopefully a smash hit with your firm!

What Is Market Shaping Anyway?

Let's back up a moment. The commonest question executives ask when we present our findings is: "What is this market shaping that you are so worked up about?" (Admittedly, we have paraphrased the question more tersely than polite clients and attendees put it, but we reckon we've captured the intent.)

Changing the definition of markets from mere exchange mechanisms to a system fostering value creation is not just semantics or purely academic debate. Think about the implications. We're claiming that, like any other human-made systems, market systems can be changed by companies, governments, and even singular individuals. This line of reasoning is radically different from mainstream strategy thinking, and opens up two exciting new options for strategists and managers.

First, if your company is operating in a market with dismal growth and profitability, you don't have to accept this as the natural world order and adapt accordingly. The near-universal imperative to adapt or die has missed the boat. If you follow the timing and techniques set out in this book, you can, under many

Figure 1.2. The Poor, Restricted View of Markets versus the Rich, Systemic View.

	Poor, restricted view	Rich, systemic view
Definition of markets	Markets defined around industries and/or products.	Markets defined as complex adaptive systems.
Market structure	Suppliers and customers in a value chain.	A system of market actors (organizations, individuals) with interactions fostering value creation.
Value focus	Exchange value: the value that is extracted by the supplier when selling a product.	Use-value: the value that is created when a product is used in the customer's value creating process.
Market versus firm	The market is external to the company. Markets are given and their development is deterministic.	The market system is an outcome of actions by market actors. Markets are plastic and malleable.
Market opportunities	A company's job is to adapt to the market, i.e., opportunities are precursors of strategy.	A company can influence market development, i.e., opportunities are created by strategy.
Role of strategy	Company level competitive strategy – how the company positions itself against competitors.	System-level value-creating strategy – how the company supports the value creation of customers and other actors in the system.
Ultimate goal	To find sustainable competitive advantage.	Continuous renewal (as competitive advantage is always transient).
Key measurement of success	Product market share. Shareholder value.	Stakeholder/shared value.
Innovation	Technological and product innovations	+ business model innovation, management innovation, and market innovation.

circumstances, innovate ways to improve the market system so that it creates more, sometimes dramatically more, value to the end customer – and pocket at least a share. Second, you can also create entirely new market systems around your novel, but currently uncommercialized, business idea or technological innovation. In fact, it seems that taking an active stance in creating the surrounding market systems for new inventions helps de-risk commercialization projects considerably. We call these two new strategic options, improving existing market systems and creating new ones, market shaping. Figure 1.3 juxtaposes these two market shaping options against the more traditional strategic moves related to markets.

The four panels left to right in Figure 1.3 show four scenarios moving from not market shaping at all to market shaping. Panel (a), taking markets as given and eking out market share, is the opposite of market shaping, because it adapts the firm to the market. Panel (b) is close but no cigar: You redefine your business by looking at other geographies or offering totally new products or services, but still assume the market is given and unchangeable.

Figure 1.3. What Counts, or Does Not Count, as Market Shaping.

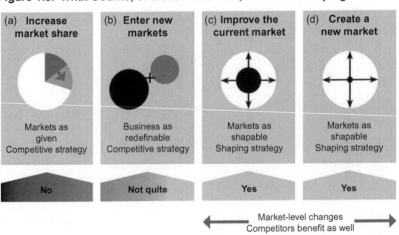

Panel (c) is pure market shaping: taking your existing market and remolding it.

Panel (d) is a special case of market shaping: market creation. Building on the theoretical insight that, unlike poets, markets are not only born but also made, this strategy takes a new product or service and aims to consciously attract or build the elements of a fully functioning market around it. Importantly, this entails more than just commercialization or "putting the product out there" and hoping a fully fledged market pops spontaneously into life. You will need, for instance, to deal with new norms and infra-structures — just as launching a car would be unprofitable or downright pointless without suitable legal and physical compo-nents, like roads, in the system.

Market-shaping Strategies in a Nutshell

Market shaping is an original, evidence-based management strategy and method of innovation that reworks your markets to fit your firm, not the other way around. Market shaping can be used to create completely new market systems (for instance, around new-to-the-world technologies) as well as to improve existing market systems. Market-shaping strategies are the practical application of viewing markets as systems for fostering value creation.

Terminology: Market shaping includes market making. Note that we see market making as a special case of market shaping. That's because claiming that any market is brand new is slippery. A newly made market could arguably be considered a rather advanced evolution of a previous market system (or systems), at least recycling its (or their) elements. However, there will be times where it's useful to distinguish making from the rest of shaping. At such times, we will expressly refer to market making. Otherwise, from now on, please take it as read that market shap-ing includes market making.

FAQs about Market Shaping

In addition to "What is this market shaping anyway?," executives typically ask us several other questions. Hence, before we go any deeper into the processes and tools related to market shaping strategies, let's rattle through the FAQs.

What are the main ingredients for shaping markets? This is a question that it takes the rest of the book to answer fully. There is no single formula and no linear progression of steps. It's about a continuous cycle. And there's a degree of art to it as well as science. Broadly though, market shaping begins with re-focusing your business definition, which also acts as your frame on the market, so that you can see the rich reality of your market system, and training it on the slice of the universe of possible markets which you want to start with. You then need to envisage a new shape for that market system that would benefit your firm more, by capturing a share of extra use value you'll help create (in other words, co-create) for customers. Whichever other players it requires to effect the change, you'll need to appeal to them by offering a share in the value creation as well. This involves pitching a win-win-win "story" or narrative about your proposed new shape. And you'll need to time the whole intervention to strike when the market is "hot" and malleable.

How is market shaping strategy different from the traditional strategy playbook? Strategies for market shaping (SMASH) differ from mainstream strategic thinking in four ways:

1. Being based on the rich reality of markets as complex systems, market-shaping strategies acknowledge that markets are human-made systems, and thus shapeable.

2. They actively seek to influence market systems, either by improving existing ones or by creating entirely new ones. Therefore, the strategic options are no longer limited to adapting and competing for more market shares.

3. As a result, market shaping brings about value-creating market-level changes.

4. Due to this, market shaping will benefit more actors in the system than just the market shaper — sometimes even the competition!

Anticipating the sound of readers wincing, we recognize that the last point is a painful realization for the ultra-competitive among our number, which we're guessing is a fair few. But keep your eyes on the prize that matters, your firm's absolute prosperity, and don't let the reflex for rivalry and head-to-head competitive plays cloud your better judgment. Given that firm performance is largely contextual, defined by your markets, market-shaping strategies will often net you greater growth and profitability obliquely than traditional competitive strategies could have. If you're not in touch with your inner altruist, you can at least treat spin-offs to the competition as a means to an end.

Do any firms already practice market shaping? According to recent Boston Consulting Group research,[34] only 9% of firms currently use market-shaping strategies. As far as we know, none of them use an integrated, systematic explanation of market shaping. We conclude they are practicing market shaping mostly intuitively. Having studied both the scholarly literature and the hundreds of firms we have partnered with for research or consulted for, we have consciously compiled replicable examples of market shaping in all sorts of settings for you to learn from. In the Nokia example, Apple was market shaping. Uber, as we saw, is all about market shaping. Spotify and IKEA are also other good examples you might be familiar with. But you'll meet more than 20 successful market-shaping firms in the course of the book.

Which firms could practice market shaping? Can I? We have developed market shaping as an integrated, systematic method. Any firm can do it. You don't have to be a giant corporation, a genius, or a jet-owning rich lister. You don't need market power in the traditional sense of monopolies and oligopolies. In fact, being big can hinder creative thinking of the kind a new strategy requires if the great idea gets tangled up in the red tape of internal processes. However, you need a good idea — a vision about how to shape your market into a better re-incarnation of that market — because market shaping works only if you are truly able to improve the market. And remember, "improving" means improvement to others as well, not just to you.

Which environments and which markets lend themselves to market shaping? Just as our view of markets applied to all markets, so the practice of market shaping can work in all markets. However, you'll see there are certain times and conditions which make any particular market more or less shapeable. Striking when the iron isn't hot could be unproductive. The good news is that we'll share with you our new range of special thermometers to take the temperature of the market iron.

In future, the practice of market shaping will probably only get more crucial as ongoing systemic changes such as globalization, the information revolution, urbanization, climate change, and population and lifespan growth increasingly carry markets across a threshold of complexity and instability that the standard playbooks cannot cope with. In terms of the Nokia example, expect lots more of 3G markets and lots less of 2G!

The Strategic Baby and the Bathwater

As we rewrite the strategy playbook, we are not throwing out the old one entirely. It offers many useful plays and even a few insights into the nature of markets, notably that it is easiest to grow in a growing market. We are not claiming that market shaping is the only way of doing strategy. On the contrary, market shapers will continue to deploy traditional strategies too. For instance, they will continue to invest in innovating technology and products. But armed with an understanding of market shaping, they will see more risks and opportunities, will time their moves better, and will less likely find the rug pulled out from under them by the market shaping plays of other firms (or governments or other organizations) the way Nokia did. And there are going to be a time and place for traditional competitive strategies when companies compete for market shares, but these strategies are limited to those periods when markets are "cold" and unshapeable, or when the current market system fits nicely with your strategy and thus is playing to your strengths. Lastly, seeing the rich reality of markets systems will alert you to market-level movements and their power to either swamp or buoy unilateral strategic actions. So, even if you're not trying to shape markets yourself, at least you'll now notice which way the tide is going. Plus, you'll be privy to the information that active market-shaping firms will enjoy and thus be able to anticipate some likely market-shaping attempts.

MAKING THE RICH VIEW ACTIONABLE: INTRODUCING THE "MARKET FAN"

If we take a simple-sounding market like the market for cars and look at it more closely in the light of social constructedness and exchange for value creation, we reveal far, far more parts and agents to the system than just the car, the seller, and the buyer. For starters, cars have no use value unless people know how to drive them, so drivers are a key actor, and driving is a core *actor competency*. There also has to be an infrastructure of roads and petrol stations, parking lots, and so on. There have to be *other actors* including service providers such as mechanics and tire repairers — even, dare we say, second-hand car salespeople and parking wardens. And as you'll know all too well if you've ever driven in one of the more lawless foreign jurisdictions, you really need commonly agreed traffic *rules* and driver norms about respecting them vehicle manufacture *standards* and *institutions* to enforce them. Plus, it wouldn't hurt to have automobile associations, lobbies for safety features like the original (Ralph) Nader's Raiders of the 1970s, and media in which to learn about the best cars on offer or how to avoid dogs and lemons, and of course there must be forums to connect buyers and sellers. Some kind of language or representation will also develop comprising not only the terms of the trade but also, for instance, road maps.

Incidentally, remember also that from a use-value perspective what you're creating is not cars but what people use them for. So it would be better to rechristen the market for cars as "the market for automobility."[35]

Now, you could just throw a big circle around all those components, draw lines between them, and call it the market for automobility — but that may not be very useful. We've gone much further and built up an illustration of a generic market called the Fan.[36] The Fan identifies all the parts and agents that can be influenced or shaped (designable elements) and systematically groups them into related layers. And you'll see that among these elements are many of the features which the product market view would have called the nonmarket environment or considered noncommercial concerns.[37] By saying all these features are "nonmarket" and "noncommercial" features, the company misses the point that they are all part of one, integrated system — the market system — and this whole system has huge power to enrich strategy. The Fan reveals that they are all bound up together.

The Fan looks beyond the blinders of the seller—buyer duo of the standard view to see the duo as part of a larger system of actors co-creating value. As you can see, there are five layers nested around the focal firm trying to influence its market. The closer the layers are to the center, the more managerial control the firm has over the design elements. However, the further away from the center the layers are, the more leverage the design elements have over the whole market system, if the firm's influence does succeed in reaching them. The layers are: (1) the core: the *business definition* that the focal firm is using when acting in and perceiving a market; (2) the *exchange* process by which the focal firm defines its product or services, their prices and finds customers; (3) the *network* that supports the exchange process and customers' use practices; (4) the *representations* that are used to symbolize the market; and (5) the *rules of the game* that guide all interactions in the market. In addition to the business definition design element, we identified two to three elements on the five outer levels that are potentially amenable to reshaping or design. This gives a total of *13 designable elements* that the focal firm can try to manage or influence.

Business definition – a designable element in itself. The innermost layer, the business definition, is the lens or frame through which the firm sees the rest of the layers and so is crucial. *Your business definition decides how many of the elements you recognize as being designable and how well you understand the ways they can be designed, as well as which slice of the overall universe of possible market you are going to position to.* Because the business definition is so crucial to seeing the market and its possible reconfigurations, it gets the whole of Chapter 2 to itself. We won't say any more about it now (Figure 1.4).

Exchange layer – designable elements: sales item, pricing and matching method. The firm must decide exactly what product or service it is offering and agree on a pricing logic, which means more than just "how much." For instance, is a news publisher selling hard-copy newspapers or the same content but online and diced and sliced? If online, will it go entirely behind a pay-wall, or offer parts free but with extra content for a charge (the freemium model), be pay per view, subscription, or fully free to the reader but with advertisements? Although a bystander to a transaction may see a widget being handed over for cash, what's valuable to the customer isn't the widget itself so much as a property right in it. The different property rights that the customer is really after include the right to access or use the widget temporarily (hire) or

Figure 1.4. The Market Fan: Illuminating the Systemic Markets.

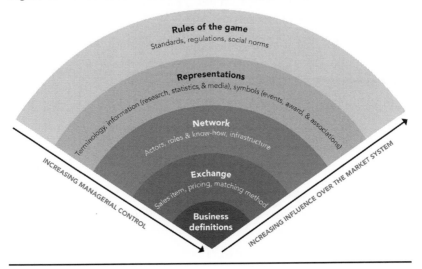

indefinitely (outright sale) and the right to earn money from using the widget (say the widget is an input you use to produce "wodgets"). "Exchange" also involves the method of connecting sellers and buyers, which gets so sophisticated it won Alvin Roth a share of the Nobel in 2012. Roth came up with ingenious ways to more efficiently match suppliers and consumers in various contexts from kidney transplants to school choice, by making it safe for them to reveal confidential information or such basics as giving them more time to decide from multiple alternatives.

Network layer – designable elements: actors, their roles and know-how, and infrastructure. A market ecosystem consists of a network of actors, each with their own roles and know-how and with established relationships between them. Together they rely on an infrastructure for the market. Securing that there are competing alternatives in the market might sound like something a firm would want to shut down, but this is exactly the kind of false conclusion you get from the flawed assumptions about markets in the traditional playbook. A 2002 study[38] found that sales of innovations really took off only after an increase in the number of firms providing the innovation, and not just because more firms had sniffed the opportunity. A market-shaping firm might be well advised to foster competition, partly to legitimize the new market as a valid opportunity. Our findings suggest that the network goes beyond a firm's immediate value chain, sometimes including non-commercial actors such as industry associations and public interest groups. An obvious element to work on is the competency of your customers, for instance teaching seniors computer literacy so they will want to buy your computers. Infrastructure means physical or technical structures that support usage of your products or services. Work is still in its infancy, but one study has looked at the impact of the grocery cart on American supermarkets.[39] Our full-worked example above, the market for cars/automobility, discussed the role of roads. From the physical highway to the technical information superhighway is a small step.

Representations layer – designable elements: terminology, information such as statistics and media outputs, and symbols such as industry events and awards. We have seen in our discussion above how availability of market statistics can form what we conceive the market to be. Market representations are arrangements of coherent but simplified illustrations of what a market is and how it works. In the healthcare market (which itself used to be labeled medical care), the shift in labels from patient to client has aimed to make the user feel empowered rather than passive and the provider sound, and (especially in the case of doctors with God complexes or state monopolies suspected of taking patients for granted) genuinely act, more accountable. Market research sometimes aims disingenuously despite the objective label which that profession in turn gives itself – research – to destabilize markets. Media are very important for picking up emerging markets. Most markets also enjoy symbols that establish them more firmly and convincingly in our mental landscapes, a process we call "legitimizing" them. Industry events, awards, and associations are the prime examples, and these, too, provide opportunities for shaping. Consider the Academy Awards for the motion picture industry. Should they also honor artistic achievement in the games sector too, as the BAFTAs have since 1998?

Rules of the game layer — designable elements: standards, regulations, and social norms. The actions of the players in the market ecosystem are guided by formal and social norms. There are activities on-going in all markets whereby these norms emerge or are consciously created. Lobbyists flock to Capitol Hill, and retired Congressmen and -women in turn emerge through the revolving doors of power as highly paid lobbyists, because influencing legal norms can change everything: keeping or abolishing a tariff against cheap Asian electronics, voting a beef and cattle farming subsidy in or out, or getting supplements like "Dr Dave's Miracle Antioxidant Super-berry Juice" included or excluded from the definition of healthcare for FDA purposes. Anyone who has tried to play a DVD only to be told their machine is the wrong zone knows how the big players influencing norms can carve up the world. Social norms are less often in writing — but just as powerful as the written ones.

Each setting of the Fan in a particular market is a snapshot in time. You'll recall that market systems change over time. The particular setting or configuration of specific elements of the Fan at a given time in a particular market provides only a snapshot of the system. It artificially freezes the system at one point in what is actually a never-ending process of evolution. That said, as an aid to strategy, the Fan is enormously powerful, as we shall soon see, when we examine it from the core outwards.

The Rest of the Book

Working from the core out, the Fan also supplies the structure for the next two chapters of our book. All the action in Chapter 2 takes place at the core with your business definition — the sole element you completely control. With a series of tools, exercises, and exemplary cases, we show why being critically aware of, and then optimizing, your business definition not only boosts growth and productivity but also frames your market more clearly and positions you better for actual market shaping. Market shaping proper begins in Chapter 3. There, with many more real-life examples, we give you practical guidance on how to explore and exploit the 12 elements in the remaining 4 layers of your market Fan: exchange, network, representations, and the rules of the game. For all these elements are by definition susceptible to a degree of influence and design by market shapers, as well as spontaneous emergence.

In Chapter 4, we bring all these designable elements together. We show how you can turn separate shaping actions into a cohesive market shaping strategy. This craft requires the right timing and a win-win-win arrangement. Additionally, we will present and scrutinize several generic market shaping moves — ready for you to be adopted in your markets. Finally, in Chapter 5, we'll take you through the leadership qualities of a market shaper.

TAKEAWAYS FROM CHAPTER 1

- The strategies in the traditional playbook are built on sand. *Poor views of markets have made for poor strategy.* We've inherited both simplistic and mystical views of markets, riddled with contradictions and kept alive by self-reinforcing definitions behind our data.

- The fact is, markets are not simply industries! Industries alone are useless — supply with no demand. And adding in a sliver of demand (the customer) for a specific product, plus maybe a place, still misses the big picture. So there are no product markets either!

- The poor view impoverishes strategy from every angle. It makes strategy reactive and defeatist because *markets are allegedly "given" — fixed and unfathomable — yet somehow also as simple as supply-and-demand graphs.* It dooms firms to compete for market share in a *zero-sum game,* but ignores the real competition. It kills originality. And it misses the main chance: *to adapt markets to the firm, not vice versa.*

- Drawing on biology, psychology, and sociology as well as economics and management, we offer the rich reality of *markets as complex systems.* That's "complex" as in ecosystems and societies, rather than merely "complicated" as in machines. The complex system view tells us markets don't obey mechanical laws of cause and effect and can't be controlled or frozen in time. *They constantly evolve, partly by unpredictable emergence.*

- Markets are complex systems of exchange for *the purpose of co-creating value, specifically use value to the customer.* And when it comes to use value, the sky is the limit. That's use value as opposed to our standard metric: exchange value — aka price. Yet growing use value can ultimately grow exchange value, markets, and profits.

- The complex view of markets has always been true. The poor views scraped by only while the world itself was radically less complex. Given globalization, technological revolution, exponential network effects, and disruption-as-the-new-normal, *the complex view is the only map that will work in the 21st century.*

- Because market systems are socially constructed, you can reconstruct them, too. For, alongside random emergence, *markets evolve also by deliberate design,* or reconstruction. Other firms will design your market if you don't!

- The pay-off for all our theorizing is design writ large: SMASH. Making new markets and molding existing ones both count as market shaping. And in answer to other frequently asked questions (FAQs): *Although under 10% of firms currently shape markets, any firm can learn to be a market shaper;* but certain market phases and environments will prove riper than others.

- To make the complexity orderly and actionable, our Fan diagram divides markets into a core and four layers. The core is your firm's business definition, which also frames its perception of the layers. See Chapter 2 for this.

- Moving outward, the exchange, network, representations, and rules of the game layers of the Fan consist of another 12 designable elements. You have less influence over successive layers, but greater impact if your influence succeeds. See Chapter 3 for this.

2

FRAME YOUR MARKET

What, fundamentally, does your business do? If the sky were the limit, what might it do?

In today's radically unpredictable markets, the one thing you fully control is what you do — your business definition. And your business definition both spells your identity and frames how clearly you can see, and shape, the rest of your market. Business identity, then, really is market destiny.

Market shaping starts by recognizing that many strategists still needlessly hamstring their firm and blinder their market view by a stale or humdrum or me-too business definition. It then sets out all the tools and incentives you need to optimize that definition. Because even when it seems all bets are off, it's a safe bet you can define a more profitable, growth-rich business and, through it, design a richer market.

UPS: THINKING OUTSIDE THE BOXES

US freight and logistics giant UPS has never been one to rest on laurels or get stuck in a worldview. Indeed, cofounder Jim Casey turned the phrase "constructively dissatisfied" to describe his own and the business's relentless questing for improvement.[1] A couple of chapters from over a century of company history illustrate how

UPS grasped the rich reality of markets and so succeeded in redefining its business whenever opportunity, or adverse changes, emerged.

The first chapter dates from the company's earliest days. What Casey jointly started in 1907 in a Seattle basement on a $100 loan was in fact the American Messenger Company.[2] As the name implied, it ran errands and delivered messages, on foot and by bicycle, as well as delivering parcels. Had the firm continued to think of its business and its market as mainly messages though, it may well have missed America's and especially the West's coming wave of growth. For, partly driving that growth was the development of affordable telephone services, a classic disruptor to the messages market. As it was, the company both looked in the mirror and peered through a new window into the future. Merging with a delivery rival and acquiring the first of a fleet of model T Fords (big enough, what's more, to consolidate all deliveries for one area in one vehicle), the company reoriented to a delivery rather than information space. To reflect this, it restyled itself, first as Merchant Parcel Delivery in 1913 and then as United Parcel Services six years later.

Fast-forward to the second illustrative chapter, in the 1990s. It was again time for UPS to think outside the box, this time the rather literal package delivery box. CEO Kent "Oz" Nelson could see that this core business was maturing. Projected growth numbers were a far cry from shareholders' expectations. Finding new and growing business opportunities was paramount.

It would have been tempting to do more of the same thing — consumer parcel delivery — only perhaps faster or in a new geography. Instead, Nelson formed a highly diverse stand-alone taskforce of senior direct reports charged exclusively with identifying new growth platforms. The team deliberately pushed beyond UPS's current business definition and kept asking "Who are we?" The answers to this question were the first steps outside the box. "We know we deliver packages, but we are also a technology company, an airline (the ninth largest airline worldwide), an insurance company, and one of the largest purchasers of railcar capacity in the world." The next soul-searching question was: "What are our capabilities, know-how, and assets?" And the answer here, essentially: UPS's unique position in physically connecting buyer and seller, combined with operational excellence, network planning, and a worldwide infrastructure.

By blinking hard and viewing itself and its universe of market possibilities through this clearer lens, the team perceived business opportunities in which UPS could commercialize these underutilized resources and capabilities. One of the first opportunities in which UPS's unique resources and capabilities showed their true value was PC manufacturers' customer-facing logistics – delivering the brand-new Dell or HP computer that you ordered online to your doorstep. UPS successfully in-sourced this activity. Later it expanded the same solution to take in other sectors that needed fast and agile supply chain management, such as medical research and health care supplies.

By analyzing its business definition and thus its market rather than mere surface products and geographies, UPS once again carved out a whole new market space: outsourced logistics. That market was worth 3.2 trillion USD by 2006.[3]

"SO, WHAT DO YOU DO?": DEFINE YOUR BUSINESS

Whereas the Fan diagram from Chapter 1 shows the mind's eye of a generic market, in practice you'll need to see your particular market, with your own eyes. You need to learn how to spot the elements of each layer in real life. And that begins with holding a mirror to the firm – your business definition – before you look outward at the other market layers. Having said all the actions in this chapter happen at the core of the Fan, let's recap what that is and why the rest of the Fan and your whole market view flows from it.

The core of the Fan consists of a single, pivotal market element: your business definition. (And remember, your business definition is part of the market; the market is not all "out there" — it's partly "in here.") Your business definition is your firm's identity. In a nutshell, it denotes your answer to that perennial cocktail party question "What business are you in?" or "What do you do?" To expand on that, your business definition should contain an element of tomorrow as well as today: an aspiration or direction in which you are heading, as well as a position report. And of course, it should be congruent with reality, otherwise known as truthful: your lived definition, not just your declared definition.

Your Business Definition Frames Your Market

Not only is your business definition your identity, bit it also frames how you see the rest of your market. Think of the core of the Fan in this framing sense as your market eye, which (a) can perceive the other 12 market elements either more or less clearly and correctly, and (b) can point in any direction you choose, carving out your desired slice of the universe of all possible starter markets. (We say starter because markets are always evolving, and, once chosen, your slice can be deliberately remolded by market shaping.)

To illustrate the framing power of business definitions, we go inside KONE Corporation. You've no doubt contemplated that odd uppercase word (Finnish for machine, incidentally) on the elevator ride up to work, as you killed those awkward moments of suspended proximity that are the minor morning ordeal of the office class. For KONE is one of the world's largest producers of elevators and escalators. And as such, KONE long held up the standard product-view mirror and saw itself as operating in, precisely, the elevator and escalator business. This same definition inevitably framed the company's perception of its market: construction companies bought the hardware, facility managers purchased the maintenance services, governments regulated elevator and escalator safety and service standards, and the competition meant the other manufacturers: Otis, Schindler, Thyssen, and Mitsubishi.

In 2007, as part of a strategic overhaul, KONE redefined itself as the "People Flow" company.[4] This subtle change of focus in its business definition transformed how the corporation perceived its market. Now, new product categories are in scope and within reach: To deliver People Flow, KONE needs to offer its customers access control solutions, for instance. Important new stakeholders have emerged, too: Architects design the overall People Flow, and application developers devise access control solutions. Relevant regulations and representations are greater in number and variety when viewed through the People Flow lens.[5] And interestingly, the competitive landscape looks very different. Because People Flow is of intense interest to all companies involved in smart buildings, of a sudden the likes of IBM and Apple are potential competitors to KONE.

Your Frame Filters and Interprets Intel

In business as in life, and whether or not you realize it, you use your mental frame (for markets, your business definition) to *filter* and *interpret* information.[6] You have to. No man and no manager has the bandwidth to apprehend everything. As the contemptuous colonel played by Jack Nicholson in *A Few Good Men* erupts when goaded under cross-examination: "You want the truth? You can't *handle* the truth!" Indeed. We have to screen some things out – to delete some of the blizzard of emails and market reports. And ultimately we have to settle on just one interpretation of the data – those emails and reports – that we do let in. No-one's market view is frame-free, just as no-one's speech is accent-free. As with an accent, if you don't think you have a frame, it just means you share the prevailing one, which makes it even more insidious!

As an example of how a frame filters information, imagine your business definition, and hence frame, is "selling mobile phones in China." The risk is that potentially relevant news about, say, youth culture in South Korea won't make it through. Business opportunities outside the business definition will go ignored. Throw in our growing technological ability to tailor information feeds, personalize search options, and turn broadcasting into "narrowcasting," and the risk amplifies. Suddenly the world's an echo chamber where your frame resonates as so natural and unquestionable you no longer notice it — if you ever did.

As a real-life example of how a frame affects our interpretation of information, we need only recall the way Nokia misinterpreted Apple's entry to the mobile telephony market. Nokia mistook the iPhone for a niche product, similar to Macintosh computers in the personal computer market. We believe this miscalculation had a lot to do with Nokia's business definition. That definition was built around the notion of mobile phones as stand-alone devices. Had Nokia critically revisited its market definition and adopted something else, such as "enabling connectivity" or "ubiquitous work and entertainment," they might have recognized the new arrival as a horse of a very different color.[7]

But frames and business definitions needn't be narrow, fixed, and misleading. Consider the UPS story. In 1912, Jim Casey could have persisted in the company's definition as — in name, and in large part — a messenger business. He could have subscribed exclusively to *Ye Olde Northwestern Messenger Digest* (OK, we made that up). He could have filtered out the miraculous ease with which his branches could now telephone through their sales figures. He could have sat back, eyes closed, in his studded leather armchair, tuning out the clattering of the recently increased automobile traffic, and dreamt only of a better bicycle, or putting a dedicated AMS runner in every Washington town. Instead, Casey looked at his conspicuously affordable, shiny new brass handset, matched this datum with the fall in message commissions in the last two quarters, and saw a moribund business definition. Conversely, he clocked the numerous clattering cars on the road and saw a nascent market for delivery by automobile. He redefined his business, renamed it, and in so doing — rescued it.

Beware! The Product View Worms Its Way in through Restrictive Business Definitions

Given that frames are inevitable but also powerful and dangerous, the key, of course, is to do your very best within the limitation. At the very least, be aware of your frame. Beyond that, to optimize the frame you have to revisit, test, and recalibrate it frequently, with constructive dissatisfaction, as UPS did both in the 1910s and the 1990s. And because your frame is your business definition, this provides an added incentive to be aware of, revisit, and optimize how you define your business. What's more, luckily the Fan teaches us that our business definition is the single element in the whole market over which we have total control.

Problem solved? If only! In practice, most business definitions are just as reflexive, reductive, and thus restrictive as our standby answers to that cocktail party question about what you do. Our research confirms[8] that the stock answer will be something like: "We sell mobile phones in China" or "We're in the mobile phone business, in China." Time and again, this crude, summative product-geography response overrides the myriad other defining characteristics of your business. Lost in summation, as it were, are distribution channels, consumer segments, price points, macroeconomic trends, raw materials, and the many other facets of your business. The business definitions these betray are unoriginal, often unconscious, and rarely examined. And a narrow, reflex answer, especially one referring only to today not tomorrow, will cramp your firm's identity, cloud your vision of the market's many layers and elements, and carve out too thin a slice of the market action for your attention.

Have you spotted what this lazy framing is doing? It is letting in and perpetuating the old, distorted view of markets from Chapter 1 as mere supply-side industries or product-plus geography. Deep in your business definition is where the poor view of markets worms its way in and clouds your vision. Fortunately, the huge upside is that, now we know where the worm lives, we know where to worm it out! If — and only if — we can eradicate the poor market view from your business definition, we can make sure you see the rich reality of your particular market.

Cast Out the Worm! Polish Your Frame for Clarity, Point It for Choice

Casting out the worm of the product view will require a combination of two processes. Think of the processes as first polishing your frame for clarity, like a lens, then pointing it to your preferred initial slice of the market as a matter of choice. (And if you prefer, you can rephrase casting out in less grandiose terms, as nipping the product view in the bud.)

So, polishing is a matter of clarity; it is right or wrong. You have to make sure you have cast off the blinders of the poor market view and are seeing clearly, letting in the full rainbow of light from all the layers of the Fan so that you become aware of all 13 elements. Thus, in our original example, Apple and Samsung saw the 3G market system clearly and correctly, while Nokia Mobile Phones was still blinkered — even blinded — by the traditional product-geography thinking.

By contrast, pointing is a matter of choice. It's up to you whether to operate in the pizza delivery space, the people flow space, or aerospace. The choice isn't right or wrong, but some choices are better for growth and profitability than others. For, contrary to traditional belief, where you operate matters more to your top and bottom lines than how you operate.

Polishing and pointing will happen at the same time. Because you can't focus a lens and check its clarity without something to train it on, you're going to be swiveling and pointing at a variety of Fan slices as you squint, blink dust out of your eyes, and learn to drink in the light.

Now, we are far from the first to say strategists should be aware of and reexamine their business definition. As early as 1960, Harvard professor Theodore Levitt[9] was urging executives to ask themselves: "What business are you really in?" and suggesting that the answer to this seemingly simple question was the font from which all strategies flowed. What we add is complexity and the Fan, and the link from the business definition to those, plus a much bigger toolkit for putting all the self-examination into action.

So, you need tools. Even before Levitt, another giant, Igor Ansoff, in 1957 had crafted a simple tool to brainstorm your future business definition. The tool was the classical *product-geography matrix*.[10] Ansoff effectively told us to brainstorm by imagining a new product to sell in the old geography, or a new geography in which to sell the old product, or new versions of both at once. But, to confine yourself to this tool is to think far too small. Although it will break your frame out of a specific product and a specific geography, the very categorization of product × geography perpetuates the meta-frame of product-geography frame. No wonder we are so hooked on product-geography business definitons, we have become Pavlov's dogs to Ansoff's matrix!

Brainstorm New Business Definitions by Zooming Out and Zooming In

To break out from product-geography business definitions into more innovative ones requires a different toolkit. The rest of this chapter is about rethinking or brainstorming business definitions – your market frames. So we could also call it "frame-storming."

There are many ways to frame-storm. However, two processes we've devised from studying a suite of real-world examples and applied successfully with executives all over the world are particularly easy to learn. We've christened them zooming out and zooming in, because they pull the focal length out and then back in, respectively, like going wide angle then telephoto. Each has an analogue in the poor, traditional product market view but takes the traditional process to a whole new level: Zooming out is like a revamped and souped-up Ansoff product-geography matrix, while zooming in resembles a turbocharged, high-octane version of market segmentation. In the rest of the chapter, we'll explain the zooming out and zooming in processes and show you how to use the two tools we've built to go with them.

ZOOM OUT: LEAVE PRODUCT MYOPIA BEHIND

Fasten your seatbelts, because zooming out is going to propel you right out of your product-geography comfort zone. It does away entirely with product-based business definitions and therefore with the simple product-geography matrix. But what's left if you can't use products in defining your business? Defining businesses around the product or service being sold is so deeply engrained that questioning it feels heretical.

Well, for starters, it's not products *per se* that we're jettisoning. Firms will continue to supply goods and services – so now isn't the time to call your broker and offload stocks in every company that ever put out a product. What we're trying to escape is business definitions that start and end with products. To find alternative concepts for business definitions, we have to look at what *functionalities* products perform for firms and consumers. First, products and services are a convenient way of communicating to customers the tangible or intangible thing to which rights are being exchanged: a haircut, a consulting project, or a diesel engine for power generation. Second, providers like clearly defined products and services, because these make their operations more efficient: You know how much time one haircut requires or what kinds of resources it takes to build a diesel engine. But more fundamentally, why do customers buy rights to products or services? To use the product or service to fill their needs or desires. Or in other words: to gain access to the fruits of providers' resources and capabilities (materialized into a haircut or an engine) as a means to co-create use value for themselves.[11]

Deep down, products and services serve as particular – perhaps arbitrary – embodiments from the set of all possible embodiments combining providers' resources and capabilities. Customers then use them to create value for themselves. Taking this compelling logic to a simple conclusion, prominent business scholars have decided that as a matter of fundamental theory there are just two broad ways of defining a business: looking at the supply (what providers can bring to the table) and the demand (what customers want and need).[12]

Now this logic digs deeper and gets far more basic and less particularized than products and geographies, but it still isn't quite enough to build a comprehensive tool for brainstorming alternative business definitions. Since markets are ecosystems of various organizations and individuals, we have to look beyond and behind the narrow transaction interface of the buyer–seller duo, or "dyad." We need to broaden our investigation to other players in the value network.

Bringing these two pairs of perspectives together – supply versus demand, on the one hand, and the immediate providers and customers versus the wider system behind them, on the other

Figure 2.1. Business Definition Radar: Zooming Out Tool for Finding Novel Business Definitions.

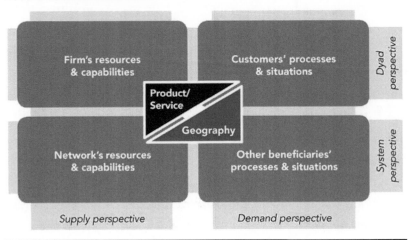

hand – we built the tool[13] for the zooming out process in Figure 2.1.

The supply perspective starts by assuming that all resources and capabilities, once purveyed by the firm, potentially unlock value for someone. Therefore, each individual resource, capability, and their combinations should be investigated as potential markets. Is it possible to re-organize the resources and capabilities of the firm or the network for higher value creation? Would someone be willing to pay for that value creation? In a similar vein, the demand perspective proposes that direct customers and other beneficiaries encompass an unlimited number of market opportunities. Thus, each direct and indirect customer should be analyzed for market opportunities. Are there needs or challenges that are so far not optimally met? What kind of business opportunities can be found from customers' situations?

Next we will box the compass, heading down all four directions of zooming out in turn.

Focus on Firm Resources and Capabilities

As we begin with the northwest direction of zooming out, you may have noticed we've already snuck in the word "capabilities" a couple of times alongside the more familiar "resources." The former needs addressing. After the word "strategy," "capability" is probably the most misused term in management literature. Capability is variously and casually tossed about as a synonym for resources, individual competences, organizational behavior, processes, and so forth. In this book, we cut the Gordian knot with a simple distinction between resources and capabilities:

- Resources are tangible and intangible things that the organization has, ranging from factories and machinery to intellectual property rights and tacit know-how.

- Capabilities refer to the organization's ability to do stuff with its resources.

Thus, the abilities to run projects, engineer factories, manage a multicultural workforce, and create compelling sales arguments are all organizational capabilities.

The resource and capability perspective can make for a powerful new frame to detect business opportunities. First, you brainstorm the whole reservoir of a firm's resources and capabilities. Then you identify individual resources, capabilities, or their combinations that aren't yet commercialized. For example, an equipment manufacturer entering a solutions business is actually commercializing its previously uncommercialized engineering, project management, installation, and risk management capabilities.

Whereas you may associate Japanese giant Toyota only with autos (it's been making them since the 1930s and overtook the iconic General Motors some time ago), the multinational is a fine example of a company that continuously and systematically scans its resource and capability reservoir to identify new business opportunities. And this strategy has earned it remarkable success.

Toyota's main capabilities are its production system and its product development system. Toyota's New Business Project Committee reviews the outputs of these systems, with an aim to find know-how, methods, materials, and technologies that could be used in Toyota's sideline businesses. Examples of Toyota's current sideline businesses are housing, aerospace, gardening, consultancy, sports, and advertising. (If slipping into conversation that you run a sideline in aerospace doesn't impress, we don't know what would.) Cars are conspicuously absent from that list.

So far, Toyota has succeeded in commercializing various innovations stemming from its core capabilities, but bypassing the product-based business definition that would start and end with entire automobiles. For example, the keyless entry system, painting methods, and shatter-resistant glass in Toyota cars are also used in prefabricated houses. In a similar vein, Toyota's production system expertise has been commercialized as consulting tools such as its signature just-in-time deliveries and the *Kaizen* system, which originally meant simply improvement but has become a watchword for continuous improvement.

The sideline businesses remain secondary for Toyota; in 2005, they made up 6% of the firm's total turnover. But everything's relative. Six percent of Toyota's turnover adds up to a tidy sum: If Toyota's sideline businesses were managed as an independent company, they would have ranked 192nd on the S&P 500 list in 2005.[14]

A similar example of the value of resources and capabilities as a business definition and market frame is the story of UPS which headed this chapter, specifically the episode under Oz Nelson in the 1990s.

Focus on Network Resources and Capabilities

Next, we turn and head southwest on the zooming out tool. Now, no matter how big the firm, the resources and capabilities within its organizational boundaries are always finite. This is especially true since management dogma in recent decades has favored specialization and focus. Highly specialized single-business companies may appeal to investors, or, if nothing else, to fund managers: They are easy to analyze and place in investment portfolios. But this orthodoxy has left the firms themselves vulnerable to economic cycles and stripped of so-called "redundant" resources and capabilities that could have turned out to be rather handy.

Luckily, zooming out to identify business opportunities based on resources and capabilities needn't confine you to those resources and capabilities under your firm's direct control. Equal, or even larger, possibilities often reside in the resource and capability base of the entire value network.

Zooming out from the network perspective starts with an in-depth analysis of the value network. What is the purpose of the network? Which actors are involved? What resources and capabilities do the actors possess? What resources and capabilities is the network missing? Armed with this information, a firm with an innovative business definition re-imagines itself by brainstorming opportunities to re-organize the value network for higher efficiency, higher value creation, or both.

Take an enterprising taxi operator. Her network is her city's transport grid. The network stars the obvious lead actors: bus and rail providers; other taxi operators; trendy cycle rickshaw outfits around the scenic, touristy bits; and a massive preponderance of private individuals in cars. If her city is like ours, the private car resources will be scandalously underutilized. Even cars in America's High-Occupancy Vehicle lanes rarely carry more than two or three occupants. (And that assumes opportunistic solo drivers aren't in fact trying their luck with wigged, dressed mannequins, or passing off articles of incorporation of a company on the seat beside them as a passenger under the principle of corporate personhood, or counting their unborn children − all three have happened.[15]) And the most jam-packed cars at morning and evening rush hour still sit empty and idle in carparks and garages the other 22 hours a day. So, why not re-conceive the urban transport network in such a way that the car resources are put to a better use? The taxi operator would do better to join Zipcap or Uber.

An almost literal "poster child" for network-based zooming out is French advertiser JCDecaux. Since 1964, JCDecaux has become the world's leading outdoor advertisers thanks to a truly innovative business model based on "street furniture." (A business model denotes the precise operationalization of a business definition.) Forty years before Internet entrepreneurs coined the phrase "monetizing eyeballs," JCDecaux looked at the tens of thousands of commuters waiting at the network of often dreary and defaced bus, train, and tram stops kept up and saw an unutilized resource: a captive audience for advertisers. The company took expensive upkeep off the hands of municipalities in return for the right to sell outdoor advertising space (that's the "poster" part) on those tired old stops, now slickly rebranded as "street furniture." Since no advertiser had the capabilities to enter the street furniture market, JCDecaux created a business model with itself as the intermediary between the municipalities, the advertisers, and the consumers. To play its role in the renewed network, JCDecaux acquired the capabilities necessary for designing and maintaining street furniture.

This business model based on network reconfiguration has flourished. Currently, JCDecaux operates in more than 60 different countries right around the world. In 2013, the company's turnover clocked 2.68 billion euro, or a smidgen over 3 billion USD. Of this, almost 45% came from street furniture, which remains JCDecaux's most profitable business with over 15% earnings before interest and taxes.[16]

Re-organizing value networks is no mean feat though. All networks have evolved over time, and the forces of inertia can be considerable. Die-hard traditions and handed-down industry recipes tend to keep the network configuration as it is. Thus, the firm seeking to re-organize value networks should ensure that the new market configuration is not just superior but far superior to the previous one. It seems few of us are willing to change unless the benefits of the change greatly outweigh the burden. As well as the dangling of rewards, the wielding of hefty market power can also help to sell the new network configuration to others.

Sometimes it takes a coalition of corporate heavyweights to dislodge an established value network. Housing and construction are a case in point example, being highly established sectors where forces of inertia are especially strong. BoKlok (a Swedish name translating roughly to "Live smart") is an innovative housing concept developed by IKEA and Skanska, a global construction and project development company out of Sweden. In 1996, IKEA's founder Ingvar Kamprad met Skanska's board chair Melker Schörling at a Swedish housing fair. They got talking about how all the new homes showcased at the fair were expensive and luxurious. Yet, the most casual observer could see a pressing need for affordable housing, no such model had materialized.

Ingvar Kamprad's vision, however, was precisely to create affordable homes for ordinary people. Skanska was a keen partner in this project, especially given that Skanska's clientele for new builds in its home market of Sweden consisted mainly of the over-50s. This demographic would be nicely complemented by IKEA's core clientele of 20- to 30-year-olds.

One year on from Schörling and Kamprad's *tête-à-tête*, keys to homes in the first four BoKlok developments were jingling in their new owners' palms. Sold at IKEA, BoKlok is as close to a flat-pack home as you can get, in keeping with the BoKlok philosophy that everyone deserves the same chance to live well. BoKlok is designed the IKEA way: first deciding the (affordable) price tag and then designing the corresponding industrialized production, efficient space use, and high-quality Scandinavian finish. In order to ensure a quick build, as well as cost-effective and sustainable building materials, BoKlok partnered with Finland's Stora Enso to develop wooden building modules specifically for BoKlok developments. Later on, the partner network was expanded to take in the Nordic finance heavyweight Nordea, as IKEA and Skanska realized that the turnkey BoKlok concept was attracting a lot of attention from "property virgins" unfamiliar with housing financing. Nordea's tailored housing loans are now integrated as an option into the BoKlok concept.

Since 1997, over 100 BoKlok developments have gone up in Sweden, comprising over 5,000 units. The concept has also debuted in Denmark, Norway, Finland, Germany, and the United Kingdom. Homebuyers in Poland may be next in line for the BoKlok opportunity.[17]

Focus on Customer Processes and Situations

Next we head northeast on the zooming out tool, to break out of the myopia of product-based business definitions in the new direction of investigating customers' processes and situations. We'll go on the record upfront here: We think no business defined around the customer is ever a mature one, since there are always opportunities to help customers to co-create more use value for themselves.

To make the discussion about customer-oriented zooming out more tangible, we have divvied this section into B2B and B2C parts.

B2B – Improving Customers' Processes

All products and services provided to B2B customers are used in some business process. No matter how commoditized the market, no firm purchases electricity, office supplies, or IT consulting for the product itself. All purchases enable the customer to do something or solve a specific problem. Electricity keeps the production lines rolling, office supplies facilitate white collar work, and IT consulting can measurably boost productivity. But the customer isn't wedded to electricity, office supplies, or IT consulting *per se*: If another suitor offers equal or better effect, the customer will have no hesitation in switching his affections to them instead. (Customers — us included — are shameless like that.)

Customer process exploration harnesses this insight for business innovation. It implies thoroughly analyzing the customer's business process to devise ways to improve or replace the process. The supplier needs a good grasp of the customer's own customer base, as well as of the existing logic by which the customer creates value for that base.

Although little-known by the public, an example of a firm that has systematically sought new businesses from its customers' processes is IBM.[18] For decades, IBM was, famously, the leading provider of IT hardware and software. As these businesses matured, IBM started investigating its customers' processes for new opportunities. The realization soon dawned that it could help its customers cut costs and raise productivity by offering outsourcing services for support processes. IBM took further steps to find new businesses from its customers' processes. It now provides business process re-engineering services to improve customers' core processes. The step from an outsourcing service provider to business process consultant was supported by the acquisition of accountancy giant PwC's then consulting practice in 2002.

When exploring possibilities for customer process enhancement, you need to analyze the customers' goals, challenges, earnings logics, and cost structures. And with B2B customers especially, your pitch must translate the new innovation into dollar gains. You might for instance show that the changes in processes you're proposing will boost revenues by letting the customer expand their operations or enhance their own customer acquisition. Customer process innovation may also aim at decreasing costs by either lowering fixed or variable costs or releasing capital employed.

B2C — From Customer Processes to Consumer Practices

If the previous examples approach business opportunity exploration from B2B, processual, and rational viewpoints, consumer practices approach the same phenomenon from B2C, experiential, and contextual viewpoints.

Practices refer to ways of doing. Think of them as a set of routinized actions which take place in a certain context. This context may consist of tools, know-how, images, physical space, and different actors. We all engage in many different practices every day: those related to sleeping, communicating, eating, traveling, and so forth. From this perspective, the role of a firm is to improve consumer practices so that they co-create more use value for the consumer. In so doing, the firm may secure a more valuable position in the practice in question — bigger, more profitable, more solid.

Practices furnish several interesting opportunities for business redefinition. First, the firm can extend its business to cover adjacent consumer practices with more or less the same product as before. The growth in the consumption of wine in so-called non-wine countries — those without a long history of producing the beverage — over the past decade lends itself to such an explanation. In the past, wine was mainly associated with fine-dining practices. Today, a glass of red or white has become a part of the everyday dinner and low-key eating out practices as well, thus expanding the overall market.

Second, the firm can seek to enhance practices in which it already has a presence. It might bring new products, services, or information to bear, or extensions across time or space.

The practice could also be rendered more valuable by bringing in new actors or new images. Take information searching. Does anyone remember having to traipse to a library and pore over filing cabinets of dusty cards, only to discover that the book which might possibly have answered your question was out? Thanks to the revolution of the Web and the evolution of successive search engines bringing in new actors, new technologies, and new know-how, the current workaday practice of googling seems a casual miracle by comparison. No wonder millenarians and digital natives gape at such primitiveness only one generation back.

When you're seeking to influence practices, keep in mind they're the results of long development processes, bound by time and culture. Consequently, they're most often path dependent and slow to evolve. While the boundaries between traceable evolution and sheer, disruptive novelty are debatable, you're far more likely to build a new practice on existing ones than hatch an entirely novel one in an empty practice space.

However, that's not to stop firms creating brand new *businesses* on these slowly evolving practices. By way of illustration, take another walk down memory lane — turn right after the library — and consider the practice of listening to music. In the 1970s, the main product business associated with music listening was LPs (translation for the younger generation: Long Play records, before vinyl became retro) on record players, although audio cassette players were a portable and drive-able alternative if you didn't mind occasionally winding an unspooling ribbon of tape back by maneuvering the reel with your pencil. Then digital happened and CDs dominated. Next, following the illegal but influential Napster interlude, the early 2000s brought the rise of iPod and other MP3 music players, until Spotify let us rent music to go. At time of writing in 2016, rapper Jay Z hopes his year-old venture Tidal will unseat Spotify,[19] but if his doesn't another probably will; and so, on the evolution goes. That's a single practice (listening to music) which has supported four or five incarnations of product businesses in a mere four decades.

Focus on Other Beneficiaries' Processes and Situations

As we finish boxing the compass and head southeast, we see that business redefinition can also be brainstormed by looking at other potential beneficiaries than the current direct customers. Zooming out from the other-benefactor perspective follows the same logic as the customer perspective, but the focal point is different. Instead of innovating value creation for the existing customers, you're doing so for others.

Innovating new value beyond the current customer base usually takes one of the following two forms: creating more value to customers' customers; and separating user and payer roles.

Creating more value to customers' customers. Many B2B companies in particular find the demand for their products and services is dependent on the demand for their customers' product and services. For example, it's quite hard to sell more than one camera lens per mobile phone — in the economics lingo, they're perfect one-to-one complements. Therefore, producers of lenses for mobile phones are by default limited to the number of annual sales of camera phones. But lens producers needn't sit tight. One obvious side-step is to innovate ways to raise the demand for camera phones. Another is to come up with new portable devices that could be used as cameras — spy-like pen cameras, anyone?

Intel, the world leader in silicon innovations, such as microprocessors, chipsets, and motherboards, exemplifies a company systematically expanding its business by supporting the value creation of its customers' customers. Even though Intel has no direct consumer customers, in 1996 it became one of the first companies to hire social scientists and form its own ethnography team.[20] Today Intel employs some 60 ethnographers, and counting. They're researching topics including digital health and technology for emerging markets.

Why the sudden ethnographic enthusiasm? Because Intel believes that a better understanding of the end users lets it innovate better solutions for its main customers. The company's organization chart tells the story, as its business areas are defined based on end uses. With considerable digital dexterity, as it were, these uses include not only "mobile lifestyle" but "digital home," "digital enterprise," and the aforementioned "digital health."

Separating user and payer roles. Although, or perhaps because, the User Pays motto has come to sound all but axiomatic, firms can open interesting new market opportunities by going against this conventional wisdom. The two-sided business models of commercial TV channels and Google's search engine are classic examples of the user/payer split. Consumers watch television or use Google to search new information for free, as the providers of these services get their revenue streams from advertisers. That is, decades on from JCDecaux's poster audience, your eyeballs just got monetized modern style: digitally.

But there are other ways to separate user and payer roles than advertisement-based business models. Oftentimes a company's business products and services offer indirect benefits to parties other than the direct customers. And sometimes these indirect benefits are so large that the indirect beneficiaries are willing to pitch in financially – if not pick up the entire bill. Bright Horizons, an international player in the childcare space, is an excellent example.[21] Traditionally, parents have been responsible for finding and paying for their children's daycare. But as any astute boss knows, moms, dads, and the kids aren't the only beneficiaries of professional and flexible childcare or the only ones who suffer in its absence. In particular, employers of young parents bear some of the impact of poor, unreliable, or inflexible childcare. Those impacts include absenteeism, reduced productivity and employee satisfaction, and increased employee turnover.

Bright Horizons has therefore forged a business model where employers pick up the tab for childcare services. And by partnering with employers, Bright Horizons has also secured a higher price point than usual in the childcare market. On top of that, changing the perspective from parents to employers has helped Bright Horizon to innovate new services, which employers can provide to their employees in order to help them juggle work and family. Currently, Bright Horizons has over 850 clients in the United States, United Kingdom, Ireland, the Netherlands, India, and Canada. They cover a wide range of industries and such big names as Johnson & Johnson, Booz Allen Hamilton, and NBC Universal.

Zooming Out Too Far: Beware Reckless Diversification

Zooming out very often unearths business opportunities that would demand radical changes from the company in question. They may require an entirely new product or business model, or you may have to start building customer relationships from scratch with unfamiliar customer segments in a place far, far away from your corporate HQ.

But should you go after even the most far-fetched business opportunity, if the upside is large enough? Well, not always. From the subjective and positively selfish perspective, a new business idea is viable only if it leaves you better off when all pros and cons are counted.

An often-overlooked risk of novel business definitions is to lead organizations to diversify unsustainably or beyond their means. The big strategy consultancies have been investigating the limits of diversification over the last few years. In its 2012 study of S&P 500 companies, McKinsey concluded that from the shareholder value perspective, diversification doesn't always pay off.[22] The upside of diversification is that when investigating the annualized total shareholder value creation in 2002–2010, diversified companies seem to be more reliable performers than their more focused counterparts. In fact, the majority of the diversified companies deliver 5–15% annual increase in shareholder value creation. However, diversification doesn't limit the downside risk. Both focused and diversified companies can destroy shareholder value. What's more, being diversified seems to cap the upside potential. We note that none of the diversified companies were able to deliver over 20% annual increases in shareholder value – even though such numbers were achievable in some focused companies.

In a similar vein, Strategy& (a combination of PwC's current consulting arm and the former Booz & Company) has recently counseled against growth strategies based on adjacency moves.[23] According to them, such strategies often blind companies to growth opportunities in their core businesses. Instead, companies slip into areas where they lack competitive capabilities, and apart from anything else, this dilutes the coherence of their business models.

So, where to draw the line between necessary and reckless diversification? The answer seems to lie in the organizational capabilities: The most successful diversified companies tend to focus on those businesses in which they can use their distinctive capabilities to the fullest. Running a reality check along the lines of "Do we have the necessary capabilities to go after this business opportunity?" can also help you to assemble a corporate portfolio in which the different parts of the business reinforce each other.

For an elegant example of related diversification which has reinforced a business, rather than stretched it too thin, consider the iPod and its relation to Apple's then core business of Mac computers. The iPod business was built on Apple's core capabilities such as the ability to create intuitive technology interfaces and excellence in product design. Over and above that, iPod enhanced the value proposition of the Mac, because it worked seamlessly with the flagship computers and just possibly also suggested an extra edge of hipness.

ZOOM IN: FIND GROWTH POCKETS AND ADJACENCIES

If zooming out dramatically widens our field of vision by pulling back from product-meets-geography business definitions, zooming in goes telephoto to reveal a more granular and nuanced view of your business opportunities. The point is to identify potential growth areas, usually in an environment that seems already mature, or hemmed in. Either those areas will be overlooked, immature pockets where you already operate but whose growth potential you can further tap by allocating more resources to extract maximum benefit from market growth, or they'll be spaces adjacent to your existing business which are viable to expand into and also promise high growth.

Zooming In as Turbocharged Market Segmentation

Traditional market segmentation slices your business opportunities along just a few dimensions, or what we call criteria; and, importantly, the resulting segmentations are often treated as strict taxonomic alternatives. In other words, you can segment by, for instance, product. Or geography. Or customer, and so on. But these criteria are mainly "either … or," rarely "both … and."

In real-world strategy you could divide, say, a hotel business by price points, yielding segments such as budget, mid-market, high-end, and luxury. But the same business could equally well be segmented by other criteria: customer group (consumer, corporate); the purpose of the trip (leisure, business); the broader geography (USA, Mexico, Canada); the type of destination (main cities, second-tier cities, other urban areas, rural); the position in the value chain (whether you own the real estate, operate the hotel, or own the brand and operate the channel); and so on. In the real world, you have to make choices along all these dimensions, not just one or two.

The point is, it is both more powerful and far more realistic to consider multiple choices and thus multiple segmentation dimensions together, and at the same time. This is precisely what zooming in achieves. And again, the purpose of zooming in, as of zooming out, is to brainstorm new business definitions and thus frames, which will in turn open your eyes to the true richness of the market ecosystem in which your business operates – the market being our ultimate target for shaping.

The Tool for Zooming In Is the Business Arena Generator

Zooming in uses the tool depicted in Figure 2.2: the Business Arena Generator, or Arena Generator, or even just Generator to its friends. This tool deliberately draws from a *large set of criteria* (the rows), each with several options (boxes along the rows), and experimentally *combines boxes from multiple rows at once*. We've used the word "Generator" because it's creative and experimental. This isn't some purely mechanical tool that lets the operator read off solutions like an old-fashioned slide rule. Rather, the Generator is a potent idea creator which requires a judicious operator to choose and then limit her criteria and options in order to produce a manageable number of likely, fruitful, and feasible combinations.

Figure 2.2. Example of Business Arena Generator for a Hotel Company.

Price point	Budget	Mid-market	High-end
	Luxury		
Focus customers	Consumer	Corporate	
Purpose of trip	Leisure	Business	
Country	USA	Canada	Mexico
Urban–rural spectrum	Main cities	Second-tier cities	Other urban areas
	Rural areas		
Value chain position	Own real estate	Operate hotel	Own brand & operate channel

When a discerning strategist zooms in using the Business Arena Generator, she is experimentally overlaying multiple market segmentation criteria at the same time to generate interesting microsegments.[24] We call these microsegments – surprise, surprise – "business arenas."[25] A good strategist can generate interesting arenas for further analysis by picking one option from one criterion and combining it with another sensible option from a second relevant criterion and then others from a third, fourth, or even more. On top of that, sometimes you can thread together more than one option per row, as the options aren't always strictly exclusive (this is real-life strategy, and in real life, categories tend not to have clear-cut boundaries). Although that may sound complicated, the resulting Arena Generator needn't be overly intricate. Figure 2.2 illustrates what an Arena Generator for our hypothetical hotel company could look like. The sample arena picked out by the highlighting in this figure, and reading down from the first row to the last, would consist of catering for high-end consumers taking leisure trips in Canada's rural areas by operating a hotel on your own real estate.

Systematic zooming in via the Arena Generator reveals multiple perspectives on the same market at the same time. As consultants, we have used this tool with dozens of clients from many industries. Every client has gained fresh insights into their business definition which traditional market segmentation, applying one or two dimensions at a time, had obscured.

In a moment, we'll explain how to build your own Arena Generator and optimize its use to your circumstances. But first, let's look at the general applications for this tool.

Three Broad Applications of the Business Arena Generator

You can apply the Arena Generator in three main ways, depending on your company's situation and strategic objectives:

1. *Identifying growth opportunities in a slow-growth business.*
   Imagine, say, an elevator business operating in Western
   Europe. Given that this region as a whole is wealthy and highly
   developed with plenty of modern conveniences and a newish
   building stock, you'd expect such a business to be very mature.
   The average annual growth rate should be in single digits. But
   zooming in would reveal at least one growth pocket. The business of modernizing residential elevators in France is growing
   well above average, so would repay additional resource. And
   likewise, in over a decade applying zooming in and the Arena
   Generator with clients, we have never once failed to find fast-
   growth pockets, no matter how mature the client's overall business looked at first blush.

2. *Detecting adjacency moves that will work in practice.* Besides
   revealing relative differences in growth and profitability poten-
   tials in your existing business, zooming in is a powerful tool for
   highlighting possible accessible diversification opportunities or
   adjacencies. Copious strategy ink[26] has flowed expounding how
   companies can grow by expanding along the value chain, entering new geographies, adding new products and services, using
   new distribution channels, and/or addressing new customer segments. As we've said before, the catch is that in practice such
   adjacency moves will seldom succeed if executed in isolation.
   For example, successfully entering a completely new geographical area — the commonest adjacency maneuver — might require
   using a new distribution channel, addressing a new customer
   segment, and modifying the offering of product and services,
   all at the same time. The risk is that you'll underestimate the
   difficulty of these requisite steps if you stick with traditional segmentation. By contrast, business arena thinking explicitly brings
   all these viewpoints together, helping you craft truly viable
   adjacency strategies by picking and mixing criteria and options
   instead of treating these growth choices as separate decisions.

3. *Bringing strategic clarity when faced with too large a business opportunity — or after zooming out.* Even though we developed zooming in and the Business Arena Generator precisely to help firms generate growth opportunities in what seemed growth-deprived contexts (and adjacency moves in seemingly hemmed-in contexts), paradoxically it has turned out also to be a great way of winnowing down strategic options for "more-of-the-same" growth or adjacency moves when these have become too many or too large. Now, having too many opportunities like that might sound like a rather luxurious predicament. Yet, with due deference to Mae West, too much of a good thing is not always wonderful, especially if you don't know how to choose. In reality, many companies in fast-growth businesses get bewildered by the sheer proliferation of opportunities and end up undermining their growth by futilely chasing all of them at once. If you aren't saying no to anything, how do your customers know what you stand for — or what you are good at? For example, we've found many software firms working in the broad ambit of e-invoicing and related process automation are operating in a market where there is still natural business growth. However, many have pretty limited resources, so they need to make educated choices on such matters as which customers to serve, which go-to-market channels to use, and whom to partner with. The Business Arena Generator helps firms to see their opportunities, analyze, and prioritize them. In a similar vein, zooming in and prioritizing the resulting business arenas can be a necessary step after zooming out in order to make the new broad-brush business definition more manageable.

Customize Your Own Arena Generator

To run the optimal zooming in analysis on your own business, follow these four steps.

Build your own Business Arena Generator out of relevant criteria rows and salient options along each row. The first task in zooming in is to come up with the criteria that could be relevant for segmenting your particular business. There is no such thing as a master taxonomy of all possible business arena dimensions, but you can get a long way by mixing and matching from the following tasty selections, so think of them as our complimentary smorgasbord (sorry, couldn't help it — we're Nordic; it was all we could do just to keep the accent marks off):

Note that you then need to come up with what we've called "salient" options along each row. Again, these often can't be exhaustive and frequently shouldn't be even if they could! For instance, a dimension like geography is infinitely divisible by using ever-finer slices: continents, countries, cities, suburbs, blocks, and so forth. But even in the finite dimensions, some divisions are more useful than others. A wise strategist who knows her business well will be able to select.

Note also that options within a criterion are allowed to overlap if need be, and you can choose more than one per row when you generate each arena (the last row of Figure 2.2 is an example) — or even skip one criterion row with all its options if it is not relevant for the particular arena that you are sketching.

- *Geography*. A key part of the classical approach to analyzing markets; divvying the market up by physical location.

- *Products/services*. Many industries already have highly institutionalized product categories, which offer a natural series of business definition partitions (for example, savings, investment, insurance, and loan products in finance or new equipment vs. after-sales services in various machinery industries). Core technologies can also serve as a dimension.

- *Customer segments*. Business arenas can offer new viewpoints on your business definition by slicing it into demographic, socio-economic or lifestyle segments, or segments based on customers' value to the firm.

- *Value chain position.* One's position along the value chain dimension often drives growth and profitability potential, so makes another natural division analytic.

- *Time.* In B2C businesses especially, one viable way of exploring the market is often to examine customers' use of time and the slots in their calendar or daily timetable. The main business opportunities might be found, for instance, in weekday evenings, minibreaks, days off, or the time used in commuting.

- *Distribution channel.* The availability of various distribution channels can also explain relative differences in market opportunities. Thus, beverage firms analyze their market opportunities separately by Hotel/Restaurant/Café, or HoReCa, on the one hand, and retail channels, on the other. To take another example, a sports apparel retailer might be interested in separating the traditional retailing market from e-retail.

- *Price.* Price acts as a natural criterion and price points as its natural divisions. Thus, premium-priced groceries often feature different market characteristics than their discount foodstuff cousins, for instance. And speaking of rich and poor cousins, consider the overload of price options you now face when flying. As the margins on air travel pinch ever tighter, savvy carriers can tell that business outlooks for first class, business class, premium economy, economy, coach, and no-frills air travel are likely to differ considerably. That's why the airline industry is constantly re-stratifying your experience of the stratosphere with finer and finer calibrations of classes and seat configurations (from the romance of cuddle class to the rigors of cattle class), accessories (you can all but fly the plane with some of the software in those seatback screens), and accompanying food and beverage and service privileges (complimentary Veuve

Clicquot Rosé opens the possibility of drinking your fare's worth before wheels-down).

- *Brand ownership.* In some industries, brand ownership is a useful partition for understanding business development and dynamics. Consider for one the distinction between branded and private label (store brand) goods in food-related markets.

- *End use or application.* Of course you can also zoom in on the various end uses or applications for the particular product or service. Examples of different applications for a certain chemical may be in water treatment, pulp production, and sluicing in mines.

A word of warning when you're brainstorming possible market arena dimensions: Beyond a certain point, more is worse, not better (again: Mae, our apologies). In most markets, you could come up with a good eight to 10 relevant dimensions and barely break a sweat, but we recommend you whittle the final selection down to somewhere between three and six dimensions. The reason for curbing your enthusiasm like this is simple math (a subject remarkably adept at inducing exactly this reaction). The thing is, the number of possible market arenas you're forcing yourself to analyze grows exponentially, not linearly, as you add each new dimension to your Business Arena Generator — remember it's a generator, or multiplier, not a table. So, three dimensions with three options each generate 27 unique business definition arenas, but adding just one more three-element row catapults the number of permutations to 81.

Identify interesting business arenas for further analysis. By now you've got your business arena map, defined by the selected criteria (such as "brand ownership") and the categories that account for the main strategic options under each criterion (such as "own brand," "private label," "third-party brand"). The next step in zooming-in analysis is to identify interesting arenas from this map for further analysis.

As just noted in our mathematical word of warning, your average five-row Arena Generator will have enough dimensions and categories to beget over 3,000 unique market arenas (five rows of five options each gives 3,125 permutations). In fact, the highest number of theoretical business arenas we've worked with was over 33 million — for a Generator that contained nine rows and between three and 15 boxes on each! No-one's going to trawl through all those. So as well as counseling moderation in the number of criteria you list to start with, we'd again preach discretion and good judgment in the combinations you then choose to run. And once more, the able strategist who knows her business will soon sniff out the most fruitful combos.

Once the rows and boxes are in place, you can choose from essentially two techniques for stringing the boxes together: elimination and combination. The elimination method starts with all possible business arenas and then proceeds to eliminate those that are logically impossible, or uninteresting for the company in question (for example, too small or too competitive), or which require capabilities that the company lacks. We tend to use the elimination method when the number of potential market arenas is in the hundreds and not the thousands (or millions). In the combination method, you run a miniature brainstorming session around each category under each dimension: "What other boxes should I combine this box with to generate something really interesting for our company?" We employ the combination method when the number of potential business arenas is too big for the elimination method.

Analyze those arenas using customized/targeted data. The upside of traditional one- (or two-) dimensional segmentation analyses is that data for those segments abounds. Research agencies, stock market analysts, and industry associations churn out more research reports than you can shake a stick at on most product categories or geographies. The downside is, this stock-standard information is readily available to all players, and the players all too readily and unquestioningly avail themselves of it. And right there, you have a prime reason why firms stuck in this old mode tend to perceive only the same few business opportunities and react with strikingly similar, not to say me-too, strategies. It's the same old: a self-perpetuating cycle of limited research, limited vision, and limited strategy. If firms all define their businesses using the same information, they will regard themselves as stuck in one industry and doomed to compete to share one, supposedly fixed market.

By contrast, zooming in offers an escape from industry group-think and a cornucopia of business opportunities your competitors are too blinkered to notice. Beware though: Novelty is a double-edged sword; the upside and downside are just reversed from those in the last paragraph. The downside of zooming in on novel business opportunities is that no research institute is likely to be generating off-the-shelf data in a format compatible with the firm's business arena framework. After all, the strength of the business arena analyses is that they're company specific! So, the price of a unique business definition is the time and effort needed to run your own analyses.

But firms shouldn't overly tremble at the task of generating data for their own arena analyses. For one thing, the number of data points needed per arena is usually quite manageable. Generally quantitative information about the arena itself (size, profitability, growth rate, and so on), the company's own business in the arena (turnover, profit, products and services offered, and so forth), as well as some qualitative information about the arena (main competitors, key trends, and their ilk) will suffice to support decision-making. For another thing, you can mostly get right-enough information by cross-referencing the existing market studies and articulating your organization's tacit know-how. Remember, you're researching to come up with a workable heuristic to inform your own action under uncertainty and time pressures, not seeking publication in an academic A* journal. So quiet your inner perfectionist voice and act on the assumption that close enough is good enough.

Prioritize the list and select focal business arenas = your new business definition. As illustrated by the Aesop fable about the fox, unable to choose among hundreds of ways of escaping from the hounds, and the cat, with only one way, extensive analysis can be futile, or even fatal.[27] So, arena analysis should always lead to prioritizing arenas and selecting the focal arenas − which will form the core of your brand-new business definition.

You need to prioritize and narrow down to a few focal arenas, then communicate these internally, so that your entire organization has a shared view on what your business definition is, which are the most important business opportunities during the next few years, and what kind of resources you require to turn these opportunities into reality. The appropriate prioritization criteria should always emulate the firm's strategy. So a company that is looking for growth inside a slow-growth context will use a different set of criteria than a firm interested in finding viable adjacencies. However, we can identify criteria for business arena prioritization that are commonly useful. In particular, we suggest:

- Arena's attractiveness from short-term business perspective (for instance in terms of size or profitability).

- Arena's attractiveness from long-term business perspective (for instance in terms of innovation potential or arena growth rate).

- Firm's market power in the arena (measured by, for example, the arena share, channel dominance, brand power, or customer loyalty).

- Competitors' market power in the arena.

- Competitor reactiveness in the arena (measured by, for example, the relative importance of the arena to the competitors' turnover and/or profit accrual).

Especially if the company has analyzed dozens of different arenas, it may be worthwhile to visualize the analysis results to support managerial decision-making. In such visualizations the multidimensional arenas are "forced" into a series of two-dimensional pictures, each illustrating different perspectives on arena data such as arena growth, profitability, intensity of competition, intensity of innovation, and so forth.

Starbucks: A Zooming In Success Story

How much could zooming in do for your firm? Well, look what it did for Starbucks. The Seattle-based roaster and retailer of specialty coffee has penetrated 50 countries, and counting, since 1971. Although we haven't sat in the boardroom and watched the vice presidents actually whiteboard a Business Arena Generator, we certainly regard Starbucks as an exemplar of the principles of zooming in. Consciously or unconsciously, it has overlain multiple business perspectives simultaneously to come up with ways to surf the global wave of coffee and café culture. Reflexively, you'd guess Starbucks' primary business definition would relate to its core product. But instead of defining its business around merely coffee or coffee shops, from the early days Starbucks took as its territory the micro-segment "luxury coffee outside home." That's a signature zoom-in, multi-criterion concept right there. Nor has Starbucks confined itself to the world's favorite caffeine delivery system. Its product range features various foods and now, riding what may be a new global beverage wave, tea.

However, product is but one criterion, or dimension, of Starbucks' multidimensional management model. Another dimension of their business definition consists of their business models:

franchising, own retail operations, and subcontracting for hotels. The third business definition dimension we would identify concerns the different coffee shop concepts, of which drive-thru' is among the fastest growing in the United States. A fourth looks at time: Starbucks' business is different during different times of the day: morning versus lunchtime versus evening, peak hours versus off-peak hours.

Finally, Starbucks overlays geography on its business definition. True to its granular approach, Starbucks' geographical analysis works at multiple levels. On the top level are countries, which Starbucks assesses by national coffee consumption, coffee shop culture, and the structure of the coffee-related industries. If the corporation decides to enter a particular country, it then analyzes the geographical market aspect in more detail. For example, its Chinese entry strategy was defined around certain residential and business districts in Beijing. The arenas get even more fine-grained though, right down to a systematic placement of new coffee shops near subway station entrances, for example, or on the sunny sides of streets.[28]

DECOUPLE MARKET SHAPING AND BUSINESS REDEFINITION

As we end this chapter, you're now equipped with the Business Definition Radar and Business Arena Generator tools to framestorm alternative business definitions by zooming out and zooming in, respectively. We hope this sheds new light on the fluid nature of business definitions and exciting new potential definitions for your business. We are confident that zooming out, in particular, but also zooming in, will have liberated your strategies from the dominant product-geography matrices so unimaginatively used to describe and define most businesses, and which so stubbornly cloud even well-intentioned firms' vision of their market.

But at this point in our presentations a tentative hand often goes up: "Do I have to redefine my business if I want to become a market shaper? My current business definition serves me pretty well — even though it is based on products, which you seem to dislike."

The answer is simple: No, you don't absolutely have to change or even challenge your business definition before you can start proactive market shaping. It's perfectly possible to see a rich ecosystem market and shape it even if your business definition never goes outside Ansoff's traditional product-geography matrix — although it's also perfectly possible to swim the Manhattan—Brooklyn commute or heat your dinner by rubbing sticks together. We do urge you, though, to spend some time truly thinking about your business definition, answering that timeless question "What business are you in?" and role-playing a little devilish advocacy against your instinctive answer. Because your business definition remains the most powerful frame on your perception of the slice of the market system that you are going to point to and then aspire to shape. And as the Nokia story shows, there's no point in shaping, say, the standalone mobile phone market if the future lies in a smartphones market ecosystem, but you just haven't seen that because you had your old product-view blinders on.

Conversely, sometimes changing your business definition is all it takes to meet your objectives. Let's say you got interested in market shaping because your growth is stagnant and your profitability level leaves your Board of Directors wanting for more. It is entirely conceivable you could fix both problems by merely redefining your business, so that your new business definition peels the product-geography scales from your eyes, polishes your vision, and points you to a market that is fast-growing and profitable. How great would that be? A home run by changing something that is completely under your control (business definition), without having to go through the oftentimes lengthy process of market shaping.

For completeness, this leaves the chance that at this stage you want neither to refine your business definition nor to become a market shaper. While this is a theoretical possibility, we've very rarely encountered it among innovative firms. (As for less-innovative firms, there is a reason why they are, and tend to remain, less innovative). Meanwhile though, at least you'll be applying the rich-market view, know your business definition inside out, and have some well-scrutinized evidence that it's the optimal definition and frame — for now. Because markets are changing faster than ever, we suggest you re-run the optimizing process in a few months' time.

Assuming market shaping is still on your agenda though, we devote the next chapter to exploring and exploiting all four layers of the Fan outside the core. Buckle up!

TAKEAWAYS FROM CHAPTER 2

- *Before you can begin shaping your market, you have to frame it so you can see it clearly.* Optimal framing is the first step in putting the rich, but generic, market Fan into practice in your own market, with your own firm's identity. It takes place at the core of the Fan.

- The core consists of *your business definition*, and unlike the four layers, *it is under your complete control.* It's essentially your answer to that classic cocktail party question: What do you do? or What line of business are you in?

- Not only does your business definition set your — actual and intended — identity, but it also frames how you see your market, by filtering and interpreting your market intel. Some sort of frame is inevitable. But with a narrow or rigid one you may either miss or misinterpret developments which a supple, diversified frame would have revealed as emergent trends in the market system or deliberate design of that system by market-shaping actors.

- *Most frames are as restrictive, reductive, and reflexive* as the commonest answer to that cocktail party question: "I'm in the [mobile phone] market, in [China]." In fact, this is precisely where the product, or product-geography, view worms its way in. Conversely, this is also your chance to cast it out.

- Casting out the product view requires, first, polishing your frame, or lens, to see more clearly. This is corrective: right or wrong. Second, you need to point your frame at the particular slice of the Fan, or the universe of all possible markets, where you want to operate. This slice becomes your starter market, which you might later choose to shape.

- Unlike polishing, *pointing is a matter of choice.* However, some choices end up better for growth and profitability than others. For, contrary to traditional belief, where you operate matters more to your top and bottom lines than how you operate.

- Every strategist needs at the very least to be aware of their business definition and to regularly ask whether they can make it more profitable and growth rich. Strategy gurus have long said as much, but without supplying sufficient tools or integrating the advice into our rich-market context. Our clients succeed in brainstorming alternative market frames, or "frame-storming," because, as well as the context, we supply very specific tools and processes. *The processes for frame-storming are zooming out and zooming in.*

- Zooming out — using our Business Definition Radar and many real-world examples — is the most potent way we know *to break you free from the product-geography myopia.*

- Zooming in — using our Business Arena Generator and again following real-world examples, such as Starbuck's — will *identify unnoticed growth pockets in your existing market and viable adjacencies you can expand into.*

- The exercise of optimizing your business definition and thus your market frame equips you ideally to embark on market-shaping proper. However, the two needn't go together: they can be decoupled.

3

SHAPE YOUR MARKET

How can you get practical leverage on the complexity of your firm's operating environment?

So far, strategy has lacked a framework systematic enough to make your firm's operating environment manageable without oversimplifying it into just-so stories and tautologies, sacrificing its rich potential.

Market shaping offers the first practical framework for leveraging complex environments. Having clearly defined the parts of a market system, the framework arrays clusters of those parts into a hierarchy of layers by order of both the firm's influence over them and their impact on the shape of the system and shows you how to design each one to achieve a new market shape. The goal is to generalize to every market and every firm and to operationalize without the need for traditional forms of market power.

STORA ENSO: MANY-LAYERED MARKET SHAPING

In 2008, the latest daring new idea was starting to gain traction, both at official strategy retreats and in unofficial water cooler discussions, at the venerable Finnish forestry company Stora Enso, operating successfully on four continents. (The "Stora" part may well be the world's oldest limited liability company, with one preserved share dating from 1288[1] — testimony to its ability to stay ahead of change.)

Earlier that year, Stora Enso[2] had invested in a cross-laminated timber, or CLT, plant in Austria. CLT is a massive multilayered wood construction product, like jumbo plywood, with each layer bonded cross-wise to adjacent layers for strength and rigidity. CLT enables building with solid wood, instead of "hollow" structures. And although it was too early for Stora Enso to be counting chickens, its customers were embracing the product as intended, using the CLT elements to replace concrete and bricks in single-family homes.

But the daring idea doing the rounds out of Stora Enso's Wood Products division was that, by capitalizing on both urbanization and the green economy, CLT just might also be the company's way into a new range of dwellings: "high-rise." We've put the scare quotes round that phrase because it's distinctly relative. Europeans deem anything over four stories high-rise, so, Guinness World Records stand down: We're not talking rivals to Dubai's 163-floor Burj Khalifa, which Tom Cruise famously dangled off in *Mission Impossible − Ghost Protocol*, or the Shanghai Tower, or even your average building in Manhattan. Standing in the way of what seemed an eminently reasonable dream, though, were the correspondingly archaic European building codes. Most countries' codes expressly forbade "high-rise" wooden housing. To study and overcome the regulatory obstacle, Stora Enso used its home turf of Finland as a market laboratory.

The corporate quickly realized that the real obstacle wasn't public or general political sentiment but that regulators acting without fear or favor don't want to be seen to rewrite the law for the benefit of a single company. So, Stora Enso rallied to the lobbying cause all the other Finnish forestry companies with an interest in wooden construction materials. Since the Finnish landscape is as picturesquely wooded as the postcards suggest, that's a goodly number. To counter the expected push back from the steel and concrete industries, Stora Enso also pragmatically broke its own traditions and joined the Finnish building industry association. There it wielded considerable clout because membership fees are based on members' turnover, and Stora Enso is a big concern and hence a hefty fee payer. With hard-to-resist reasoning and a little adroit wording, the company convinced the association to change its stance from "pro concrete and steel" to "material neutral" — read: open to wood.

In 2011, the offending regulations were finally amended, which raised the legal ceiling on use of wooden frames to eight stories. Job well done and market shaping over, you might think. But Stora Enso's overall market-shaping strategy was multipronged and, to borrow our Fan language again, targeted other elements and layers as well.

In addition to changing the regulations, Stora Enso had to ensure that all the other actors in their market system knew about the change — and that they had sufficient know-how to work with wooden building systems. To raise awareness, they combined a publicity campaign and a nation-wide roadshow, showcasing not just the regulatory change (alone surely a soporific PowerPoint if ever there was one) but also beautiful and functional reference buildings. For specialist know-how, Stora Enso and its compatriot forestry companies collaborated intensively with the local universities to ensure that the country's future architects and structural engineers knew how to design wooden high-rise buildings.

Educating and encouraging customers, as well as the large building companies and developers, to love the new technology also required savvy strategic moves. First, because customers didn't want to find themselves stuck with a sole provider. This holds in general, too. For customers, competing alternatives are a must to ensure safe supply and reasonable prices. So, Stora Enso rolled up its sleeves and created an open standard for wood element building that is available to everyone — including its fiercest competitors. The customer bonus from the open standard is that they can buy different elements (walls, ceilings, roofs) from different provides, confident that tab A will still fit slot B at the building site.

Second, because Finland's builders and developers are responsible for all hidden flaws in their buildings for a 10-year period post completion, you can't expect them to dance in the streets over new, untested technologies. A typical response would be more like: "Call me again when you have reference cases with zero defects that are over 10 years old." Putting their money where their mouth was, Stora Enso decided to temporarily extend their role to become a co-builder and co-developer wherever their wooden building elements were used. In practice this meant that if any problems in the wooden building elements emerged during the 10-year liability period, Stora Enso with its deeper pockets would pick up the bill — thus considerably lowering the risk of adoption for the inherently risk-minimizing builders and developers.

In just a matter of years, Stora Enso's market share in the Finnish high-rise market has gone from 0 to 4%. Sounds insignificant, but against the conservatism of the sector, even this is a considerable shift. Besides, a company that's been around since Kublai Khan (grandson of Genghis) was a cowboy knows that change takes time — even when you are the one promoting the change. In this case, you might say they nailed it.

EXCHANGE: WHAT IS SOLD, HOW IT IS PRICED, AND HOW BUYERS AND SELLERS FIND EACH OTHER

Through buying and selling, exchange frees us from isolating self-dependence and unlocks our shared resources. Not surprisingly, exchange is the foundation of all market ecosystems. But first, buyers and sellers need to find each other and agree what's being exchanged and how to price it. These are the three elements of the Exchange layer, and we explore each in turn.

Sales Item: What Is Being Exchanged, Exactly?

An ordered market has to singularize and specify the sales item. This means answering the questions What am I buying? and What's in it? (For example, am I getting the old house on this farm, or just the land? And does "the house" mean that period chandelier too?) Customers can then assess the value of the sales item and compare items.

Three types of sales item changes may conduce to favorable shaping of the broader market system: improving functionality, bundling or unbundling, and altering the property right that gets exchanged.

Improving the functionality of the product or service. Innovating new or improved products and services in small increments often reaps direct rewards. For instance, bringing out a turquoise shirt to replace last season's baby blue might secure an uptick in quarterly sales. But most market-shaping strategies aim to make a whole market wider or more profitable. For that, your sales item changes must enable customers to create significantly more value for themselves. Unless your product or service innovation can deliver that, it's not a market-shaping play.

One field famously displaying the type of fundamental functionality improvements required for market shaping has been solar power generation. Thanks to revolutions in both the energy conversion and conservation of solar cells, installed photovoltaics capacity worldwide leapt from a meager 100 megawatts in the early 1990s to over 230,000 megawatts by 2015.[3] (By way of comparison, a nuclear reactor puts out a good 1,000 megawatts.) The plummeting price of solar cells has also played a part, but we'll leave pricing till the next section.

Trouble is, leaps in functionality enough to spur the growth of the entire market system are fiendishly hard to sustain. As we saw in Chapter 1, Apple understood the systemic nature of smartphone markets and laughed all the way to the bank with its market-shaping iPhone and the App Store. Some researchers say the functionalities of earlier iPhone generations could also count as market shaping. Thus the iPhone 4 brought a multi-tasking system for apps, and iPhone 5 opened the door to apps developed with other developer tools such as Xcode.[4] But the iPhone 6 just might herald the end. Bigger screen? Accessing your email by pressing instead of tapping? Not really market-shaping functionality jumps, we'd say. And Apple's saying as much itself. In January 2016, it projected a revenue fall for 2016, the first time in more than a decade. "Apple is grappling with becoming a maturing tech company and is now entering a period of slow growth."[5]

Bundling or unbundling. James ("Jim") Barksdale, CEO of US computer services company Netscape, once tossed this one-liner to an audience as he hurried to wrap up a presentation: "Gentlemen, there's only two ways I know of to make money: bundling and unbundling."[6] Barksdale's quip is informative as a first step for aspiring market shapers. For two decades, the music world has been driven by unbundling. Nowadays you no longer need spring for an entire CD to get your favorite song, and you can even craft your own music channel. This is a trend among media generally. Over the same time, we've migrated from newspaper subscriptions to pay-per-view models. It's even happening in our other line of work besides consultancy: higher education. From various MOOCs (massive open online courses) like Khan Academy, HarvardX, or Coursera you can tailor your own Ivy League education without ever laying an admiring eye on the actual ivy.

Not all unbundling is digital. Low-cost airlines have unbundled their — very tangible — services, from check-in baggage, to in-flight meals and reserved seating. The stripped-down offering is so mini-mal, it's almost deceptive — must I pay extra if I want to bring, say, my nose? And if you rebundle you may end up paying almost the same fare as with the flagship carriers. But at least it's your choice.

Unlike consumer businesses, business-to-business companies tend to bundle up from stand-alone products to solutions. For instance, many equipment manufacturers bundle machinery and the related maintenance services into convenient one-stop-shop solutions. Swedish corporate SKF, the global leader in the small but perfectly formed matter of ball bearings, has a long track record in creating comprehensive solutions around productivity improvement, preventive maintenance, and life-cycle management of factories.

Time-poor business customers will often reward you for solution offerings. The pitfall we've found is clients failing to communicate clearly what is and is not included. B2B customers need to know what they're buying and what's in it just as much as purchasers do in any well-functioning market. And solution speak has other limits. A realtor marketing houses as "domestic habitation solutions" is unlikely to tap into the feel-good factor of the first family home.

Changing the rights being exchanged. Legally speaking, transactions in the marketplace are minicontracts, and what we are exchanging are property rights. And dry as it may sound, a little knowledge of property rights and how to switch among them can unlock considerable growth and profitability potential in your market.

With a little pinching and prodding, not to mention some wincing by legal purists, we can shoehorn the property rights relevant to most businesses into two boxes: ownership and access. When you buy a car without a financing deal, you acquire ownership rights. You can use the car at your discretion, for instance to generate a sideline Uber business and pocket the profits. And you can on-sell it when you please. Alternatively, you could acquire access rights to the car for some period by leasing instead of buying. Leases typically put constraints on the use of the car, such as stipulating service agents, and obviously you can't sell the car in your own name. Extending the analogy, you could think of the property rights in most service businesses as access rights. When you buy a haircut, you briefly access, rather than permanently own, your hairdresser's skills and equipment.

Many successful companies have grown their markets by switching their offering from ownership rights to access rights. For example, traditional equipment manufacturers have systematically changed their sales items by transforming investment goods into long-term lease contracts. The classic example dates from the 1960s. "Power-by-the-Hour" was Bristol Siddeley's nifty name for a support service for jet engines. Instead of selling the engine, the company leased both engine and accessory replacement service, chargeable by the flying hour. Airlines could now forecast operating costs without having to finance the capital expenditure. Rolls-Royce reinvented and trademarked the program in the 1980s, although rivals like Pratt & Whitney offer similar programs.

From a market-shaping perspective, this kind of sales item redefinition commands several advantages. Chief among these is to increase the size of the available market through sheer affordability. Sometimes demand grows further still, because customers can turn a long-term capital investment in equipment into an operational expense. Meanwhile, instead of parting forever with the product, the supplier gets to monitor, and often measure, the value which the customer creates from it downstream − all grist to the supplier's data mill.

The same shift from ownership to access is afoot in information technology under the name XaaS, or Everything-As-A-Service. XaaS is driven by cloud computing. The big idea of cloud computing is outsourcing of IT processes. The cloud gives the buyer access to software functionality and to the collective R&D power of many organizations, without owning the software. An example is Salesforce.com, which has collected all the resources necessary for sales management into one software-as-a-service package, making them available globally over the Internet on demand. And everything-as-a-service thinking doesn't stop at software products. Music (Spotify), movies and television series (Netflix), legal services (a Finnish law firm we'll discuss shortly), and even chemicals (the United Nations Industrial Development Organization's Chemical Leasing initiative) can all be purchased as a service.

Pricing: How Much Is It Worth?

No exchange goes ahead without a common understanding of the value of the sales item. But as we saw in Chapter 1, outside commodity markets there is little credibility in the neoclassical model of supply and demand. That model posits a mathematical function whereby perfectly rational buyers and sellers with unchanging tastes and perfect information are guided inexorably by an invisible hand to a single market-clearing price. Yet, in reality, price formation is socially situated and contingent: think relational, not just rational; perceived, not only real; more *homo* and less *economicus*.

Social factors turn on such arguably "irrational" variables as trust, provider status, and the consequent perceived quality of the product; social norms and expert opinions; regulations and institutions reducing buyers' uncertainty and risk (such as warranties and consumer protection); and a whole complex of psychological dynamics. Behavioral economics codifies these and thereby proves that sneaking suspicion some of us skeptics have held all along that market actors are secretly humans and thus less than perfectly rational. More than that, it turns out they – we – are prone to systematic errors. The 2002 Nobel economics laureate Daniel Kahneman surveys our many built-in cognitive biases in his bestseller, *Thinking Fast and Slow*. The brain's automatic system of heuristics, or mental shortcuts, is fast and in many contexts a good enough approximation, but in market decision-making, it is apt to send us confidently off in the wrong direction. Going some-what beyond Kahneman's book, widely documented systematic errors relevant to pricing include:

- *Anchoring*: referencing by available numerical cues — even if the number in question is completely unrelated to the sales item and the situation at hand.

- *Denomination effect*: spending more when denominated in small amounts (100 paltry cents feels so much more affordable than one dollar!).

- *Hyperbolic discounting*: excessively preferring short-term payoffs.

- *IKEA effect*: overvaluing objects that you've had a hand in assembling.

- *Loss aversion, endowment effect*: feeling losses more than equivalent gains, so we demand more to give up an object than we'd pay to acquire it.

- *Sunk cost fallacy* (or irrational escalation): overinvesting in a decision based on cumulative prior investment; more plainly known as throwing good money after bad.

Given how far, and how systematically, consumers fall short of paragons of rationality, the plays and ploys of pricing are a natu-ral element for market shaping. The two simplest pricing levers for market shaping are altering the price level and changing the "price carrier." (For dynamic pricing, value-based pricing, and other recent insights see the ample literature.)

Change the price level: lower — or sometimes higher — price leads to growth. Intuition, and in this case neoclassical econom-ics, rightly predicts that lowering prices will usually raise demand. This strategic play often goes hand-in-hand with chang-ing sales item functionality and unbundling. Take low-cost air-lines. Between the launch of the first low-cost carrier, Southwest

Airlines, in 1971 and 2013, commercial passenger trips per year soared from just over half a billion to well over three billion worldwide.[7] Back on the ground, India's Tata Motors has slashed the cost of cars, launching the low-cost Tata Ace truck in 2005 and the Nano city car in 2008 — at 2,000 USD, the world's most affordable mass-produced auto.

Counterintuitively, higher prices can grow markets, too. For this, thank the availability heuristic: the decision-making short-cut that overvalues easily available information, such as price itself. Heuristically — some might say superstitiously or even snobbishly — high prices signal high quality and so can raise demand. You can particularly exploit this in fields where it is hard to objectively assess quality before purchase, or even perhaps after use. Many professional services, legal advice — and management consulting! — included, fall into this category. Other things being imaginarily equal, which lawyer would you trust with your company's merger: the one who charges $50 an hour or $300?

Surprisingly, you can also help shape markets for some very tangible and easily sampled products with a higher price point. When BreadTalk,[8] an international bakery chain founded in Singapore in 2000, started to create a market for Western-style bakery products in Asia, they deliberately priced their products 80 to 120% higher than locals. This signaled not only superior quality but a brand new market niche.

Change the price carrier. The price carrier is the element that determines the price of your product or service — what carries the price tag. Where you're exchanging ownership rights to a product, the commonest price carrier is the product itself. Likewise, many services use a single service as the price carrier. There is a price tag for a haircut or for your vacation flight to Cancún. But in businesses which give customers access rights to tangible products, or where customers' usage of the service is difficult to predict, the typical price carrier is time. Thus, customers pay a fixed sum each month to lease a car, or to use Spotify or Netflix.

Once you, as market shaper, realize these typical price carriers are mere social conventions, you know the drill: you can socially reconstruct them. Price carrier plays are of course particularly powerful if the new carrier better aligns the interests of the providers and customers. Better-aligned interests grow trust and thus, over time, markets. Consider legal services. In-house legal departments, where the firm effectively owns its lawyers, are the preserve of big corporates, and even in-house teams outsource on specialist matters. Now, law firms generally charge by time taken to solve your problem, denominated in six-minute units. This price carrier poses a *prima facie* conflict of interest. The firm profits from solving the problem slowly; the client wants it solved quickly. Moreover, it is extremely difficult to measure the skill and efficiency of a profession specifically versed in an arcane art with obscure language and no guaranteed outcomes. Even the most skilled and diligent lawyers can lose.

As ever, an innovative market shaper has alchemized the lead of trouble into the gold of opportunity, by changing the price carrier. Fondia, a business and corporate law services firm operating in Finland, Sweden, and Estonia, offers the Legal Department as a Service or LDaaS business model.[9] Clients pay a fixed monthly price for unlimited access to their team. The team takes care of the clients' legal needs whenever they arise. The clients get the security of knowing their legal costs in advance, and it becomes in Fondia's best interests to solve their client's problems efficiently. In 2015, Fondia acted as the substitute internal legal department for more than 140 companies and came home second in the *Financial Times*'s "Top Game Changers in the Past 10 Years (non-UK)" category. Lawyers: Is this market-shaping opportunity going begging in your country?

Matching Methods: How Do Sellers and Buyers Find Each Other?

Another Nobel economics laureate, Alvin E. Roth, shows that functioning markets must:[10] (1) provide "thickness" by bringing together enough potential buyers and sellers; (2) make it safe for them to act; and (3) give market participants the means to choose when faced with alternatives. So, standing on yet another giant's shoulders, we'll argue that the Matching Method element of the Exchange layer in our Fan must fulfill these same criteria.

Matching methods range from seller-finds-buyer and buyer-finds-seller to auctions, clearing houses, middlemen, and physical or virtual catalogues. As the world digitalizes, matching methods are changing. For instance, although picking up the phone at dinner time may still expose you to a telemarketer's scripted friendliness, sales calls are giving way to self-service via websites.

You need to assess matching methods by cost effectiveness in your market context. While personal selling does cost far more than using a website, it can also be more effective. In many fields, the matching process is a huge cost. In management consultancy, it swallows up as much as 40% of a senior consultant's time and thus a goodly portion indeed of the total cost mass.

The value and frequency of exchanges importantly drive matching method selection. Low-frequency and low-exchange value favor catalogue-based matching; high-frequency and high-exchange value favor personalized matching. And like all elements in the Fan layers, matching methods, too, can be innovated. We'll now show you two ways to innovate.

Digitalization offers opportunities to innovate new matching methods. Market shapers can learn from New Zealand. Holiday homes hold a special place in the Kiwi psyche, and a special name: the "bach," derived from "bachelor's cabin" and hence pronounced "batch." This scenic nation – the cinematic embodiment of Tolkien's Middle Earth, among other things – boasts over

185,000 baches, scattered across an area equal to the United Kingdom. They range from humble railway cottages or beach-side huts worthy of the derivation and kept in the family for generations, to immodest nouveau riche palaces. That's one bach for every 25 people, so almost 12% of New Zealand residential houses are used as holiday homes.[11]

Before the Bookabach service launched in 2000 (www.bookabach.co.nz), it wasn't easy finding renters for the subset of 7,000 baches, which Kiwi owners can bear to part with on lease. Bookabach provides a matching method that fulfills Roth's three criteria. It brings together a critical mass of renters and owners. Its standardized descriptions of the homes and backgrounders on the renters let buyers and sellers transact safely both. And both sides have the means to make satisfying choices. As Bookabach expands into Australia and the Pacific Islands, it exemplifies how a new matching method can improve the market and make it grow like Topsy.

Another example of creating new matching methods with the help of digitalization is Dow Corning. This specialty chemicals company caught its competitors napping in 2002 when it launched Xiameter, an Internet-based discount sales channel. Xiameter's role was to both take home new business and retain cost-conscious customers.

Traditionally, Dow Corning supplied silicone to diverse clients, but wrapped the product around with information, service, and support. However, experienced and knowledgeable customers were exiting their traditional, high-touch relationship, because they found technical services on silicone application surplus to their requirements and just wanted basic products at low prices. Dow formed Xiameter as a separate business to meet these low-end market needs. The Xiameter brand offers the same quality silicone product unbundled from the services and at considerably lower prices. Beforehand, Dow Corning had no online matching method; now 30% of its sales originate online, nearly three times the industry average.

Xiameter defied industry prognostications that the two-tiered pricing system would simply undermine Dow Corning's core business. The parent company recouped its investment in three months.[12]

Don't forget bricks-and-mortar matching methods. Innovations of matching methods needn't be digital. Bricks-and-mortar offers interesting opportunities – especially if someone else supplies the bricks and mortar.

A firm which clicked that traditional matching methods could grow its market is FRANK by OCBC in Singapore.[13] This venture is an outreach to Gen-Y by $200 billion giant OCBC, the Oversea-Chinese Banking Corporation (*sic.* – they drop the s), who were not content to control 26% of the Singaporean youth market. The full slogan is "FRANK, The New Way to Bank." Frankness of course conveys honesty, sincerity, and simplicity. And simplicity is what multifaceted research told OCBC that Gen-Y wanted. OCBC had assumed that the way to millennials' hearts would be some novel digital channel. Surprisingly, the research revealed that Gen-Y customers want a branch office, but one located in their favorite mall and which they feel comfortable entering.[14]

Driven by the insights but eschewing the fuddy-duddy term "branch office" came the FRANK retail store. There customers can browse, touch, ask questions, and discuss their banking needs. A particular hit was making another aspect of banking more tangible: an in-store display of postcard size FRANK Debit and Credit cards sporting over a hundred designs. The cards function as merchandizing in-store, but more importantly, they allow customers to experiment and express themselves: Which card design describes my personality the best? All of a sudden, old-hat debit and credit cards become tantalizing designer offerings, which the name FRANK by OCBC even implicitly likens to a haute couture clothing label or a sexy perfume: Think "Rive gauche by Yves St Laurent."

Naturally the FRANK retail stores are complemented by various digital channels fit for digital natives. Hence, for example, a new FRANK website, frankbyocbc.com and a conversations blog for Gen-Y customers. But OCBC is convinced that it would never have established such a strong foothold among Singaporean youngsters without creating the new retail stores.[15]

NETWORK: RIGHT PARTNERS, RIGHT KNOW-HOW, RIGHT INFRASTRUCTURE

For a market to work and develop, more actors than sellers and buyers are needed: sub-contractors, providers of complementary products or services, intermediaries, information providers, market research agencies, media, various interest groups and regulators, to name just some.[16] Actors play certain roles. To execute these roles, each actor requires certain know-how and to be configured or connected in certain ways. Market ecosystems also require various forms of infrastructure, ranging from simple and often self-evident things like roads and electricity to more sophisticated things such as reliable data-communication links and fuel distribution systems.

The thing is, the current state of other actors and infrastructure in your market may not be as healthy as it could be. More relevantly to a strategy book, it may not be as healthy as it could be *for you*. Because your optimal market might benefit from more, or fewer, or different actors, playing different roles, in different configurations and equipped with different resources. And your optimal market might require more, or less, or different, or differently supplied, material and immaterial infrastructure. Indeed, if your market is still mostly the twinkle of a brilliant innovation in your eye and you have yet to create the market itself, you certainly won't have enough actors or infrastructure yet! You'll have to populate that space.

Happily, all these different elements — the actors, their roles and know-how, and the infrastructure — can to some extent be indirectly influenced, supplied, or brought into existence. Companies with an ambition to create new market systems or shape existing ones need to do exactly that. And we'll be distinguishing here more between making new markets and shaping existing ones.

Actors: Do We Have the Right Actors in Our Network?

As a market shaper, you have to ask yourself three key questions about actors: Do we really know who the other players are, what resources they have, and how they connect? Can we add or remove players from the network to enhance value creation? And are there — do not adjust your set! — *enough* competitors, and can we collaborate with them?

Draw the map of the network — because shaping the market requires seeing it first! We often see companies struggle to conceptualize their business network beyond relationships with customers. Understandably. Customers take up lots of time and the company can't control customers' own customers or their other upstream suppliers. But time spent influencing such players will repay the effort.

First, map your wider business network as it stands today:[17]

1. *Identifying the actors.* Jot down all commercial and non-commercial actors involved in your market. Start with the value chain from raw materials to end consumers: your suppliers, their suppliers, and all players between your immediate customer and the final consumer. Then look laterally. What other products and services do your customer use that relate in any way to your line of business? What are the associated value

chains? What about the other value chains linked to your customers' customers, suppliers, or suppliers' suppliers? This exercise turns linear value chains into complex value networks. These are more compatible with the systemic view of markets.

2. *Fleshing out actors: what do they do, what resources do they have?* To decide whether your business network could be re-designed, you need to flesh out what kind of players supplier X, media partner Y, and so on are. Usually two analyses suffice: What are the actors' main activities (what do they actually do — for instance, a hospitality company can operate hotels and restaurants themselves or else just manage the sales channel and the brand) and what resources do the actors have (does our hospitality company own real estate, what are its main employee groups, and how strong are its brand-related assets?). Go wide on resources. If your supplier is a pulp and paper company, its obvious resource is plant-making pulp and paper. But it may also have, say, a considerable in-house R&D department with numerous fiber-related patents, or something else that distinguishes it.

3. *Joining the dots: What are the main relationships between the actors?* Actors' business linkages may be closely held information, potentially subject to restrictive nondisclosure agreements. Where publicly available data runs out, reasonable assumptions, tacit information — and even industry gossip — must take over.

Changing the structure of the network: adding or removing players. Armed with your comprehensive — albeit never complete — map of the wider business network, it is time to brainstorm ways to change it. The two main ways are eliminating unnecessary players and adding new, value-creating ones.

Business literature brims with examples of companies effectively shaping their markets (albeit not in so many words) by eliminating actors. In particular, as it did for innovating matching methods, digitalization opens doors for disrupting wider business networks. A classic case is Dell Computers. Dell's business model is based on Internet-enabled disintermediation. That means bypassing traditional wholesale and retail channels. Likewise Nestlé's wholly owned daughter company Nespresso was its first business to sell directly to the end user. Nespresso shook up the fairly stable world of coffee by switching from selling packets of your daily grind through retail channels into selling proprietary coffee pods through direct channels. Simultaneously, it changed the pricing logic to recurring revenues.

Sometimes disintermediating leads to vertically integrating the value chain. One such case is global retail fashion giant Inditex, from Spain. Inditex boasts over 6,390 stores in 88 markets. Its eight brands include Massimo Dutti, Bershka, Oysho, Pull and Bear, Stradivarius, and, topping 60% of total sales, Zara. The company almost wholly self-designs and manufactures. A first-class logistics system in Spain delivers new products twice weekly to all stores. Crucial to Inditex's success is their use of purchasing data from the point-of-sales terminals to steer the production facilities. Controlling the whole value chain chops months off the group's response time to market changes. While the industry's average time from design to finished product is six to nine months, Zara's is 15 days. Zara commits on 50–60% of production in advance, whereas the industry average is 80–90%. Zara's inventory turns over 12 times a year (industry average: three or four), and the unsold stock accounts for 10% (industry average: 17–20%).[18]

But once your lens on the market Fan is polished, you'll realize that *adding actors* furnishes as many, if not more, opportunities to shape markets than elimination. For example, intuitive market shapers we have studied are swift to unblock supply bottlenecks throttling the market system. A company called International SOS[19] has done so systematically and singlehandedly. Founded in

1985 by French physician Dr. Pascal Rey-Herme and his childhood friend Arnaud Vaissié under the name AEA International, SOS supplies medical assistance services to expatriate communities and multinational companies in Southeast Asia. Dr. Rey-Herme first sensed the potential while working at the French Embassy in Jakarta. As Western companies expanded into Southeast Asia, staff demanded medical care and emergency assistance comparable to at home. International SOS first opened an assistance center and clinic in Jakarta. It flew difficult or overflow cases to Singapore to partner hospitals of international standards. The corporate clients were doubly pleased. For emergency treatment in Jakarta or Singapore turned out not only considerably cheaper than evacuating to Europe or the United States but often better, due to more rapid access.

To meet demand, International SOS had to develop a global partner network. Beyond employing reps in its call centers and its own hands-on medical professionals, the company required various external service providers to deliver Western-level medical care throughout Southeast Asia. It had to enlist and accredit specialist doctors, external hospitals, ambulances, charter aircraft, and security professionals.

Thirty years on, International SOS's partner network has kept pace with the company. Nowadays, International SOS operates from more than 900 affiliated medical services sites in 92 countries, employing some 5,600 medical professionals, but with a network in excess of 77,000 accredited external healthcare, aviation, and security providers.

Fostering emergence of competitors for new markets to take off. Via network structure, competition drives market development. For new markets to develop, you need suppliers offering competing alternatives. The mutual benefits of competition to the competitors themselves must not be underestimated. Long-term lack of competition both bespeaks and begets poor business opportunities. And customers often hesitate to enter single-provider markets, especially in business-to-business. Professional procurers often require two or three alternative providers for each product and service.

Studies repeatedly show that markets take off on surges of supply. For demand to emerge, there has to be sufficient and credible supply.[20] The competing firms collectively legitimize the new market. More suppliers enhance sales and distribution channels, spur infrastructure development, and improve promotion efficiency, eventually convincing prospective buyers that all that new market development must be producing value. So, to make a new market you should invite competition in, not fight it off. Apple did precisely that.

Apple was established in 1976. Whereas hobbyist computers sold as electronic kits, Apple I came as a fully assembled computer circuit board with some 30 chips. Even though Apple helped pioneer personal computing, it literally welcomed IBM when that company launched the IBM-PC in 1981. A full-page ad in the *Wall Street Journal* read, patriotically and just a shade patronizingly:

> *"Welcome, IBM. Seriously. Welcome to the most exciting and important marketplace since the computer revolution began 35 years ago. [...] When we invented the first personal computer system, we estimated that over 140,000,000 people worldwide could justify the purchase of one, if only they understood its benefits. Next year alone, we project that well over 1,000,000 will come to that understanding. [...] We look forward to responsible competition in the massive effort to distribute this American technology to the world. And we appreciate the magnitude of your commitment. Because what we are doing is increasing social capital by enhancing individual productivity. Welcome to the task."[21]*

While even Apple underestimated computerization, history suggests IBM's input was necessary to make a mass personal computing market. There has been plenty of room for both players, and more.

Roles and Know-How: Is Work Division Optimal; Does Everyone Know What They Need to Know?

Short of wholesale elimination or addition of actors, simply altering their roles will sometimes set the market on a new growth trajectory. Alternatively, if you already have the right players playing optimal roles, you might still need to make sure everyone has optimal know-how to fulfill their role. We now address those two methods in turn.

Modifying the roles in the network: making work division clear and optimal. In an effective and stable market, actors' roles and role boundaries are clear. Division of labor allows specialization, which drives cost effectiveness and new value for all stakeholders. By contrast, continuous change or development also destabilizes actor identities and roles. How you influence roles and work division very much depends on whether you are making a completely new market or shaping an existing one. In *new markets*, all roles for all actors are unclear and evolving, and actors entering the markets are more at ease with this: What else could they expect? A new market typically follows a sequence.[22] First, actors try to orient themselves as to what this new market really is ("What is being sold – and to whom?") and what to do there ("Am I a buyer, a seller – or a middleman?"). Next comes a stage of contraction. Actors who cannot find an appropriate role exit, while remaining actors become stronger and develop a more persuasive view of the future market that others buy into. During these stages, the sales item and the matching method are still unclear and work division is blurred. As new actors emerge, incumbents can specialize. Finally, the market system reaches a state of cohesion – still complex, but "ordered." By now, matching methods are established and sales items agreed. Actors start to enjoy shared frames of reference as to how the market works and should develop. From the market-making perspective, the key question is: Can we accelerate this "ordering" process?

By contrast, if your firm wants to *shape an existing market*, then factor in the inertia around established roles and shared frames of reference. Few people innately hunger for change. Getting your business partners to unlearn comfortable existing roles and take on new ones requires a very convincing value proposition.

Nevertheless, Fair Dinkum Sheds, a distributor of residential garages, barns, farm sheds, and industrial buildings in Australia, New Zealand, the United Kingdom, and South Africa, has managed to do just that. For readers unversed in Antipodean English, "fair dinkum" is Australian pioneer slang for fair, true, or truthful, like "the real deal." And well after pioneer days, yore and yesteryear, in modern colonial culture unglamorous, makeshift sheds and garages manage to retain something of an iconic place. Fair Dinkum Sheds[23] have shaped this plain-sounding market by canny use of digital tools and smarter work division in their partner network.

Until recently, modern Australians either hired an engineer to draw a new shed according to their specifications and to ensure structural integrity, then rolled up to the local council for a building permit. Or they bought a box-standard shed from a shed reseller with ready-made structural integrity calculations – then rolled up to the local council for a building permit (there was and is no way out of step two). The customized option took time and money. The box-standard alternative was cheaper, but undistinguished.

Fair Dinkum Sheds spliced the two, "mass-customizing" with minimal engineering costs through so-called span tables. Engineers certified a range of designs, small through large, with different numbers of doors and windows. Upon request, Fair Dinkum then designed custom variations to suit, using software that was itself certified. Live human engineers still have to double-check the results of the software – but the automation slashes costs.

Inevitably, Fair Dinkum have now created a free app, functionally titled Shed Designer, that lets customers design their own sheds. Customers can design the dimensions, roof pitch, configuration of windows and doors, color, and so on before even visiting a Fair Dinkum Shed distributor. The app integrates with the engineering software and turns around a quote in a matter of hours. What's more, because certified drawings precomply with local building codes, rolling up to the council has become less of a chore.

While engineering companies are still key partners in the shed market system, their role has transformed. Where once they drew, calculated, and certified one-off shed designs, nowadays they help customers design the 10 to 15% of sheds requiring more than span tables and continuously refine the design and engineering rules in Fair Dinkum's software.

Educating customers and other partners: helping others to do their thing. If your customers or other stakeholders have suboptimal information to play their roles, the market system will create suboptimal value and be smaller and/or less profitable than it could. In that case, and specially where you're asking business partners to change roles like Fair Dinkum's engineers, you'll find it much easier to reshape the system if you – tactfully – educate the other players.

New Zealand's giant dairy exporter Fonterra recognized the need to do exactly that if it was going to, as it were, milk the market system in China.

Westernizing palates had created a vast appetite for fast-food restaurants, Italian restaurants, and Western-style bakeries – all big dairy users. But often locals didn't know which dairy products to use or how. The very language failed them. By itself, the Chinese word for cream, pronounced năiyóu, encompasses all cream-like products, dairy and non-dairy. Moreover, many non-dairy creams in China are sweetened and inappropriate for savory dishes. And the price-based preference for non-dairy creams left kitchen staff unprepared for dairy's temperature sensitivity, short shelf-life, and other idiosyncrasies.

Fonterra Foodservice,[24] a sales division dedicated to business-to-business customers who are neither food retailers nor manufacturers, like restaurants, hotels, and bakeries, has had to educate customers. Specially recruited native-speaker chefs had to demonstrate to their peers in all the establishments above how dairy inputs create better quality end products, so justifying higher prices and differentiating them from the competition.

This strategy of chef-led customer education has paid dividends. In 2014, Fonterra's foodservice business clocked over NZ\$1.3 billion (USD 860 million) in revenue, mainly from China, other Asian countries, and the Middle East. And as of early 2016, Fonterra's group strategy relies heavily on foodservice for growth.

Infrastructure: What Do Customers Need to Use Our Products and Services?

The final element in the Network layer of the Fan is infrastructure, both material and immaterial. For material, think: transportation, water, and electrical distribution. For immaterial, think: information communication technologies. Whether provided by public or private sector, infrastructures are crucial for well-functioning markets, and thus for market making and shaping.

Imagine the value of cars without paved and lit roads, driving schools, street maps, traffic lights, and fuel distribution networks, even the humble parking warden. Just as market systems struggle in developing countries that lack infrastructure, new market systems anywhere highlight the same need. If the current infrastructure doesn't support your market vision, you have three alternatives (once we rule out the do-nothing option): create the necessary infrastructure yourself, turn the creation of the infrastructure into a separate business opportunity, or influence others into developing the infrastructure for you.

Invest in the infrastructure — even if it doesn't generate direct revenues for you. If government or other dedicated industries haven't stepped up, infrastructure just might have to become your business. Innovators typically learn to accept infrastructure development as a cost of commercialization.

Alongside technological and tax issues, and no doubt muscling out by Big Oil, one limiting factor on the electric car market is lack of standard charging infrastructure. (Rail faced a similar problem 150 years ago with nonstandard gauges.) In Europe, BMW, Bosch, Daimler, EnBW, RWE, and Siemens responded with Hubject[25] and eRoaming in 2012. Targeting electric vehicle (EV) manufacturers and providers of charging infrastructure and e-mobility services, eRoaming brings thousands of charging points under one contract. It bridges national boundaries, different station owners/operators, and types of charge point used. Drivers no longer need to subscribe to multiple networks. EV owners look for the "intercharge" logo and read QR codes on the terminals with a mobile app device for details linked to that particular charge point. A new protocol developed by Hubject communicates between the terminals. And while eRoaming is underway in Germany, Belgium, Netherlands, Luxembourg, and Austria, in the United States, ChargePoint and ECOtality have likewise formed a partnership called Collaboratev to allow access to the charge points of different operators.

Turn the lack of infrastructure into a separate business opportunity. Development and maintenance of your missing infrastructure can become a profit-generating venture in its own right through either a temporary or permanent role extension. You might aim to sell the new venture once it's mature.

Wärtsilä has extended its role to develop the market for liquefied natural gas (LNG)-powered engines. LNG takes gas where pipelines don't reach. By cutting the gas's volume 600-fold, liquefaction enables transport over long distances by specially designed ships. Wärtsilä's engine technology supports LNG and meets new EU maritime emission rules. Wärtsilä also provides ship owners with solutions to convert engines from heavy fuel oil to LNG.

The bottleneck for this market has been the smaller scale distribution infrastructure of LNG from the massive terminals to a number of smaller users. This would require new small-scale shipping operations, with so-called LNG feeder ships. This role is a new one in the network and it has not been self-evident, which existing actor – ship operator, ship owner, gas selling company, gas end user, or technology supplier – should take it on. Who invests and who guarantees gas supply? Wärtsilä has provided all actors with intelligence about the importance of this role, hoping that this will help the creation of a new cohesive market.[26]

Influence others to start building the infrastructure for you. Rather than lobby government to invest in roads, rail, or undersea cables, you may well need to consider appealing to other actors in your wider business network.

In India, Unilever's Shakti[27] program has used customers to bridge yawning chasms in support infrastructure. In rural India, multinational giants cannot count on their normal distribution networks. Distances are great, roads rudimentary, and the usual retail partners absent. What was present, abundantly, was underprivileged potential customers for Unilever's hygiene products. The Shakti program, launched in 2001, trains women in rural communities to become microentrepreneurs, selling Unilever's hygiene products door to door. Today, Unilever collaborates with over 70,000 *Shakti ammas* (Shakti Moms), covering over 165,000 villages and five million households in India. Shakti has been win-win-win, producing sales for Unilever, jobs for *Shakti ammas* and income for communities. Unilever has replicated the program in other developing countries.

REPRESENTATIONS: HARNESSING LANGUAGE, INFORMATION, AND SYMBOLS

If actors can't talk to each other about the market, it will grind to a halt: a seller can't cry her wares, a buyer can't name a price. Moreover, if we can't talk about potential changes to the market, we'll be at a loss to shape or make it. Communication is as much the currency of the market as money. Arguably, without the right language, we can't even think about the market. Indeed, we'll show that a market which no one talks about is like the philosopher's tree falling in the forest: It might as well not exist.

Hence the representations layer — this covers all the forms of verbal and nonverbal language, information, and symbols that let us represent to ourselves and others the layers, elements, and shape of a market system. Thus, representations include the spoken and written word, numbers, even images. Examples range from product names and labels and dry technical and commercial terminology, through catchy advertising slogans and logos, to formal statistics and market research reports, informal gossip on social media, "old media" profiles of your exciting innovations, all the way to the fancy award ceremony celebrating achievements in your market.

We all make representations. For a few actors, notably the media, it is their business. But in our opinion, far too few firms deliberately use representations to augment their market-shaping strategies. Intangible they may be, but that does not render them ineffective — quite the contrary. Market shapers' representational toolkit features three main devices: (1) actual language that you have coined or adopted to name, explain, or familiarize your product or service offering; (2) information — about the offering and more importantly the wider market — purveyed by sources such as market research companies and media, but which you can feed into or otherwise influence; (3) and new symbols to legitimate your envisaged market such as awards you found, events you set up, and associations you create.

Your Language: Naming, Describing, Familiarizing

Shapers and makers of market systems are also authors of new meanings. To borrow sociological terms, having made sense of the new shape they must then give that sense to the other actors involved. Representations – language – are the medium. Most obviously, market makers need to name their offerings, which will be entirely novel product categories. As an ancillary, though, market shapers more generally must also explain and sell the offerings and associated changes in the market system. We'll give tips on those two processes in turn, before advising on representational ways (applicable to both processes) to make change more palatable. First, though, let's observe that language is its own complex system. And it's probably subject far more to spontaneous emergence than to deliberate design. Even the acknowledged literary masters of a language wouldn't claim to control it. We'll see similar humility befits corporations, too.

Make your new product category name accessible – even to competitors. When it comes to names, market makers and shapers launching an invention or other novel offering can feel understandably proprietorial. But for all new product and service categories we recommend using a name that, while ideally catchy, first and foremost is accessible and available to everyone in the market ecosystem. That includes competitors. The perverse fates of trademarks show the risks of trying to corner a market in a name. Trademarking is the ultimate attempt to not only design, but own, language. Yet, language's emergence can bite back. Hoover™, Band-Aid™, and Velcro™ are famously now used as generics in practice. But did you know the same goes for Bubble-wrap™,[28] Dumpster™[29], and Zipper™[30]? Escalator[31] has even lost its status in the eyes of the law.

On the one hand, all these marks are victims of their own success: if they hadn't been so popular, the vernacular wouldn't have assimilated them as common nouns and even rudely "verbed" them. On the other hand, genericization may tarnish your hard-won reputation through cheap knock-offs; it sacrifices uniqueness and control practically and sometimes legally; and it wastes your IP investment.

Perhaps the greater danger, though, is that you won't corner the market with your trademark but paint yourself into a forgotten corner with a bad one. If you don't supply good, catchy, generic names, and your trademarked name happens not to take off, you're risking suboptimal growth for the category. Now consider the generic names that were intended for Bubble-wrap™, Dumpster™, Escalator, and Zipper™: air bubble packaging; mobile garbage bin; conveyor transport device or moving stairway; and separable fastener. Ever used them? Would you? They don't trip off the tongue. The Dempster Brothers, Otis, SAC, and UFC should thank their stars that their marks were more honored in the breach. But what history doesn't tell us is how many less-fortunate market makers doomed great new products or services by a misstep in naming.

What's more, although you sometimes get the chance to rename, names tend to stick – for better or for worse. A name may persist even if the core product or service undergoes radical technological or business model innovations.

Deploy ancillary language and concepts to explain and sell the new market shape. Alongside product category names, successful market shapers will coin or commandeer ancillary terms, phrases, or whole concepts, to explain and sell the change in their market systems. You'll recall International SOS, whose innovative medical business exemplified influencing the Network layer. In well-turned phrases, the company also created or co-opted concepts to describe the developments necessary for a new, but allied market system: its security wing.[32] This was astutely added after rebellions ended the 31-year dictatorial rule of Indonesia's President

Suharto in May 1998. With civilian airports closed, it fell to International SOS to evacuate Jakarta's expats.

In broadening their market from medical evacuations to medical and security assistance, International SOS has educated its customers about every firm's "duty of care" for its employees' security, both medical and operational. That term of art from the law of torts exudes legality but is simple enough to be intuitive – unlike, say, "incorporeal hereditaments." Meanwhile, deftly recasting SOS customers as "members" has achieved a connotation of long-term stability. And finally, they have christened "return-on-prevention" as an analogue of "return on investment" to convince said members to invest in planning, so a crisis doesn't become a disaster.

Sometimes, fortune smiles on you and offers linguistic aides that have sprung, un-designed, from sheer emergence, even if you weren't trying to shape the market yourself. Grab them with both hands! Consider the international accountancy market. In 1960, writing (somewhat serendipitously) in *Fortune* magazine itself, commentator TA Wise coined, or at least popularized, the term "The Big Eight" for the developed world's eight biggest accounting firms.[33] The phrase and the idea stuck in the press. What matters for our purposes is that, in a gesture of market sharing, the firms wisely embraced the description. They could have disavowed it and competitively struck out for more singular pre-eminence. But instead they self-identified as being "one of the Big Eight." Membership of this exclusive club conferred not only cachet but a measure of protection against shrinkage, even though the market was still consolidating. That's testimony to the sheer power of representations.

When the Big Eight did shrink to the Big Six in the 1990s, the Big Five in 2002, and – finally? – the Big Four, it wasn't dispassionate counting based on revenue or other stat's that heralded each new number. It was an announcement by an influential source that took hold in, and shaped, our perceptions. Today the grip of Deloitte, PWC, EY, and KPMG is stronger, because many companies are legally obliged to use these Big Four. And the benefits keep flowing. In a self-fulfilling prophesy, cachet boosts contract volume, lures the best workers, and blocks industry players from ousting or joining the anointed four.

Familiarize the unfamiliar with metaphors, conceptual extensions, and boundary concepts. "The two most engaging powers of an author are to make new things familiar, familiar things new": So wrote 19th-century English novelist William Makepeace Thackeray. Let's look at three devices by which market shapers can enlist Thackeray's first power to ease their market actors into change: metaphors, conceptual extensions, and boundary concepts:

1. *Metaphors.* Metaphors use a word or phrase literally denoting one thing in place of another, to suggest a likeness. Consider the main maker of the energy drinks market, Red Bull. The tagline "Red Bull gives you wings" is just one aspect of a sustained metaphor of flight which has served the company well. Red Bull also sponsors family-fun Fly Days where the public try out their home-made flying machines. And Red Bull's highly innovative multifunction center called Hangar-7 at Salzburg, Austria's airport, is effectively a temple to the metaphor. It even displays a Flying Bulls aircraft fleet.

2. *Conceptual extensions.* Conceptual extensions employ an established concept in a new, surprising, or challenging way to nudge market actors into thinking to the new market shape. Thus, "water footprint," for instance, which extends "carbon-footprint" (itself an extension of common or garden "footprint"), measures the total freshwater that goes into a product. It includes the water consumed and polluted along the supply chain. The Water Footprint Network,[34] an NGO created after companies such as Unilever, Heineken, and Nestlé became increasingly aware of their water-related risks, deploys the concept to engage companies, investors, research institutes, and

government in assessments as a first step to sustainable development through water stewardship, resource efficiency, and
governance.

3. *Bridging concepts.* Broadly, both bridging and boundary concepts use shared but ambiguous terms to stimulate dialogue
   between different market audiences about the new shape. Take
   Slow Food. Launched by Italian Carlo Petrini in 1986, this
   movement to preserve regional cuisine and local food production has gone global under a nifty name bordering "fast food"
   that unites growers, restaurateurs, and diners against that very
   concept. Back in the United States, a strategically deployed
   bridging concept has brought the most concrete benefits for 30
   million Americans suffering from 1,300 disparate, very uncom-
   mon diseases. Sufferers were long left to battle alone, with no
   customized treatment options. Low numbers made their conditions simply uneconomic for pharmaceutical companies to
   invest in research and meet strict testing and trialing regimes.
   But an ad hoc patient coalition, the National Organization for
   Rare Disorders,[35] rehomed these "orphaned" diseases as a
   numerically large family in their own right under the simple,
   single concept "rare diseases." Consequently, the Orphan Drug
   Act of 1983 created financial incentives for the development of
   treatments for rare diseases by relaxing statistical burdens –
   thus effectively creating markets for these medicines.

Information: Helping Others to Make Sense of the Market

Picture a couple preparing to buy their first home. They inform
themselves by, among other things, monitoring media and scruti-
nizing statistics about the latest sales prices. Would they take the
plunge into a mortgage – sometimes described as the unwelcome
third body in the marital bed – if these information sources didn't

exist? Or if they only portrayed industrial, commercial, and residential real estate as one big aggregate block?

Even when not being shaped, healthy market systems require not only promotional representations but more solid information that explains what the market is all about, how it is developing, and how to operate in it. It's about breeding familiarity, confidence, and trust, as much as knowledge. And of course information, too, comes via representations. Prime sources are media coverage, research reports, and statistics. Surprisingly, these information representations are also malleable and offer opportunities for deliberate market shaping.

Influence media to set the agenda for attention and to legitimize new markets. Representations are the stock in trade of media organizations. Despite what we may think, the representations created by media do not report the market neutrally, simply holding a mirror to it. Rather, they open up potential for the media's content creators themselves – and market participants who have their ear – to select, slant, polish, or tarnish the images conveyed. (All this, without even considering firms' traditional ability to place paid advertisements.) Thus, media organizations are important information distributers, helping potential customers and other new actors wanting to enter the market to learn about the market.

Market shapers can benefit from media in two ways. First, media substantially set the agenda for discourse. While they may not dictate *what* their audience thinks, they certainly influence what their audience may think *about*. So, say you want to shape your market toward renting or as-a-service business models. It might be advisable to encourage media to write more about the rise of sharing economy.

Second, media can legitimize a new market definition. As a third party or fully fledged fourth estate and guardian of the public interest, old media in particular – print and broadcasting, whether online or offline – provide a supposedly impartial view on the potential benefit of the mooted market for customers and society.

But media are a ticklish element to influence. For starters, they traditionally guard their independence with jealousy. More pragmatically, most nonstate run media face their own commercial imperatives – how to monetize content and win eyeballs. Fortunately, though, their resulting predilection for the new, the surprising, and the controversial often fits well with a firm's attempt to create new, or shape existing, markets.

Swedish-based e-commerce food delivery service Linas Matkasse (Lina's Food Bag) has played well in the media for just these attributes, with the birth, and boom, of the market for home-delivered ready-made grocery bags. In a particularly homely touch, the bags of nutritious ingredients come complete with recipes planned by Lina herself. As a new and exciting variation on a basic necessity for the time-poor modern consumer, Linas Matkasse has garnered attention from both national broadcasters and tech and business media, making Europe's 100 hottest start-ups list in *Wired* magazine in 2012. This honor conferred coverage and credibility in the eyes of customers.[36]

Ensuring apt market research and statistics – especially if you work in B2B. Representations by market research and statistics also enhance the perception of a legitimate market and channel information to potential customers and business partners. This information includes facts and figures on the size of the market, its growth, the main players, and their respective market shares. Such data especially inform companies' strategic decisions and are often a prerequisite to institutional investors committing funds.

We are not suggesting sinister, undue influence. Given that market systems are increasingly in flux, market research companies are struggling to keep up: they need your input. A direct, good-faith, evidence-based discussion about your view on emerging product or service categories to research and important attributes for customers in the future can be win-win. And if you as market shaper are betting your strategy on your views, you can't get much better faith than that.

Basware, an international software company that develops solutions for procurement and financial process automation, exemplifies the harnessing of market research as part of market making. The company's task was two-fold: to induce research companies such as Forrester Research and Gartner to acknowledge the existence of the novel eProcurement market and to get Basware short-listed as a provider in their analyses. This two-pronged market-making strategy has seen Basware grow between 18% and 44% annually since 2005, with double-digit operating profit. In 2008, Forrester put Basware at the head of the pack in the young and specialized Accounts Payable Electronic Invoice Presentment and Payment (AP-EIPP) market.[37]

New Symbols to Legitimize Markets: Events, Awards, and Associations

Industry events, awards, and associations not only shine the spotlight on the firms or individual actors they bring together or honor, like media and market researchers, they also implicitly legitimize the whole market. This legitimizing role is symbolic. Picture February 28 at Hollywood's Dolby Theatre. The Academy Awards or Oscars are an event, organized by an industry association, to present awards. The most obvious symbol is the winners' gold statuettes. But the red carpet photo ops, the hushed opening of envelopes, the name-checking of motion picture industry doyens, also symbolize high artistic standards of the industry as a whole and the rigor and expertise in being ranked by one's most-venerated peers. Not dissimilar are the prestige and professionalism connoted by, say, the famously rigorous medical and bar associations.

However, there's a twist in this section. Whereas media crave novelty, events, awards, and (especially) associations can solidify the status quo and thwart change, or at least slow it down. So creators of new markets and shapers of existing ones very often have to deliberately align fresh such symbols with the intended new market system.

Build alternative events and awards aligned with your market vision. Events and awards are worthwhile subjects of strategy, not just PR fluff. And fortunately, there is no natural limit to their number. So if your market vision is dramatically at odds with the picture painted by the current events and awards, it's safer to create an alternative than try changing the existing ones.

The benefits of this strategy often outweigh investment cost, for two reasons. First, most managers and firms are competition-aholics. The lure of a prestigious new award will raise engagement among your customers and other key stakeholders. Second, media gladly cover events and award winners, because they're news.

The example of KONE Corporation showcases how events and awards are linked to other representations. Rather than being "in the elevator and escalator market," KONE have defined themselves around the bridging concept of People Flow. People Flow is intuitive but usefully ambiguous – and thus acceptable to builders, architects, developers, office managers, and consumers alike. KONE's People Flow strategy has impacted representational terminology in its market system. Even though KONE has trademarked the People Flow slogan, it has wisely refrained from contesting similar concepts and phrases among competitors. Thus, when Otis claims to be the world's leading people mover, or Schindler proposes mobility systems to manage the flow of people, KONE counts it as a win for its language and its story. This fits with our advice to make your product category names accessible, even to competitors.

KONE has launched a new event to promote People Flow. On People Flow Day, teams of KONE employees pick up clipboards and ask users and customers exactly how, where, and why people move in buildings during a typical weekday.[38] Besides feeding into internal R&D, the People Flow Day is a good way of engaging the media. Despite these advances, KONE could have been even more active in promoting People Flow. Examples of such actions could be to donate People Flow professor chairs to selected universities and hosting annual People Flow awards. Take heed if you were still inclined to snub such things as fluff.

Fight to change industry associations. An industry association promotes an ordered market that is hospitable and less risky for participants. It does so not only by standardizing market elements but by creating a confident common language. Furthermore, governments prefer to deal with associations rather than with more nakedly self-interested individual firms.

However, like events and awards, industry associations generally favor the status quo. Worse, a reactionary association might actively oppose market-wide changes if detrimental to some members. And, unlike events and awards, industry associations derive authority by being exclusive. So, if your market-shaping strategy is clearly at odds with the current association's agenda, our advice is to prepare for conflict.

Stora Enso, the Finnish company, from the opening section of this chapter that reshaped the construction industry away from steel and concrete and toward wood, manipulated industry associations among other elements. First, the company helped redefine the Finnish Timber Council's (Puuinfo's) role from generally promoting wood toward establishing an open standard for wood element construction. Second, they secured the creation of Finnish Wood Research. This nonprofit joint company planned and implemented research, development, and innovation projects essential for the business operations of wood product companies. Most importantly, Stora Enso joined the Confederation of Finnish Construction Industries and proactively influenced it to push standardizations and building codes toward a more technology-neutral stance — read: less wood-averse. And serendipitously, standards are part of the next layer, Rules of the Game, to which we now turn.

RULES OF THE GAME: INFLUENCING STANDARDS, REGULATIONS, AND SOCIAL NORMS

As we've worked our way outwards on the Fan, the stakes have been mounting. The Rules of the Game layer is outermost because it is the hardest for your business to influence but also the most influential if you succeed. Rules of the Game, whether formal standards and regulations or informal social understandings, effectively write the rules of the market game which the other layers play out. Indeed, regulations literally write them. Without Rules of the Game, including a vast number of noticed or unnoticed regulations, there would be no functioning, stable market systems. For one thing, consumers and investors would lack predictability and hence confidence. And if you ignore Rules of the Game, you risk finding your otherwise-excellent product or service rendered either incompatible and hence inoperable, undesired by culturally imprinted consumers, or plain illegal.

Although you need Rules of the Game for a functioning, stable market, truth is, you can also have too much of a good thing. Rules of the Game can either lubricate the wheels of commerce or throw a wrench in the works. They can either enable or stifle the market system. New markets may, for instance, need new standards in order to start developing, such as the 2G and 3G standards for mobile communication which Nokia co-developed. But too many, strictly enforced standards and regulations, combined with deep-seated social conventions, may "deep-freeze" a market, making it very difficult to shape. This could well prevent gains to not only the would-be innovators but also consumers, the market as a whole, and the wider economy. Ironically, those are the very interests that governmental regulators are charged with guarding as part of their own, supposedly even-handed strategy. Nowadays digital disruptors and practitioners of the sharing economy are feeling particularly stifled.

Next, we'll address in turn the peculiarities of standards, regulations, and (especially consumer) social norms: what we're dealing with in each element and how to spot it; what the element typically addresses; how clear-cut it is; and how the Rules of the Game are made, monitored, and enforced, so you can figure out how to unmake or remake them.

Standards: Without Them, Nothing Fits Together

Standards are easily spotted. For starters, they often travel under abbreviations that make large mouthfuls: "ISO 9000" may trip off the tongue, but less so "UTS ANSI/ASME B1.1," a Unified Thread Standard for screw threads. You'll know – or should know – the standards your industry has to comply with, anyhow. Standards can be national, regional, or international. Somewhat limiting the degree of true standardization, there will, for instance, be different building codes in different nations, and sometimes even in different regions. Like regulations, standards can be used strategically by industries and governments for purposes other than sheer compatibility. One such ulterior motive of national and regional standards is to create trade or entry barriers, protecting an area from competition.

From the market-shaping perspective, standards are of utmost importance as they ensure compatibility. Without compatibility, stuff doesn't fit together. Markets become inefficient. And your fab new product no longer plugs into the local power sockets. Next, we'll cover some differences between de jure and de facto standards, the tendency among the latter to escalate to full-blown standards wars and the interesting strategy option of relinquishing valuable IP to create favorable standards.

De jure versus de facto: building coalitions versus pushing adoption. Deriving from the Latin for "by force of law," de jure standards are approved, and often also enforced, by formal authorities. By contrast, de facto standards prevail only "as a matter of fact," by widespread uptake. Standards authorities for the former can be international, such as the International Organization for Standardization (ISO) or Internet Engineering Task Force (IETF); regional, such as the European Committee for Standardization (CEN: *Comité Européen de Normalisation* – whose site supplies a lexicon of its own 300-plus acronyms: Brussels bristles with initials); or national, like the American National Standards Institute (ANSI). Well-known examples of de jure technical standards are TCP/IP (transmission control protocol/ internet protocol), the IETF-endorsed standard communication language or protocol of the Internet. Without that particular standard, the information superhighway would be a maze of rutted footpaths and dramatically less traveled.

Making or changing a de jure standard takes a vast amount of time and effort, and often force of numbers. The prerequisite is usually to prove the need for the standard. Industry-wide coalitions fare best at that. For instance, all major European mobile technology firms joined in developing the GSM standard (under the umbrella of the European Telecommunications Standards Institute) for 2G digital cellular networks used by mobile phones. GSM was first deployed in 1991 – fully nine years after work began – and by 2014 was well and truly the default global standard for mobile communications, with over 90% market share.

Because de jure standards take so long to cement, many firms try for de facto standards. The secret there is convincing customers to prefer your technology. The de facto route wastes no time in standard-setting cabinets. Better still, sometimes official standard organizations anoint popular and beneficial de facto standards as de jure ones. On the other hand, promoting widespread and fast adoption of a new technology can be devastatingly expensive.

Adobe's PDF format is a classic case of building a de facto standard that eventually became de jure. From 1993, Adobe worked hard to popularize PDF into the de facto industry standard by providing the Acrobat Reader programs for free. In 2005, PDF/A became ISO's de jure standard (ISO 19005-1:2005) and in 2007, PDF 1.7 followed suit (ISO 32000-1:2008).

Standard wars: ally with the biggest faction. Multiple firms promoting rival candidates for a de facto standard can escalate into a full-blown standards war. Typically the combatants whittle down to two factions that battle on for some time. Remember video? One classic standards war was that between BetaMax and VHS in the late 1970s, won by VHS. Another pitted Toshiba's HD DVD against Sony's Blu-Ray. Toshiba conceded in February 2008.

Standard wars mostly break out in market systems where consumer products or services have to inter-operate seamlessly with other industries' offerings. So, if you work in B2B or your products are relatively stand-alone, with few complementarities, then competition for de facto standards needn't escalate into wars.

Luckily, if hostilities escalate, there's a relatively simple tip for picking winners. On analysis, winners of standards wars have shared one commonality – and it's not technological superiority or ease of use. It seems to come down to sheer numbers: the faction with the most companies backing it. As in military strategies, alliances hold the key to the victory.

Trade off your IP for a favorable (de facto) standard. Most technical standards stem from intellectual property (IP) rights. An inventor patents something clever in the hope of a nice, long revenue stream. The paradox, of course, is that IP rights wall off a technology, whereas de facto standardization requires throwing open the gates and sharing it.

Reconceiving your innovation not as the exclusive IP fruits of your labor but as common seed sown for a future standard opens up market-shaping opportunities. For example, Tesla, the trailblazer of electric vehicles, has opened up its entire IP portfolio to all electric vehicle manufacturers to use. The purpose is to sow de facto standards compatible with the company's technologies and wider aims.

A similar example concerns shipping containers. Containerization has done for shipping what the assembly line did for car production.[39] By integrating rail, road, and sea transport, it revolutionized efficiency in cargo handling. Today, a skilled crane operator loads a 20-ton container into a slot on a container ship in less than a minute.

Progress turned on not only the container itself but a series of inventions by Californian Keith Tantlinger. The Berkeley-educated engineer came up with ways to stack, ship, and transport containers across the world without their ever being touched by a human hand. Tantlinger's inventions included such non-household names as the twist lock, the corner post slotted eyelet fittings, the cell guide, and the spreader bar (sounds painful). Tantlinger was working for a supplier of Sea-Land, a shipping company founded by Malcolm McLean. Dubbed the father of containerization, McLean sold port authorities, shippers, crane manufacturers, and others on his brainchild's efficiency benefits.

By the early 1960s, a standards war had thrown up numerous incompatible designs for containers and lifting gear. In 1965, Tantlinger convinced MacLean to give up Sea-Land's patent rights to the twist lock and corner post, which let the ISO define a slightly altered version of their design as the world standard. McLean's generosity was itself strategic: As Sea-Land's major shareholder, he stood to gain handsomely from a large-scale adoption of containerization.

Regulations: Defining What Is Legal

Regulations and laws literally set the rules of the market game. Even the "free-est" market has general laws in the background. Such legal regimes may protect consumers, labor, or the environment, or serve other purposes. More fundamentally, regulations also enable market stability and confidence. A complete absence of regulation would turn the market over to the laws of the jungle rather than the benevolent invisible hand. Knowing this, even the most ardent libertarian stops shy of calling for, say, abolishing the laws of contract. As the former World Trade Organization CEO, Mike Moore — a keen deregulator and incidentally a Kiwi — has often said, a market with no rules is a black market, not a free market.[40]

Typically, the most important market-related regulations take the form of either specific government regulation or industry self-regulation. Not all of them are enshrined in legal instruments, but all regulations are written and formal. With a few exceptions, most are also binding and carry sanctions for breach. And whereas some standards and all social norms are relatively bottom-up, regulations are clearly top-down.

When it comes to regulations, the strategy playbook for a market shaper aims to achieve one of two basic outcomes: to change existing regulations to free up bottlenecks (sometimes called deregulation — even though it more often softens regulations than actually scraps them) or to introduce more regulations to further stabilize the market. Examples of the specific plays to achieve those aims follow.

Changing existing regulations in cooperation with regulators: coalitions and the force of facts. Traditionally firms and industries influence regulation by working with government. Nowadays, anti-Washington sentiment paints lobbyists as faceless multinationals buying the votes of conscience-less politicians and selling consumers, workers, and/or the environment itself down the river. But the partnership is considerably more good-faith in reality.

If your market-shaping strategy requires regulatory change, make the necessary alliances with as many of your competitors as you can persuade by a win-win value proposition. Government officials balk at being seen to favor – or even talk to – individual companies. But ears prick up and doors open when a coalition of companies comes knocking. Consequently, industry associations are a popular vehicle to influence existing governmental regulations.

You must also arm yourself with facts showing the proposed change benefits as many other market actors as possible, including your competitors, customers, suppliers – and wider society – is indispensable. A sufficiently compelling "national business case" alone sometimes carries the day, even without allies.

The breakthrough of Finnish power source supplier Wärtsilä in India illustrates the power of convincing facts.[41] Back in 2008, Wärtsilä's inability to sell a single "peaking" power plant in a market where outages abounded and the average electricity deficit hit 16.6% during peak hours made no sense.

The company traced the glitch to India's Electricity Act 2003. The Act's so-called "cheap-electricity-for-all" agenda perversely incentivized very large plants for base load provision – but not investment in new peaking capacity.

Wisely, Wärtsilä armed themselves with facts before weighing in on the debate on tariff policy. They commissioned a pan-India analysis from a well-reputed Indian strategy consultancy firm on how residential and commercial consumers cope with recurring power cuts. It emerged that Indian consumers had invested over USD 20,000 million in backup systems, with annual operating expenses of over USD 6,750 million. The actual cost of power paid by consumers was much more than needed for reliable electricity nation-wide. The study also indicated that both residential and commercial consumers were willing to pay more for reliable provision.

Suddenly, Wärtsilä, a relative outsider, found doors opening to crucial regulators: the Ministry of Power, the Central Electricity Authority, the Central Electricity Regulation Commission, the Bureau of Energy Efficiency, the Planning Commission, the Ministry of Petroleum and Natural Gas, the Ministry of Environment, and the Gas Authority of India Ltd. There followed three years of tireless networking, meetings with target groups, media sessions and seminars, an avalanche of press releases and a blizzard of white papers, and high-profile events such as the annual Wärtsilä Mantosh Sondhi Awards. Finally, in 2011 Wärtsilä hit pay dirt. The Central Electricity Regulatory Commission asked the Finns to draft the regulation governing peak and non-peak tariffs. The game-changing "peaking tariff" was written into the National Electricity Policy in 2012 and came into effect in 2013.

Changing existing regulations by breaking them: advocacy by customers and other stakeholders. Cooperating with regulators to change regulation is a long haul – perhaps too long if your market environment is fast moving or you're seeking change across multiple jurisdictions. One high-risk strategy is to work against officialdom by flouting the problem regulations. And you might just pull it off, if the existing framework is under-serving customers and other actors in the market system. Provided your solution fixes that, advocacy by your customers and other stakeholders may just tip the regulators into rewriting the rules.

Uber appears to be using this strategy to change onerous and deeply country-specific taxi regulations worldwide. In almost all jurisdictions, the Uber juggernaut has collided with, or at least had to steer around, regulation.[42] The company faces ongoing protests and legal action from taxi drivers, taxi companies, and governments on the grounds that it competes unfairly against taxis because it pays no taxes or licensing fees; endangers passengers; runs unlicensed, untrained, uninsured drivers.

One of Uber's strategies has been to engage the law, using ordinary courtroom argument to distinguish itself from traditional taxi services and thus exempt itself from the attendant regulation. For instance, Uber argues its business model is qualitatively different and actually safer, in that passengers get to choose and rate their driver and vice versa, with a history building up on each. And Uber represents itself as purely the broker in market transactions between independent drivers and passengers. The company's stronger argument, though, may well be a purely commercial one: "The market has spoken — deal with it!" Uber's looks like a deliberate strategy not to wait for slow and uncertain regulatory change before launching, but to force change after the fact by weight of popularity with the voting public.

Whether the goodwill holds and rewrites regulation by popular demand remains to be seen. At time of writing in 2016, there are some weak positive signals that this might happen. For instance, tech-savvy Estonia has decided to join what it can't beat. President Toomas Hendrik Ilves has publicly said that the country was "looking for a solution instead of prohibiting a new form of business."[43]

Introducing new regulations to stabilize the market: industry self-regulation as a viable option. Shaping regulations is not always about de-regulating or removing legal roadblocks to new and innovative business models. Sometimes your envisioned market would require more, and more stringent, regulation. This is especially the case in new markets, as due to their newness they tend to lack the necessary regulations. Insufficient regulation can deter otherwise interested customers, suppliers, and investors. Some level of regulation is needed to breed trust!

If so, a relatively united, or unite-able, market, should consider self-regulating instead, for a couple of reasons. First, developing — and later on altering — industry self-regulation tends to be faster.

Second, assuming your allies are likely to know the drill already, they won't feel caught off guard. Industries from healthcare and higher education, through food, fashion, advertising, mining, fishing, and professional sports, to nuclear power have established self-regulatory processes to govern industry practices.[44] Finally, governments (especially of a non-interventionist persuasion) may sigh with relief at an attempt to self-regulate. Credible industry self-regulation takes the problem off the hands of thinly resourced official regulators. We also note in passing a defensive use of self-regulation. Governments wanting to reform an industry will sometimes threaten to regulate it from outside unless the industry self-regulates. This defensive play can also be made pre-emptively to stave off such a threat. Of course, making it credible again requires having your alliances solid and your facts straight.

Social Norms: Making Things Acceptable and Desirable

Unlike standards and regulations, social norms are informal understandings, conventions, and beliefs that inform members of social networks on how they should behave in a specific context or culture. They are therefore a much trickier beast to spot and to shape. With a few exceptions like the rules of clubs and gallant attempts like Emily Post's famous rules of etiquette from 1960s America, you won't find social norms written down. Rather, they reside in what the 19th-century French sociologist Emile Durkheim termed the collective consciousness. They emerge over time from somewhat misty forces rather than being deliberately and openly developed.

To grasp the subtle dynamics of social norms, we borrow from innovation diffusion theory.[45] This predicts that the path by which a customer population adopts new products, ideas, norms, and preferences follows the normal distribution curve, aka the (Gauss) bell curve. It follows that market penetration can be described with a so-called S-curve. Adoption starts slowly through small groups of innovators or early adopters. Next the early and late majorities adopt. Finally, a few extreme laggards catch on. Therefore, in order to help form a norm, market shapers need to specifically work with the innovators and early adopters. These groups hold greatest sway and offer opinion leadership.

In markets, social norms affect diverse players. But they especially help mold consumer tastes and expectations as to what is acceptable or desirable. As well as modifying consumer preferences, though, market shaping may require shifting entrenched industry conventions.

Making your product or service category desirable by influencing customer preferences. If you're versed in traditional marketing and competitive strategies to modify customer preferences, now's the wrong time to trust your intuition. Because (forgive the repetition) market shaping isn't about making customers desire your product or service more than the competition's. It's about making the entire product category more desirable or changing what "desirable" means right across that category.

For a recent case of reshaping customer preferences, we turn to a subject close to our hearts and current home: wine, specifically the wine industry "Down Under." Wineries in New Zealand (where we live) and Australia have succeeded where others had failed, in setting a trend for sealing wine bottles with screwcaps instead of corks.[46] With centuries of tradition behind it, the cork method was a classic social norm: functionally somewhat arbitrary, even inferior, but embedded in custom and hence expectation. Wine drinkers took for granted that any decent drop would come sealed with a cork. And beloved practices and rituals had grown up around uncorking, together with a range of apparatus from basic corkscrews with wooden handles to the sommelier knife, wing corkscrews, twin prong cork pullers and expensive titanium corkscrews. Each was accompanied by its own satisfying sound effects.

Yet industry insiders had long known that corking wine was functionally flawed. Some 2– 8% of the seven billion bottles produced yearly had deficiencies related to cork, chiefly mustiness due to a chemical called 2,4,6-trichloroanisole (TCA). Objectively, screwcaps eliminate the problem. Social norms, though, are notoriously subjective. A screwcap especially adapted for wine bottles had been around since 1959 and had passed later testing with flying colors. Yet, commercial uptake languished due to such subjective resistance from consumers and the retailers who knew their tastes. Although Switzerland had made greater inroads, even there consumers associated screwcaps with only mid-priced wine.

By the turn of the millennium, the Kiwis had said "Enough." Leading producers, mainly from the South Island's premier Marlborough region, resolved to stop their excellent wine getting degraded by a lousy closure mechanism sustained only through myths and misplaced snobbery. Interestingly, even though the objective was to change consumer preferences, no consumer advertising took place. Instead, the Kiwis deployed a (once again) multipronged strategy to educate opinion leaders. To wine critics, they explained the science and held comparative tastings (tasting the same wine under cork and screwcap). To big retailers, they emphasized improvements in customer satisfaction and logistics: eliminate cork = eliminate corked wine = eliminate consumers having to return the corked wines to the store. Commercial clout aided the cause, because Marlborough sauvignon blancs were hot property. Therefore, the de facto alliance of most Marlborough wineries rather forced the retailers' – and consumers' – hand.

In the following five years, the movement gained momentum internationally. European wineries including Chateau Margaux started conducting trials with screwcaps. By 2007 some UK retailers were requesting screwcap closure as a standard for imports, because they considered it less risky. By 2016, the screwcap battle was largely won, excepting a few hold-outs like the United States and China. In the United Kingdom, acceptance by consumers has more than doubled, from 41% in 2003 to 85% in 2011. Even in swanky restaurants, nobody blinks when a sommelier unscrews a bottle. Oh, and the total marketing budget dedicated to make this global change happen? Five figures, at the low end – in NZ dollars.

Industry conventions as an obstacle to shaping customer preferences. Our analysis reveals industry conventions are often more of a sticking point than consumer preferences. Consumers may take a chance on new products and business models more readily than relatively reactionary producers. Producers have bigger interests at stake. And they may well be risk averse if they have not embraced an ethos of abundance through market growth. However, if not a prerequisite, winning over industry peers greatly facilitates modifying customer preferences about a product or service category.

Industry conventions proved an obstacle to shaping customer preferences in the screwcap case just discussed. Winemakers and wine merchants even defended their positions with the argument, discredited by scientists in Bordeaux in the 1970s that wine had to breathe through porous cork to age properly. All the oxygen needed for aging is already in the bottle when it is closed.

Three events critically won over industry sticks-in-the-mud. First, the screwcap advocates convened a special meeting for wine producers and writers in 2001. In attendance was Jeffrey Grosset, a famous Riesling maker from South Australia's Clare Valley. Grosset had put his Rieslings under both cork and screwcap for long times. As well as showcasing the collected scientific evidence all in one place, the meeting let participants experience it themselves with tastings of the same wine under cork and – sometimes for many years – under screwcap. The outcome was enthusiastic acknowledgment that the wines under screwcap not only were high quality but aged very well. The Screwcap Wine Seal Initiative (SWSI) was born.

The second big event was the London Wine Fair in 2002. To persuade industry influencers and critics, the SWSI promoted the new closure with a blind taste test and a very simple trial of putting corks into glasses of acidified water. Every glass suffered some color and flavor taint except the glass containing no cork.

The game-changing event, though, was the First International Screw Cap Symposium, held on home turf in Marlborough in 2004. The symposium was attended by 250 delegates from 12 countries and further manifested the need for an industry-wide approach to sharing information and expertise related to screw-caps. To do so, the International Screw Cap Seal Initiative was established. Key to the successful sharing was the publication of a well-crafted book covering all aspects of sealing wine under screw-caps, wittily titled *Taming the Screw – A Manual for Winemaking with Screw Caps*[47] and published in 2005.

So, breaking the grip of obstructive industry conventions is not dissimilar to breaking bad habits: It takes time and tenacity and is best achieved by replacing the old convention with a fresh one, since simply eliminating it and leaving a blank space is nigh impossible. Despite the slog required, changing industry conventions is a must for many market shapers. After all, we are trying to shape complex market systems – and competitors with their habits are very much part of the complexity.

TAKEAWAYS FROM CHAPTER 3

- Radiating out from the core of the Fan are four-ranked layers, or clusters of elements, which a market shaper can explore and potentially mold. These layers we label, in order: *Exchange, Network, Representations,* and *Rules of the Game*

- The first two layers flow from the firm's chosen business model, affording the firm *more managerial influence.* The latter two rank as harder to influence, but *more influential* if you succeed.

- *Exchange* is the minimum foundation of all market systems. Buyers and sellers must find each other and agree on what's being exchanged and the pricing. Here, market shaping options to explore are: redefining the *sales item* (improving functionality, bundling or unbundling, carving out different property rights to trade); changing the *pricing logic* (altering price levels, switching price carrier); and/or devising fresh *matching methods* to connect providers and customers (digitalizing platforms, or building on existing bricks-and-mortar methods).

- For a market to run smoothly and develop takes more actors than just buyers and sellers. The *network* needed may run to sub-contractors, providers of complementary products or services, intermediaries, information providers, market research agencies, media, interest groups, regulators, and more. Here, market-shaping options to explore are: enhancing the *set of actors* (adding or removing actors, securing a healthy level of competition); *redefining actor roles* (clarifying and optimizing role division, educating customers and other actors to play their role); and/or fostering material and immaterial *infrastructure* (investing in infrastructure even if it earns no direct revenue, extending your role to infrastructure provider, or inducing other actors to build it).

- *Representations* cover all the forms of verbal and nonverbal language that let us represent to ourselves and others the elements and shape of market systems. Here, market-shaping options to explore are: coining or adopting facilitative *language* (making product category names accessible, deploying ancillary language and concepts to explain a new market, and familiarizing the unfamiliar via metaphors, conceptual extensions, and boundary concepts); fostering confidence-encouraging *information* (setting the agenda for media attention to legitimize new markets, ensuring suitable market research and statistics); and/or promoting *symbols* that legitimize new markets (events and awards aligned with your market vision or industry associations for their cachet of authority).

- *Rules of the Game*, whether formal standards and regulations or informal social norms, define what are acceptable plays. Here, market-shaping options to explore are: influencing de facto or de jure *standards* (building coalitions and/or pushing for adoption, allying with the biggest faction in standards wars, forgoing your IP for a favorable standard); securing *regulation, de-regulation, or re-regulation* (persuading regulators with hard facts or surrogate advocacy by customers and others or industry self-regulation to stabilize a market); and nudging *social conventions* (influencing customer preferences, challenging obstructive industry conventions).

4

LEARN SHAPING PRINCIPLES AND PLAYS

When should you make your market-shaping move? How do you pitch your desired market "shape" to other actors? And are there any classic combinations of moves every shaper simply must have?

Advancing in any strategy modality requires gaining a bird's-eye view seeing beyond ad hoc moves to cohesive patterns.

Market-shaping's rich variety of moves share common principles about timing and win-win-win outcomes. Timing your move to proven signs of shapeability makes the difference between striking while the iron is hot and repeatedly striking your head against a brick wall. Moreover, every pitch should specify and ideally quantify – in the right language and in good faith – likely wins to those actors you need to move with you. Likewise, every shaper will repeatedly profit from a handful of generic go-to combinations.

LES MILLS INTERNATIONAL: WORKING OUT WITH WINNING TIMING

In New Zealand, the name Les Mills conjures images of greatness: decorated track and field athlete, revered coach, high-flying politician, and successful businessman. As an athlete, Leslie Royce Mills represented New Zealand in four Commonwealth Games and as many Olympic Games in shot put and discus throw and took his place on the medalists' podium five times. He served as mayor of Auckland, New Zealand's largest city, for the best part of a decade. And in business, he accumulated successes in retail, property development – and running gyms.[1]

However, it has been Les' son, Phillip, who finally made Les Mills into a household name outside New Zealand. Phillip also represented New Zealand in track and field and an athletics scholarship took him to the University of California, Los Angeles (UCLA), between 1974 and 1978. The timing couldn't have been better for his business prospects. Phillip was able to witness first-hand the birth of the modern aerobics industry. Aerobic exercise as a concept had been coined in the United States in the late 1960s, and by the late 1970s, aerobic (or cardio) exercise classes were all the rage. "Peak aerobics," you might say, was reached in 1982 when Jane Fonda's big-haired, long-legged, and – to modern eyes – nostalgically coarse-grained workout routine started twisting and spooling around the heads of the world's multiplying millions of video cassette recorders.

Back in New Zealand, having joined the family's gym business full time in 1980, Phillip applied his mind to systematizing the American group fitness phenomenon. At that time, the commonest group exercise to music was aerobics, and its commonest form was the so-called freestyle. Freestyle instructors selected their own music, choreographed the routines, and, if necessary, tweaked those routines to suit the assembled individuals' stretching, bending, flushing, and puffing in front of them. Unfortunately, the intersection set of brilliant choreographers and charismatic instructors (not to mention super-fit human specimens) is a decidedly slim and select one. Its small size limited the quality and therefore ultimately also the quantity of the aerobics market.

Phillip's stroke of market-shaping genius was to eliminate this supply bottleneck by creating standardized classes that are updated regularly by top-notch choreographers (to save the fashion forward from sweating uncoolly to the beat of a song that is "so last year") and setting up a system for training instructors. This combination of standardized classes and teacher training ensured a simultaneous excellence in class content and instruction which enabled more instructors to get into the choreographed music exercise scene. And with more high-quality instructors, more excited customers were soon signing up.

Les Mills (the business, not the person – though Olympic athletes are capable of impossible-sounding feats) was floated on the stock market in 1984. This enabled the family members to exit the business – but after the 1987 stock market crash, Phillip bought it back. At which point, cue another canny move when it comes to timing. By the late 1980s, interest in aerobics was on the wane. Leotards and legwarmers didn't cut it anymore, and there was some disappointment in the fitness outcomes – the low-intensity training just didn't deliver the improvements in muscular strength, endurance, fat burning, and aerobic fitness that health-conscious self-improvers were striving for.

In 1990, Les Mills launched the massively popular BodyPump class. BodyPump,[2] then just called Pump, brought weights and high-intensity training to group exercise to music. It utilized the same bottleneck-busting features – standardized classes, teacher training system – on the supply side that the company had perfected in the 1980s. Only, this program aimed to widen the market of group fitness further still. The high-intensity and deliberately masculine look and feel got men along to the studio, while breaking female customers free from the assumption that women shouldn't or couldn't do weight training.

With the reinvigorated fan base of BodyPump enthusiasts already forming long lines outside studios in Australia and New Zealand, prospects beyond Down Under's gorgeous shores beckoned, too. Les Mills International was born. This current company focuses on developing and licensing Les Mills programs around the globe. Since 1997, its internationalization has relied on independent distributors. Les Mills International sells regional distribution rights covering one or more countries to a distributor who then sells local gyms the rights to offer Les Mills programs, such as BodyPump or BodyBalance, to their customers. However, the distributors play a more significant role than that of a passive re-seller: they often translate the materials into the local language and add a necessary twist of the local flavor. For example, because France's fitness sector is comparatively academic, the French distributor is responsible for beefing up local marketing and product information materials with extra technical and scientific details. In addition to distributors, Les Mills International's success[3] relies heavily on the community of deeply engaged instructors – for many customers will pick up their gear and follow their favorite instructor from gym to gym, even from one exercise program to another. So, each time a charismatic instructor defects to a non-Les Mills gym, or switches from offering Sh'bam to Zumba classes instead, the company loses his or her loyal consumers, too.

During the last 20 years, Les Mills International has gradually finessed its business model so that every actor in the equation feels that they are winning.[4] For example, there is a buyout provision for the distributors. Since the distributor agreement is not a freely sellable asset, a clause ensures that after a specified number of years, the distributer can sell their business back to Les Mills International for an agreed multiplier – giving the distributors an incentive to grow their business. The gyms feel that they are winning as well, because Les Mills programs consistently draw the crowds. For their part, instructors win with Les Mills International, because they're guaranteed access to the latest music, the best choreography, and rock-solid teacher training – the wherewithal to make them look like rock stars when in front of their classes. And being among the tightly knit Les Mills instructor clan doesn't hurt them either, especially seeing how many instructors are self-employed and thus lack the collegial and social network for which we often rely on our places of employment. And the consumers? They are (positively) addicted to the BodyPump experience and know (in great detail, if they're French) that there is scientific evidence that this program improves their measurable fitness from bone density and muscle strength to endurance.[5]

Now Les Mills International is attempting its third move to shape its market by offering BodyPump workouts digitally, via Les Mills On Demand,[6] direct to consumers in their living rooms. Time will tell whether this new, wider matching method will write yet another happy chapter to the company's success story.

TIMING IS EVERYTHING

In market shaping as in comedy, timing is everything. If your timing is off, even a crystal clear vision for your market and a shrewd strategy for which Fan layers you will reconfigure to realize it may in fact realize nothing other than lost time and resources.

In this section, we'll address the three main questions around timing your market shaping. First, shapeability: is your market system currently hot and malleable, or frozen stiff? Second, if it is shapeable, should you follow your competitive instinct and bravely play first mover, or let someone else blaze the trail? Third and alternatively, if your market is not shapeable at the moment, how do you turn your enforced waiting time to best advantage? The answers to these questions provide the first of this chapter's two principles undergirding market-shaping plays.

Understanding When Your Market Is Shapeable: Striking While the Iron Is Hot

The theory of complex systems that we sketched in Chapter 1 predicts markets will always be in a process of "becoming." Even in instances where a firm seems to be shaping − or making − an entirely new-to-the-world market, there will have been some adjacent market or some predecessor system by which consumers met needs similar to what the "brand new" market will supply. And empirically, mapping the life of market ecosystems over sustained periods, our work has confirmed that markets can behave quite differently over time. Long eras may exhibit relative calm and stability — some gradual development, perhaps, but more or less constant basic structure and rules of the game. Punctuating the stability, however, come times of turbulence. At such points, the market undergoes rapid changes — and perhaps becomes a completely different market ecosystem.

Savvy market shapers seek to time their efforts to coincide with these latter periods of instability, rapid change, or discontinuity. The reasons are two. First, in market ecosystems as in physical systems, the static coefficient of friction is much larger than the kinetic one. Translating the physics speak, you need less market shaping elbow grease to nudge an already-mobile market into your favored direction than to stir a static one into motion in any direction. Second, a market-shaping initiative which promises a credible end to current instability with a new equilibrium will appeal to the natural human — and commercial — craving for stability. People and firms are creatures of habit. Thus, market systems which are turbulent, discontinuous, or just unstable are more malleable — more shapeable.

But how can you tell whether your market is in one of those unstable, malleable phases or not? Well, you can try shopping for such information off-the-shelf among conventional research. A 2012 McKinsey study[7] investigated the "malleability" of different industries. Let malleability stand in for our term shapeability and despite our known misgivings, let "industries" substitute for markets. McKinsey ranked healthcare products and services, other consumer services, food products, energy equipment and services, and gas utilities as the most malleable industries on a continuum. At the other end, office electronics, tobacco, and automobiles came in as the most stable and least malleable. Trouble is, of course, the research shelf is often bare of your particular market of interest. Even when not, the advice is generic and equally available to your rivals. More importantly though, the shelf life of these studies resembles that of a periodical — or frankly, a dairy product. One unexpected event — a natural catastrophe, a regulation added or removed, a breakthrough technology — and your stable market erupts into a turbulent one literally overnight.

While acknowledging the issue of timing is as much art as science, we offer three more generalized and enduring signs of shapeable markets. First, any major shock or crisis brings turbulence. For an example from the natural world, the devastating earthquake in Christchurch, New Zealand, in 2011 has disrupted local construction and related market ecosystems. This discontinuity has initiated a very deliberate national conversation around whether New Zealand as a whole should move from concrete to wood as its building material of choice. (They don't call it The Shaky Isles for nothing.) Short of obvious shocks or crises, a second sign of a shapeable market is rising dissonance or debate in the market — from controversy to simply a buzz abroad that "something should change." Such dissonance is an especially strong indicator of a market-shaping window if it is sustained for a long period of time or if it seems to be increasing in intensity rather than gradually subsiding. Finally, the recent history of the market ecosystem may also divulge clues about its malleability. Recent studies[8] suggest that markets which have assumed their current form through a government-led process or the deliberate market-shaping efforts of a particular firm are more susceptible to continued market shaping than those which have evolved organically, without strong influence from any particular market actor.

Systems theory also teaches us that random emergence will unpredictably co-shape market development. And practice bears that out. In practice, assessing shapeability is often a process of educated trial-and-error. You may remember from Chapter 3 Stora Enso, the global forestry giant that's shaped the Finnish market to allow for wooden high-rise buildings. Truth be told, though, success didn't happen first pop. Stora Enso had already tried to seize the moment of a short but definite increased interest in using more wood in residential high-rise buildings in the late 1990s. The company encouraged its builder customers to use wood whenever the regulations allowed. However, the interest waned quickly, and Stora Enso's efforts weren't enough to revive it. In their self-assessment of why this early market-shaping venture didn't come off, Stora Enso freely admit that their wooden high-rise strategy in that decade lacked certain important strengths of its re-incarnated version in the late 2000s. For example, the regulatory bottlenecks went uncleared and the company stuck to its comfort zone as a provider of raw materials rather than bear the burden of element development and temporarily extend its role into a co-builder and developer offering pre-fab construction components rather than raw materials. Yet Stora Enso management also told us that the market system itself felt somehow different and unreceptive so that any market-shaping play was less likely to take and stick at that time.

By contrast, a decade later a downdraft from the black cloud of the GFC brought a record 8.3% plunge in Finland's GDP in 2009. But the cloud had a silver lining. The strapped Finnish government rushed to embrace any initiative which promised jobs. That included re-regulating to allow wooden frames in taller buildings. Meanwhile, the US-led downturn in sawn timber forced Stora Enso itself out of its comfort zone into a range of other plays. Among many cost-cutting moves, the market-shaping initiative shone brightest and actually promised new topline growth.

Although the signs of shapeability may be subtle, and the intrinsic systems phenomenon of random emergence rules out predicting precisely how long a shapeable or unshapeable state may last, the secret of course is to maximize the art and science of reading markets and to minimize the error in your trial-and-error. But luck plays its part. Half of executives from 21 diverse firms we analyzed told us they put their firms' success in market shaping down partly to luck or serendipity. On closer analysis, that "luck quotient" was higher for success in identifying timing, in general, and market systems' shapeability, in particular.

Shapeable Market: First Mover or Fast Follower?

If your market is shapeable, the next question becomes: Should you aim to be the first mover or let someone else do the heavy lifting and opt for a fast-follower strategy?

Whether out of pure competitive reflex, or a scarcity mentality that latecomers will have to fight over scraps, many executives seem innately to prefer being the first mover. Yet, first mover advantages in market shaping occur much more seldom than you might think.

The elusiveness of first mover advantages is especially true when talking about creating an entirely new market ecosystem. In such instances, firms may benefit from being first mover only if they can answer "yes" to the following three questions. Are high levels of customer lock-in likely? Do we have a sufficiently flexible core technology and/or business model to accommodate changes when (not if) the market takes an unanticipated turn? And most importantly: Does the new market exhibit pronounced network effects − of a kind we can control and benefit from? Exhibiting network effects[9] means that the value of the core product or service in the market ecosystem rises exponentially with the number of people using that particular product or service. A classic example of network effects is the telephone. Except, say, to a hypothetical shy and reclusive collector of communication devices, a "network" of a single telephone is valueless because you can neither place nor receive calls. But telephones assume exponentially increasing value as more and more telephones are connected to the network. Even in the presence of clear network effects, though, the advantage, let alone necessity, of being the very first mover is somewhat unclear. Take social networking sites. During their coexistence, Myspace (launched in August 2003) was initially much more popular than its rival Facebook (launched in February 2004). However, in 2008 Facebook overtook Myspace as the most visited social networking side worldwide. So, at least in this case, being a first mover and building a strong initial position did not protect Myspace from Facebook. It'll be intriguing to see whether being "one of the firsts" will guard Facebook against later entrants such as Instagram or WhatsApp in the social networking arena. The billions Mark Zuckerberg spent acquiring these two companies in 2012 and 2014, respectively, might just pay off.

In many instances, then, it may be better to quell the urge to move first and instead opt for a fast-follower strategy in creating new markets. The fast-follower alternative is especially suitable in market ecosystems where the value creation to the customer is dependent on complementary actors or resources. (Note the difference from network effects, where the presence of more of the *same* products and services turbocharges the value.) To realize how important that dependence can be, let's compare the portable music player market in the early 1980s with the early 2000s. The 1980s was the golden era of Sony Walkman. Launched in 1979 in Japan, Sony Walkman was the first of its kind with the portable cassette player and compact headphones. The product was an immediate global hit, and despite competitors such as Sanyo and Panasonic following fast with similar or superior products, Sony managed to maintain its dominant position. In 1989, 10 years after the launch, Sony Walkman still controlled around 50% of the US and Japanese markets — while collecting a price premium of around 20 USD per device.

Although portable CD players to some extent supervened during the 1990s, the next big thing in the portable music player market was MP3 technology. The first mass-produced MP3 player, MPMan (a clear nod toward Walkman, which had become a catchall term for the entire category of portable cassette players) was launched in Asia by South Korea's SaeHan. However, the market was much slower to gain momentum with MP3 players than it had been with portable cassette players some 20 years earlier. In 2001, there were some 50 companies providing MP3 players in the United States, sharing a meager market with annual sales of less than 250,000 units. Then in October 2001, Apple launched its iPod – which became the holiday season hit with 125,000 units sold in less than three months. By 2009, Apple had sold over 200 million iPods worldwide and still commanded around 50% of the MP3 player market.[10]

Why did Apple's fast-follower strategy prevail in the market system whose previous iteration had so recently rewarded Sony's first-mover strategy? The answer lies – exactly as you no doubt anticipated – in complementary actors and resources. When Sony launched Walkman in 1979, consumers had no trouble getting their hands on the cassettes; cassettes had been widely available since 1972, so the world was awash with that resource. What's more, consumers were already thoroughly accustomed to playing cassettes in other devices, so no one had to educate them about, or familiarize them with, the technology. Contrast the landscape of complementary resources for MP3 players in 1998. As the world edged toward the millennium, an Internet infrastructure built on crackling, hissing 28.8Kbps dial-up modems did not yet facilitate downloading of MP3 files. Further, before Napster (launched in 1999), there were no actors that provided MP3 files for consumers on a mass scale – and the ones provided by Napster were of dubious legality. So, the users of early MP3 players had to be very technologically adept, patient with slow download times, and willing to bend the law. Apple timed its entry to the MP3 market well. For, by 2001, many of these market-level bottlenecks were being unblocked. Additionally, the compatible and intuitive iPod hardware and iTunes software made the use of MP3 files much easier for the consumer, further lowering the adoption threshold. And the final, master market-shaping move from Apple came in 2003 when the iTunes store was launched to the public, allowing consumers to purchase MP3 files legally and conveniently. Not surprisingly, the sales curve of iPods really steepened only after 2003.

There is, however, one truth about timing in the broadest sense that holds equally under first-mover and fast-follower tactics: Market shaping takes time. In the ongoing research project where we have analyzed 21 successful market shaping cases, the period from the initial idea to an observable change in the market system is typically counted in years. Rich as the payback from successful market shaping often is, it is vain to think that one can reap this payback – and reconfigure a vast socio-material system such as a market – in a matter of months.[11]

Non-Shapeable Market: The Art of Active Waiting

What do you do if you're bursting with an inspired vision for a future market ecosystem but the market seems persistently unshapeable and stubbornly resists your most energetic market-shaping efforts?

Even though you can sometimes overcome a high-static coefficient of friction, you may be wiser to postpone the active market shaping until the market shows signs of becoming more dynamic and malleable. But don't think of the delay as inaction. View it as what management scholars in a more general context have called "strategy as active waiting."[12] The central tenet of this thinking is simple: True strategic action is needed only when the operating environment poses a golden opportunity or an existential threat. Whenever such opportunities or threats don't exist – or are too vague to decipher – the task of the strategist is to wait patiently, head down, and mind focused on operational and tactical tasks. Under this philosophy, deciding to postpone a decision is a decision – and a very valuable one.

In a market-shaping context, active waiting can be the period when the firm perfects its readiness to launch the shaping strategy. Perhaps now is the time to shed that excess organizational fat and invest in operational efficiency, for instance? Additionally, intending market shapers may be well advised to build up a war chest while they wait. We've seen how handy Uber's war chest has already come in when faced with litigation and regulation, and just how deep a chest the Silicon Valley giant appears to consider necessary. (The difference is, this corporate juggernaut had not been actively waiting so much as actively waging the beginnings of the war.[13]) Not that war chests are sufficient, though. You'll recall from Chapter 1 that even 7 billion euro couldn't save Nokia Mobile Phones, a non-market shaper, from its market-shaping rivals Apple and Samsung.

Now, as long as active waiting only involves plans and PowerPoint presentations, you can't lose much other than time. But what about investments? Money spent based on a faulty strategy is usually money wasted. How, then, to make clever investments while waiting for your market to become more shapeable?

In the general context of investments under uncertainty, strategists talk about "reserving the right to play." Such investments help the organization to stay in the game while avoiding premature commitments. Much the same applies in the market-shaping context. And right now, companies in various sectors are developing their digital capabilities in order to reserve a right to shape their increasingly digital future market systems. These investments are made today, even though the period of active market shaping may be 10–20 years into the future in several of these sectors.

Three rules of thumb help identify possible "reserving the right to play" investments. First of all, be as low cost as possible. You are merely securing the option. When the time comes, you will most likely have to invest heavily in the actual shaping. Second, minimize lock-in. A shapeable phase may be years off (unless one of those surprise events like natural catastrophes, regulatory shifts, or a game-changing technology supervenes). By then, investments that shackle you to a technology, geography, or support infrastructure may well be obsolete. Finally, you'd be surprised how often such low cost and low lock-in investment opportunities are sitting right under your nose, among your own organizational capabilities. So, please, as we've cautioned before, don't overlook capability development as HR fluff. Take the time to consider whether such investments — via either internal development or targeted, small-scale acquisitions — could reserve you the right to shape your market in the future.

MAKE YOUR STRATEGY WIN-WIN-WIN

Besides getting the timing — deliberately or by sheer luck — right, successful market-shaping strategies follow a second undergirding principle: They benefit more than just the shaper. Market-shaping strategies couldn't be more different from zero-sum games in this respect. They aim for win-win-win outcomes, and you have to sell them as such.

In this section, we'll look into the delicate and elusive art of win-win-win: why it is necessary, who should be "in it" to win it, and how to quantify the wins for respective actors. We'll end by addressing the fine balancing act of collaborating with your competitors to shape markets and then competing with the same players to share them — without becoming anti-competitive.

Ensuring Win-Win-Win within the Minimum Viable System

This section addresses those first two questions: why win-win-win is necessary and who should be in it to win it. Let's begin, though, with an ethical detour. One of the greatest concerns that clients and students typically raise with us about market-shaping strategies is the notion of entrusting commercial organizations with major influence over the development of markets. If companies care only about their bottom line, the argument goes, ought they wield the power to make and shape markets? Should everything be for sale? Will this lead to a winner-takes-all, corporations-rule-the-world dystopia? And who will speak for the powerless — the environment, children, the oppressed?

Rest easy. Without going deeper into the moral limits of markets,[14] we are cautiously optimistic about avoiding dystopic futures even if more companies wake up to their potential influence over their market ecosystems. The reason may surprise you. It is the very fact that most market systems are increasingly complex, networked, and — key to present purposes — transparent. This trinity of features democratizes and dilutes power rather than concentrating it. For, any single would-be market shaper must first convince numerous other actors of their vision's merits. So even if one willing accomplice would abet a cynical rogue actor at (further) pillaging the oceans, raping the landscape and marching children of the poor into sweatshops, odds are that some other actor will say No — for whatever reason, including their own self-interest. In fact such systems do better than democratize. They confer veto power, so tyrannous majorities can't carry the day. As we'll explain, any enduring market-level change must be embraced by all actors in a certain minimum subset of that market.

The flipside of consensus is win-win-win. (Readers versed in game theory or group dynamics might know it as cooperative games, games without losers, or non-zero sum games. But by any other name the rose smells as sweet.) What drives win-win-win is simply having to sell other, basically self-interested actors on your market vision. If you've ever worked in actual sales, you know the amount of appealing required to close a deal, even when the customer's landing themselves a doozy of a product for a snip of a price. Now multiply the effort up for market shaping. Your pitch now also has to convince all the other actors who are necessary for the customer to extract value from your products and services.

Picking up on those necessary actors, the first step in promoting a market-shaping vision is to figure out the "minimum viable system[15]" of your market. What channels are needed to reach the customers? What happens between your customers and the end user? What kind of sub-contractors and business partners will you require? Working out the requisite value chain is only half the job, though. In addition to the physical value chain, your future market system most likely needs other actors in it. Should you be stalking the corridors of power and knocking on the door of policy-makers? Getting down to tin tacks with the organizations that devise and maintain technical standards? Winning over special interest groups of consumers? And what about media, research organizations and the education system?

Okay, so you've identified the actors in your minimum viable market system. Now do some math. How does the envisioned change impact each respective actor? Who stands to gain? Who will lose? Will some actors remain unaffected? Anecdotal evidence suggests that those market-shaping initiatives which both (1) create a positive change to all actors involved and (2) distribute the added value relatively evenly across the network enjoy the best chances of succeeding. Conversely, just as you'd expect, it seems a very tall order to coax anyone possessed of an alternative into accepting a market innovation that either (1) leaves them worse off than the status quo or (2) lands the vast majority of the benefits into the lap of the market shaper. Our evidence suggests that relatively equally distributed win-win-win best ensures success.

The Finnish healthcare sector bears testimony to the power of such egalitarian, multi-win market-shaping strategies — and not in the way you might expect. A couple of years ago, the country's number one insurance company, OP Group, grew tired of fighting the sector's endemic ills. Yes, the technical quality of care was top-notch. But the systems weren't nearly as patient-centric as popular discourse would suggest. For we've all shared those dinner party conversations about social problems where someone ends up playing he Nordic trump card of an ideal solution: "Well, in Finland/Sweden/Norway, they just ...." Thing is, no discrete actor was truly interested in the obvious societal good of getting people back on their feet and back to work as fast as possible. The respective incentives of hospitals, doctors, nurses, pharmaceutical companies, and the other players simply never quite aligned with that macro goal. At first, OP Group tried pushing against the big institutions like university hospitals. When these refused to budge (static coefficient of friction being up somewhere through the roof), OP Group decided to set up its own hospital, with just two objectives: maximizing patient satisfaction and patient outcomes – in other words, getting people back on their feet and back to work. Not surprisingly, shaping a national healthcare market was a herculean task. (After all, the government itself hadn't pulled it off.) Undaunted, though, OP Group have come out and publicly questioned established practices in the medical community, starting with who is best equipped to determine the length of sick leave. They've also pressed on the sore point that the private sector performs a lot of unnecessary surgical procedures. Yet, despite the odds, OP Group's healthcare business is growing fast. From a single, orthopedics-only hospital in 2013, they're on track for five full-suite hospitals by 2018, and they've racked up a country-wide chain of medical clinics to boot.

The good people at OP Group attribute this coup to their win-win-win-win concept (yes, they threw in a fourth "win," just to be on the safe side). Patients benefit from better and faster outcomes, and the service still comes with a smile. Employers benefit from reduced absenteeism. OP Group benefits from better outcomes, faster, and thus smaller claims. And the whole of Finnish society benefits from a healthier workforce. No wonder that OP Group's current hospital is continually laying out the welcome mat for delegations from all around the world. They are hoping to translate the success formula to the benefit of their national healthcare systems and, perhaps, to reassert the Nordic trump card in dinner party conversations among the worried well.

Note the limits to spreading your market-shaping love, though. *It's only the actors in your minimum viable market system whom you have to treat nicely and fairly!* Market shaping can, and does, generate losers! That's why ignoring market shaping just isn't an option. And it's half the reason we've urged you to shape markets yourself – lest some other player who doesn't need you in their minimum viable system gets in first and forces you out. Some market-shaping strategies have, in fact, bankrupted companies. And while the word "disruption" may inspire dreams of deliciously unreasonable wealth in the minds of would-be disrupters, it will strike fear into the hearts of the professions and sectors that would be disrupted. The reason Nokia Mobile Phone was a casualty of market shaping is that it was dispensable to the market vision of Apple and other smartphone manufacturers. Nor is the mighty Apple in the form of the iPod/iTunes business model immune to losses inflicted by others' market-shaping efforts. Because music streaming services like Spotify simply don't need Apple on side in their minimum viable system any more than Apple needed Nokia. So look lively. Market shaping is about not only thriving, but simply surviving. Note some strategy implications in this. You can raise your chances of both thriving and surviving by making yourself indispensable, or at least very desirable, to other potential market shapers. Stay closely and amicably connected to as many players as possible, so that would-be rival market shapers figure either that you are a key partner in your own right, or that they can only reach key partners through you, and/or they simply prefer to partner with you because you are so helpful and such a pleasure to work with. Continuously scan and probe the market for emergent trends so you are not blindsided. Foster nimbleness, with differentiated capabilities and as few irretrievable commitments as possible, so that you can pivot to new market developments. And consciously consider what complementarity you could offer to the emergent product or service even if you can't offer the product or service itself.

Quantifying the Win-Win-Win to Get Others on Board

Thus far, we've explored why win-win-win is necessary and who needs to be in the circle of winners — namely your minimum viable market system. Now let's get more specific about how you sell your market vision to those core actors. The answer, in short, is to quantify the benefits. It's simple. Telling a business partner that your market view benefits them is a good way to open a conversation about collaborating. But showing them they will lift their sales by 50 million USD each year for five years is more likely to close the deal.

We can't overstate that lesson. Too often we meet disheartened market shapers who have given up, not because their proposition encountered actual resistance from the other market actors, but because merely lukewarm responses damned it with faint praise. "Yeah, sounds kind of interesting" makes for heart-breaking feedback if you believe your market-shaping brainchild could save the world. Yet, tantalizingly, retrospective analysis revealed that many of these "neither rejected nor embraced" ideas were actually win-win-win, capable of creating plenty of value to all actors in the minimum viable market system.

So, why the indifferent responses to these basically valuable ideas? Too often, our disillusioned market shapers simply hadn't done their homework properly. It's about due diligence. You've got to investigate in detail what kind of value the reshaped market would generate to each particular actor. In order both to open fruitful dialogue about your vision and to close the deal, you've got to be able to paint every prospective partner a clear, compelling, realistic, and specific picture of what's in it for them.

Say your vision promises to revolutionize the residential construction market. Simply reciting like a mantra "My vision is win-

win-win" or enthusing that your market innovation will leave "everyone better off" won't cut it. For one thing, it's just not specific enough. "Better off" means different things to the home owner, the construction company, the master builder, the architect, and the insurance company. To get more than a foot in the door, you must be able to spell out the benefits of market shaping in each actor's context, using their language.

This is especially true since market shaping — like all win-win-win strategies — requires a so-called abundance mentality.[16] You and your partners must believe there will be rewards aplenty for everyone. And the cornucopia you evoke must be doubly plausible and compelling to sustain collaboration over the long haul, since market shaping typically takes years, sometimes even a full decade or so. Multiply up the degree of convincing required if your market's starting position is more like austerity or frugality than abundance. Such states foster a scarcity mentality and zero-sum game thinking.

Numbers talk and so does money. So as well as becoming an expert on each collaborator's likely win and framing it in their language and their context, get specific, quantify it, and, in particular, count the dollars wherever possible. As an instructive example, let's take a look at how quantification worked in large-scale shaping of the massive European market for e-invoicing. Over 30 billion paper invoices are sent in that continent every year. Would you believe, though, that as late as 2008 only a paltry 3% of the invoices were electronic?[17] Until very recently, the process of sending and paying invoices was overwhelmingly a manual one.

The manual processing of invoices is slow and costly. First, the paper invoice is received via mail. The envelope containing the invoice must be delivered to the right person and the person must open the envelope (we never claimed it was rocket science — just cumbersome). After this, the invoice will be inputted to the accounting system as an account payable. The actual payment usually takes place in an online banking system, which requires both entering the data and approving the transaction. After this, the invoice must be archived and sent to the accountant for balancing. All in all, this process takes on average 14 minutes for each invoice and costs almost 30 euro. (And in other news, there are people whose day job is conducting time and motion studies of paper invoices.) E-invoicing slashes the time to one minute and the cost to a shade over three euro per invoice. Now scale that up to EU level. European trading would save 238 billion euro per annum by switching from paper invoicing to e-invoicing. Such value quantifications have been instrumental to the likes of banks and ITC companies pushing e-invoicing and the real-time economy. Since the mid-2000s, the EU has made great strides toward facilitating e-invoicing, boldly going where no Eurocrat has gone before by simplifying cross-border VAT red tape and creating the Single Euro Payments Area (SEPA).

Don't be put off if you can't project wins with 100% accuracy. No one can. The thing is, your value quantification still serves to make the benefits tangible and to demonstrate that you have thought about the opportunity from the other party's perspective. Honesty is the best policy, anyway. Being transparent about possible sources of error and assumptions used both garners you trust and is very often an excellent way of engaging prospective partners in a dialogue about your market view and its benefits. And that is a conversation from which you, too, can learn.

So, what kind of benefits to quantify? Obviously, monetary measures lend themselves to value quantification: Does the new and revamped market system increase your partner's revenues, lower his costs, ease his capital expenditure, or lower his risks? But you needn't limit yourself to profit and loss and balance sheet statements alone. Very often improvements in sustainability or well-being can also be quantified. For example, our innovative Finnish health insurer OP Group went to great lengths communicating its ability to improve patient outcomes. The hospital was able to show that it had shortened the typical period of disability from 62 days to 23 in meniscus tear incidents and from 160 days to 104 in shoulder injuries — just because of its faster and more patient-centric care procedures.

Collaborate to Shape, Compete to Share

If explaining the necessity for win-win-win furrows brows among our more competitive consulting clients, then breaking it to them that the winners will include some of their sworn rivals does worse than raise hackles. Backs get arched. Dummies are sometimes spat: "Are you seriously suggesting helping our competitors? What have our competitors ever done for us?" Now believe us. We feel your pain. But our answer remains a sturdy "yes." For theory and practice are in agreement here. A market-shaping strategy that helps your competitors win as well will significantly improve your chances of success.

There are three main reasons why you should keep your friends close and enemies closer — in win-win-win relationships — when shaping markets. They are variations on a theme: personal advantage, if not necessity. First, all too often even giants lack the power to shape their market systems alone. You can close the "oomph deficit" by partnering with a competitor who shares, or could be persuaded to share, a similar vision for your market system. Consider, for instance, two Scandinavian companies which rent out construction equipment, Cramo and Ramirent. The pair sport relatively similar fleets of equipment, portfolios of additional services, and geographical footprints. So no wonder that Cramo and Ramirent compete cut-throat in Northern Europe. Russia, though, is a different beast. The Eurasian colossus offers a vast opportunity for both companies. Its construction output is estimated to be fivefold that of Finland, the home country of both Cramo and Ramirent. Inevitably, there's a "but." Rental penetration (the ratio of rented to owned construction equipment) sits at only one-fourth of the Scandinavian level. Long story short, Russian construction companies like to own equipment, not rent it. Separately, both Cramo and Ramirent had tried without much success to preach the gospel of renting to their Russian clients: less tied-up capital, no maintenance hassle, top-of-the-line equipment. So in 2013, the two companies joined forces and started a 50/50 joint venture with a deliberate aim to shape the Russian and Ukrainian construction markets toward more rental. The joint venture, Fortrent, has a distinct brand, so that the market-shaping collaboration in these two places doesn't hinder the companies' competitive actions in other regions.[18] The events of 2014 − annexation of Crimea, shooting down of MH17, economic sanctions between Russia and EU − make it too soon to tell whether Fortrent has been truly successful in changing construction practices in Russia and Ukraine. But the venture had at least got off to a good start before then.

The second reason for collaborating with your competitors to shape markets is to prevent painting yourself into a niche corner. Say you have a brilliant idea to improve your market system. Unaided, you manage to change some elements of it. The new channels are there, new terminology has been created, the media embraces the new concept, and some customers are keen advocates as well. Despite all these achievements, if none of your competitors embraces these new developments, your "market shaping" will probably just create a new niche sub-segment, with you as the sole provider. *The inconvenient truth of market shaping is that, barring monopolies, for true market-level changes to occur, the majority of the competing providers have to change their ways.* Little wonder, then, that a CEO of an ecological fashion company told us in a recent interview: "We [the providers of ecological fashion] are competitors only when we are competing for the same deal − when we submit competitive proposals, that is. But in the grander scheme of things we are collaborators. We are all driving a similar change in the marketplace, promoting the same ecological values."

Finally, there's a third reason to collaborate with competitors. In some instances, collaboration is a plain prerequisite for any change in the market system. This is especially likely in market systems characterized by few providers and much regulation – such as airlines. Consider Air New Zealand. This strategically shrewd national carrier plays a central network role in the domestic economy, particularly the all-important tourism sector. A recent strategy statement[19] recognizes uncontrollables like fuel price fluctuations, natural disasters and weather conditions, global and regional recessions, and unpredictable exchange rates. Rather than try even to forecast these, the statement says Air New Zealand will target controllables: the fleet, the "product," safety of operations, firm culture, and particularly the network, where "network" means both routes and network alliances.

New Zealand's "open skies" policy to boost tourism has forced Air New Zealand into alliances to make the overall market structure more hospitable to them.[20] Its new cooperation agreements with other airlines go beyond being a member of the global Star Alliance. They extend to immunized revenue-sharing arrangements, in which two airlines join forces on a specific route and share the revenues based on bilateral agreements.

The first bilateral alliance came on the competitive and unprofitable trans-Tasman routes, to Australia. A separate alliance with Virgin Australia in 2011 granted access to each other's national network (routes) based on revenue sharing.[21] Both actors made profits. Since then, similar arrangements have been forged with Cathay Pacific for the Hong Kong route and Singapore Airlines for the Singapore route.

These alliances required new capabilities for dealing with governmental and regulatory actors at both ends, with a collective pitch on how customers would reap lower prices and access to more routes. For example, on the Singapore route, the alliance was authorized for an initial four years from 2014. The airlines will have to demonstrate that the alliance has delivered real benefits to consumers, without adversely impacting competition in other markets.[22]

And finally, after all that talking up of collaboration, we turn as promised to competition. It's a short but important coda. Having extolled the benefits, and sometimes the plain necessity, of involving competitors in your market-shaping strategy, let's sound a note of warning. Such collaboration should be limited to market shaping. Once the market has been shaped, it's time to slip into something that traditional strategists will find more comfortable: the normal practice of competing for market shares. Indeed, if you don't you risk tipping onto a slippery slope down to the anti-competitive "dark side" of market shaping: illegal, or at least unethical, collusion.

USE GENERIC PLAYS

There's no point reinventing the wheel. By consulting and teaching widely across both hemispheres and researching back in time, we have identified many members of the exclusive international "club" of intuitive market shapers. And we've broken down their intuition into a common, learnable system, isolating 13 designable elements of our market Fan across its core and the four layers. Working a tad mechanically from the core outwards, Chapters 2 and 3 walked you through those elements and how to shape them one by one, with tips wherever possible on when and where to target each. But we can now go one step further. Our knowledge of the field is now wide enough to distill (so far) *five generic plays — and variations within them — which ought to feature prominently in any market shaper's repertoire* (see Figure 4.1).

By definition, all these plays — like the great majority of market-shaping strategies — increase market size and/or profitability. But note another feature of our plays: They are combinations, usually with a shared starting point (such as pricing logic). For, as foreshadowed, in real life, market-shaping moves seldom

Figure 4.1. Generic Market-Shaping Plays.

occur in isolation. Market shapers more often need to combine elements either sequentially, like a series of moves in a sporting play, or simultaneously, like a musical chord. The plays in the next pages thus *tend to be sequences and chords rather than single notes*. Finally, these five plays are also *generic*: you can employ them pretty much as-is in a vast number of contexts. Hence, the metaphorical wheel that we can now supply to you ready-made and road-tested to spare you from reinventing it.

For the two or three combinations under each of our five categories, we'll explain which Fan layers to combine for each market-shaping play and the dynamics that explain their power to increase market size or profitability. And as usual we'll give you real-world examples.

Relocate the Exchange Interface

As markets are complex systems of exchange, it's unsurprising that the first arrow in our quiver — the first generic market-shaping play — turns on altering this core function. Many savvy market shapers aim to move or manipulate the interface where the monetary exchange — buying and selling — takes place. The commonest variations of this play consist of putting a price tag on a previously non-monetized activity, bundling offerings into larger solutions, or unbundling them into smaller stand-alone products and services.

Put a price tag on a previously non-monetized activity. We business people suffer our very own strain of the cognitive bias that Daniel Kahneman christened What You See Is All There Is, or WYSIATI. At least when thinking with our business brains we tend to apprehend only those human activities that have so far been monetized into tradeable products and services. This, even though once we leave work behind for civilian life at the end of the day (and admittedly the science is still out on whether the modern, hyperconnected executive can ever leave work behind) we engage as ordinary human beings in a host of activities that so far carry no dollar value — but could. Taking our business blinders off opens our eyes to the first variation of this generic market-shaping play. It involves deliberately looking beyond the currently monetized world and attaching a price tag to a previously non-monetized activity — thus hatching a brand new market. This play plies the exchange interface by pushing out the envelope of market exchange to include what used to be non-market.

The world of activities that resides outside monetized markets is vast. Take a humble example, housework. In addition to supplying a goldmine of resentment for domestic quarrels, the US Department of Commerce Bureau of Economic Analysis estimated that taking into account household work — which is currently excluded in all official national statistics — would have increased the US Gross, "Domestic," Product by 26% in 2010.[23] So, a single group of non-monetized activities (cooking, odd jobs, gardening, shopping, childcare, and domestic travel were also included in this study) is worth more than a quarter of the entire national output of the world's largest economy!

In consumer businesses, this market-shaping play starts by identifying things that people do without paying anything – instead doing them themselves, via voluntary work, by asking for favors, or using barter. In the business-to-business context, shrewd market shapers can find opportunities to monetize previously non-monetized activities by analyzing what their customers do using their own staff – and whether some of these activities could be insourced to the market shaper.

Coor from Sweden provides a great example of such a play in B2B. In the late 1990s Skanska, a Nordic construction giant, lit on an interesting new business opportunity: offering its B2B customers facility management services. At that time, large businesses such as Ericsson used to manage their facilities themselves. But cleaning the toilets and manning reception was hardly core business for any of these companies. So, the ears of Skanska's clients pricked up when Skanska suggested they outsource all this annoying ancillary activity back to the construction company. And Skanska made a natural discussion partner. After all, Skanska had built the facilities in the first place, so – the thinking went – it ought to know how to run them. In 1998, Skanska decided to spin out this promising new sideline, and Coor was born.[24] By 2016, in less than 15 years, Coor had grown into a leading Nordic facility management company that is listed on NASDAQ Stockholm and earns revenues of nearly 900 million USD.

Coor also illustrates nicely what it takes for this particular market-shaping play on the different layers of the Fan. First, you have to define the sales item. What is included and what is not: just cleaning or everything to do with facility management? And what property rights are being exchanged? (It is access rights in this case, since selling the ownership rights to staff like your cleaner jars with newfangled notions like human rights.) Second, you have to decide the appropriate price carrier. Will you charge by the hour, or per service? Or will you perhaps offer fixed-price contracts with certain performance level guarantees? By definition, insourcing activities that were previously conducted by your customers also changes the work division between you and your customers. So you'll more than likely have to ensure that your customers have got the necessary know-how to operate now that reception and cleaning have been outsourced to you, an external facility management company. Finally, monetizing a previously non-monetized activity often requires adjusting social norms and industry conventions. In this instance, it means making the case that it is an acceptable business practice — if not in fact best practice — for busy firms to outsource their facility management and other non-core activities so they can focus fully on their core businesses.

Bundling and unbundling. Our next variation of the exchange interface relocation generic play is bundling and unbundling of the sales item. Again, both occur at the exchange interface, and specifically the sales item. Let's take unbundling first. Examples already noted in Chapter 3 are turning music albums into individual songs and breaking down all-inclusive air fares into components such as checked-in baggage and reserved seating. Such unbundling of larger sales items into smaller ones — can be a market-shaping act (in other words, expanding the overall market or its profitability) if it creates more use value to customers.

In a similar vein, bundling separate products and services into turnkey solutions can sometimes be the main move in a market-shaping play. Now, most bundling examples come from B2B sectors. Hungry for a slice of after-sales services action in those sectors, providers of equipment from copying machines to nuclear power plants have started to bundle equipment, spare parts, and maintenance services into one-stop-shop solutions. But bundling for market shaping is not limited to B2B, as our next example brings home.

The last decade has seen the rise of food home delivery services
that provide not only the right ingredients but matching, easy-
to-follow recipes. In Scandinavia, a pioneer of this business model
has been the Swedish venture Linas Matkasse (literally Lina's
Food Bag). The company was founded in 2008 by Carolina
Gebäck ("Lina" to her friends and customers), who is a trained
dietitian and nurse, and her brother Niklas Aronsson.[25] The idea
for the business sprang from a series of seemingly simple but fundamental realizations. First, Niklas' wife questioned the time-
stealing rigmarole of traditional grocery shopping: "Why can't I
just order up my meal ingredients on the way home and have
them handed through my car window like in a drive-through?"
Second, it clicked to the siblings that, for all the well-publicized
patriotic pride in unique national cuisines, most folk in most
countries of our homogenizing world fancy remarkably similar
meals. Third, news flash: It turns out your average time-poor
homemaker brings less expertise and rigor to meal planning than
would your average quantity surveyor. Meal planning is tricky,
and an unseemly fraction of the ingredients you sprang for on
that out-of-your-way supermarket trip, from spuds to spinach to
spaghetti will wind up in the garbage. Enter the food bag. This
big little idea is a literal bundle of products and services which
solves all these problems in one go. Simply select your food bag
type – how many dinners per week (typically 4 or 5), how many
adults' and children's portions, and any special dietary requirements (vegetarian, lactose-free, gluten-free, easy-to-cook, you
name it). Hey presto, the precise bundle of ingredients and the
recipe to prepare them to arrive on your doorstep once a week.
And since your friend and ours, Lina, is a dietitian by training,
you can also rest assured that the recipes have enough fruit and
veg – and not too much of the bad stuff.

Unbundling and bundling by nature require redefining the
sales item: what is being exchanged, what is included and what
is not. Additionally, at the Representations layer, these market-

shaping plays tend to necessitate new terminology, like "maintenance services" in our B2B example, or "food bags." And at the Rules of the Game layer, you'll need to influence customer preferences: "Yes, in homemaking etiquette it is entirely respectable and *comme il faut* (may even become *de rigueur*) to get food delivered to the door — and good gracious no, the tomatoes in the bag won't be rotten." Moreover, bundling usually requires some changes in the pricing logic element of the Exchange layer. At the Network layer, there'll normally be adjustments to the work division between the company and its customers, since for instance customers used to manage their own internal bundling of equipment, spare parts, and maintenance services. Network structure itself might have to change, too. For example, food bag operators often partner with grocery retailers and logistics companies to source their ingredients and complete those last-mile deliveries.

Getting back to basics, how do unbundling and bundling lead to improved market systems, which were the prerequisite of market shaping? On the one hand, unbundling seems to be a double-edged sword as a generic market-shaping move. While in some cases, it may expand market size by enticing customers to use the service more or more often, in other cases, it can actually shrink markets.

Bundling, on the other hand, invariably grows market size. This growth commonly steals from adjacent market systems, though. For example, the growth experienced by the equipment manufacturer from its solution business tends to eat the lunch of stand-alone maintenance service companies, leaving them smaller market "pies" to slice up amongst themselves. The only exception to this rule are market shapers of the ilk of Linas Matkasse, where the growth comes from bundling non-monetized activities such as housework. No one in the adjacent, unpaid domestic duties system complains about having to split a smaller quantum of chores.

Directly Deliver Step-Change in Use Value

All market-shaping strategies raise use value for the customer —
that's a prerequisite for growing market size and gaining customer
acceptance for new market systems. However, not all market-
shaping strategies promise to boost customers' use value equally.
The second generic market-shaping play picks out two varieties of
use value creation: commercializing a new widget and improving
customers' use environment.

Commercialize a "new widget." In a business context, the textbook definition of "innovation" is the process of turning an invention into a good or service that has willing customers. In short,
innovation subs as a synonym for commercializing "new widgets," both tangible and intangible. Until now, we have confined
product and service innovations to the background in order to
foreground market shaping. Yet, interestingly, market shaping is
also called market innovation. It's now time to ask squarely: Do
product and service innovations relate to market shaping? And, if
so, how?

We have defined market shaping as the deliberate molding of
market systems which somehow leaves the market system better
off: bigger, more profitable, or more efficient in terms of resource
use. Drawing on this definition, the answer to our double-barreled
question is "yes, but." Yes, commercializing new products or services can shape markets — but only if this new widget increases
the use value that the customer derives from it. Hence our classify-
ing the commercialization of new widgets under the heading of
"Deliver step-change use value."

A marked — or in some cases massive — increase in use value is
absolutely crucial for a product or service innovation to count as
a market-shaping action. It's not rocket science. Without added
use value, there can be no increase in market size. Why would the
customer spend more — or why would new customers flock to the
market — if the new widget is just old wine in new bottles? And

thus, without more or higher-paying customers, the game remains an old-fashioned competitive quest for market share rather than a true market-shaping endeavor.

In Chapter 1, we used cars as an example of an innovation that helped to create a completely new market. The underlying activity, moving from point A to point B, had long since been monetized by the time Daimler, Benz, Rolls, Royce, Ford, and their less-celebrated colleagues came on the scene. A fleet of already alternatives awaited the aspiring traveler: horse-drawn carriages, trains, boats, bicycles, and so forth. But cars afforded unique benefits, greatly augmented customers' use value and created a new market system. Microchips, mobile phones, and X-ray machines are further qualifying examples of market-shaping product innovations.

When aiming to shape markets by commercializing a new product or service, you've got to ask yourself one key question is: Is your innovation wholly new-to-the-world, like the original patent mousetrap of 1879 that first disturbed rodent paradise? (It was a ghoulish-looking, fanged, spring-loaded jaw like a shark's snout, by the way.) Or is it, as they say, just a better mousetrap (like the iconic spring-loaded bar mousetrap which superseded the shark's snout in 1899)? New-to-the-world innovations offer the opportunity to create completely new markets à la cars or microchips. In these instances, the market shaper has to work on all the layers of the Fan diagram: from defining the exact sales item and pricing to molding the network to ensuring relatable representations and favorable rules of the game. The shaper need only offer "marked" extra use value.

Better mousetraps, however, are another matter. The good news is that most of the Fan layers of the existing market system will probably work in favor of the incremental innovation without full-blown market shaping. While you might have to tweak the sales item, representations, and standards, otherwise it ought to be relatively plain sailing. The bad news is that most "better mousetraps" aren't better enough. That is, they don't offer sufficient uplift customers' use value – and by sufficient we now mean not merely marked but massive. We have it on no less an authority than Google Inc. (the company itself, as in When Larry Met Sergei, not just its search results) that innovations must be at least ten times better than the current solution to pack a punch.[26] All those poor patent mousetraps that manage only, say, a ninefold increase will fall short and thus fail to shape the market. Their creators end up as mere niche players despite their technological superiority. And indeed, too often we meet confused entrepreneurs whose great innovation failed to shape a market. In an age of syndromes, our diagnosis is mostly to Better Mousetrap Syndrome – securing only incremental improvement in customers' use value. So, approach this variation of generic market-shaping plays with exceeding caution. Easy though it appears, it is one of the hardest to pull off!

Enhancing customers' use environment. There is another way of augmenting use value for customers besides commercializing new and improved offerings – one which again hinges on boosting use value. We approach it with mousetrap metaphor still in hand (gingerly, of course, so as not to guillotine a digit). Customers' use value depends not only on the mousetrap itself, but on the context in which it is used. Should customers not know how to deploy mousetraps or should some other element crucial to meaningful functioning (say, cheese) be absent or in short supply, then mousetraps don't generate much use value to customers. And this will inevitably limit the size of the market (not to mention potentially cost the users a finger or two). Luckily though, one firm's problem is another firm's market shaping opportunity, as we're about to see, and commercial creativity flows in to fill every such gap.

Sometimes improving customers' use environment starts from infrastructure. Textbook authors are fond of a pair of case examples: the invention of shopping bags and, later, shopping carts.

Both literally helped customers buy more than they could carry. In a similar vein, early bicycle and car manufacturers were very active in promoting the idea of building paved roads.

Even more opportunities for enhancing use environment dwell in exploiting customers' know-how – or lack of it. Time and again, the customer is simply not the best or most engaged expert on a vital preliminary matter: how to use a product or service. (Fear not: the customer will still always be right – just, not yet.) That holds especially true if the offering in question fails to set private consumers' hearts on fire or it is not utterly central to a B2B customer's business operations. In this vein, you might remember from Chapter 3 the New Zealand dairy giant Fonterra and its ventures into China. Fonterra's foodservice business spotted the gaps in local know-how and has very profitably filled them by educating Chinese restaurateurs and bakers on the correct use of dairy products to guarantee the most delicious end products.

Enhancing customers' use environment as a generic market-shaping play kicks off at the Network layer: ensuring that customers have the right know-how and infrastructure at their disposal. These activities usually have to be complemented at the Representations layer by ensuring the most apt, accessible terminology. For it helps if customers can ask by name for shopping carts and trip the same label off the tongue when enthusing to friends about their benefits. Similarly, Fonterra Foodservice skillfully drew a new nuance in the Chinese language, explicitly introducing a crucial distinction between non-dairy and dairy creams that had previously gone lost in translation.

Use Market-Widening Pricing

And so to the next generic play in our repertoire of generic market-shaping plays: market-widening pricing. You needn't drink the neoclassical Kool Aid and reduce humankind to mere *homo economicus* to grant that price wields considerable sway over market systems. The main variations of the present play, as-a-service pricing and disruptive economics, achieve more frequent consumption by more customers through making the offerings more affordable – or by aligning incentives of customers and providers.

As-a-service that lowers capital expenditure – or aligns incentives. One more generic market-shaping play kicks off from the sales item element of the Fan framework: what we've dubbed simply "as-a-service." Whereas we most readily associate the term as-a-service with software and other digital goods, businesses producing tangible goods or traditional, non-digitalized services can likewise shape their markets with this particular play – but the details vary slightly with context.

When aiming to shape markets with the as-a-service play in the tangible goods context, your key question becomes: Does the transition from selling the ownership rights to exchanging access rights (the theoretical basis of this whole play, as you'll recall from Chapter 3) help customers to shed a lot of capital expenditure? If the answer is yes, as in the case of jet engines (Bristol Siddeley's and Rolls-Royce's Power by the Hour concept) or most investment goods, then the as-a-service play rates a good chance of spurring market growth. And this play doesn't only apply to business-to-business customers. Consumers, too, will gladly consider leasing as an alternative to buying with big-ticket items such as cars, major appliances – or even art. More customers of both stripes will be lining up if they can access the good by leasing and thus spare themselves the hassle of financing and the liability of a ballooning balance sheet. That said, the laws of accounting do not currently allow the twin necessities of financing the manufacturing of tangible goods and keeping these goods on someone's balance sheet, somewhere, to vanish into thin air. Both these necessaries will land up in the supplier's lap. So, if you're contemplating an as-a-service market shaping move in the tangible goods context, check you have the strength to take this financial burden upon yourself.

Here's a puzzle. How, if at all, might the as-a-service move play in a service context? Service as-a-service sounds distinctly tautologous, and peddling it would sound like, in old language, the benchmark marketing feat of "selling ice-cream to Eskimos." You're already exchanging access rights instead of ownership – and investments in services are very seldom considered as capital expenditure. So, where could this strategic lever get purchase? In an Orwellian twist, while services may all seem equal, some are more equal than others. There turn out to be degrees of service-ness, as it were. Those services which customers buy infrequently, which are delivered as projects, and which carry a hefty price tag are better candidates for market shaping via the as-a-service play. Such are often professional services like management consulting or legal advice. Do you remember the northern European legal services firm we introduced in Chapter 3 which bucked the tradition of charging by billable six-minute units? Fondia's pioneering of LDaaS or Legal Department as a Service is a textbook example of an as-a-service play in the service sector. The secret ability of their move to expand market size comes from aligned incentives – and thus increased trust between customers and providers. This secret generalizes. In a raft of professional services that are sold as projects, the customers' and providers' interests are out of sync. Customers want their problems solved as quickly and efficiently as possible, whereas it is in providers' vested interest to make these problems appear as complicated as possible – so that the client's eyes don't pop out of their head with disbelief and their temples throb with outrage when they receive the bill. As-a-service contracts, which usually have a fixed price per month, elegantly resolve this conflict of interest. What's more, such as-a-service moves can offer a pleasantly surprising win-win. Bumpy, lumpy sales are a curse of professional services businesses. Since the business model sells projects, cash flows are a devil to predict. Even the longest projects face a 6- to 12-month horizon — after which, the order book of any law or consulting firm reveals only blank pages. Locking in long-term as-a-service contracts smooths providers' cash flows, while putting smiles on the faces of the bill-paying customers who know their service provider is not taking them for a long and very costly ride.

Like we said, the as-a-service move is based on defining the sales item: what is being sold. On top of this, a successful as-a-service move also requires redefining the price carrier. The price tag no longer attaches to a piece of machinery or an hour of a lawyer's time, but to a specified time period and agreed service level. As the sales item and the price carrier are modified, the customer typically has to learn new ways of dealing with the provider. In particular, new know-how about purchasing as-a-service contracts is needed. And to support the monitoring of as-a-service contracts and the cross-comparison of as-a-service providers, some new representations are likely to be needed. What will be the metrics of "success" and who'll collect the data for these metrics? Finally, a full-scale transition toward as-a-service markets usually necessitates some changes in industry conventions. The market-shaping firm has to convince clients it's safe and smart to buy legal services as a service, while combating any stigma or self-stigmatizing of their lawyers as somehow bulk-bought commodities in a market where boutique carries a premium. Status anxiety enters our business calculations more often than we'd care to admit!

Lower prices for disruptive economics. Lowering of prices is probably the only market-shaping act that neoclassical economics acknowledges. Little wonder, given that such disruptive innovations, often spurred by technological advances, have been around for centuries and are hard to gainsay. Consider, for example, the invention of the printing press —which happens to be a classic example of market shaping using disruptive economics. Invented by Johannes Gutenberg in 1436 — it was on all the front pages —

this breakthrough German engineering of its time dramatically lowered the production costs, and thus price, of books and other printed texts. Until then, manuscripts and whole books had been painstakingly copied by hand, mainly by bored and tetchy monks resenting their data-entry job status. (Amazingly, we know their state of mind from their surviving bitchy complaints in the margins, which rather detracted from the sanctity of the subject matter: "I am so cold," "Oh, my hand," "Won't someone please invent Typex™?" — though one of these is thought to be apocryphal.[27]) This new technology and the resulting lower prices increase the size of the medieval book market beyond belief: in mere decades, presses had spread to a dozen European countries (the medieval equivalent of going viral — only the plague, albeit actually a bacterium, managed it anywhere near literally). And the same time span saw more books printed than in the whole of human history before then — a staggering statistic, anti-medieval jokes aside.

The market-shaping dynamic of disruptive economics is simple, but powerful. Slashing prices makes the product or service available to completely new groups of customers — and lets existing customers consume radically more of the product or service in question. Just think of the poster children of low-price disruptors: budget airlines like Ryanair and fast-food restaurants such as McDonalds. The only thing we do more often than scoff at them is use them. Many passengers on low-cost airlines are taking to the skies for the first time, no longer grounded by the hefty prices of flagship carriers. And these cut-price operators let everyone fly more and more often. Anyone for a weekend shopping in Milan or a clubbing trip to Berlin? In a similar vein, many youngsters first eat out — with their own money, that is — at McDonalds or some other low-cost fast-food joint. Indeed, having a low-cost restaurant on every city block has made eating out a much more prevalent part of contemporary lifestyles — to the point that in many large cities, prospective tenants and apartment buyers will sometimes forgo a kitchen.

Harvard professor Clayton Christensen has made his name investigating disruptive innovations, especially the low-price ones. Interestingly, he finds that such low-cost disruptive innovations start out ignored, even laughed at, by incumbents (we already mentioned the scoffing), but become the dominant business models in most industries.[28]

To shape your market via disruptive economics, you'll need to orchestrate changes in the market system beyond slashing prices. Disruptive economics isn't just about low prices; it's also about low costs, since the business model has to be profitable for the provider over the long term. Slashing costs in turn usually translates into using new, cheaper channels and altering work division — either shifting responsibilities onto the customer the way IKEA turns us into unpaid but willing assembly workers or reshuffling the supplier network to drive as much cost out of the production as possible.

Widening Customer Catchment Area

Whereas the previous generic market-shaping play encourages more participation by more customers through making the products and services more affordable, the fourth generic play pursues the same ends more directly: by turning non-users and non-payers into paying customers and innovating wider and safer matching methods.

Turning non-users or non-payers into paying customers. Our next market-shaping play shares a family resemblance to disruptive economics, but is nevertheless its own individual. We saw that the market-shaping power of disruptive economics stems from two sources. Lower prices both (1) put the product or service within the grasp of new groups of customers and (2) let current customers use the product or service more copiously. Its relation, the generic move of turning non-users or non-payers into paying customers, taps into the former of those sources, namely bringing new customer groups to the market system. But it does so by other means than lower prices. So, same growth level, different methods.

BreadTalk, an international bakery chain, illustrates this move nicely. When George Quek and Katherine Lee founded the company in 2000, the demand for Western-style bakery products in their native Singapore was minimal. This, despite English heritage, Singapore having been Britain's "Gibraltar of the East" before the shocking defeat to the Japanese in World War II. In fact, in most Asian countries bread simply wasn't a staple item. The founders of BreadTalk would need to cultivate their own demand by making Asians fall in love with this baked doughy European mainstay. Two actions carried the day and ensured the suitor successful wooing. First, BreadTalk modified the traditional Western bakery products slightly to fit local Asian tastes. For example, pork floss (equally picturesquely known as meat wool) is a favorite in Chinese cuisine, either alone as a snack or wound as a topping over various savory foods.[29] BreadTalk's stroke of genius was to create a pork floss bun. The bun was an overnight hit and gently acclimated Singaporean (and other Asian) palates to Western bread. Second, BreadTalk assiduously educated consumers about baking, bread, and the ingredients therein. To this day, if you visit a BreadTalk retail outlet, you'll see an open kitchen where the bakers are a-baking and displays like those in an interactive museum explain such curiosities as how live yeast works. BreadTalk now boasts over 850 bakeries in Singapore, China, the Philippines, Vietnam, Thailand, Malaysia, Qatar, Kuwait, and elsewhere.

Not uncommonly you'll find this generic market-shaping move following on the heels of the very first one on our list: commercializing a previously non-monetized activity. That's because such commercialization normally arises within a rather clearly defined and specifically targeted customer segment — leaving plenty of untapped potential outside that segment if you're prepared to look further afield. Coor, the Scandinavian facility management company, showcases this point. Coor began life as a provider of facility management services to large commercial organizations the likes of telecom heavyweight Ericsson. After Coor had successfully created this new market in outsourced facility management, it looked around for fresh growth from other customer segments. Its wide-ranging exploration was rewarded. Small- and medium-sized companies, on the one hand, and large public organizations, on the other, turned out to make suitable new customers for outsourced facility management. Coor has been successful at bringing both these previous non-customers under the tent of payers for monetized activity.

Turning non-customers into customers, of course, calls for substantial customer education. Being new not just to the company but to the entire market, these customers are bound to lack some of the necessary know-how about the products and services, both how to purchase them and how to use them. Additionally, you might have to massage or modify the sales item to fit the needs of the new customer groups — the way BreadTalk did with its pork floss bun. Finally, the original matching methods may need enhancing to win you access to completely new customer groups. And to that wider topic, we turn next.

Wider or safer matching method. Sometimes what is holding back your market is not the limited number of prospective customers nor the lackluster appeal of providers' offerings but an inadequate matching method for bringing customers and providers together. Connecting willing sellers with willing buyers is an entrepreneur's most basic opportunity — almost a duty.

In the last two decades, a whole crop of successful market-shaping ventures have mushroomed out of some new digital matching method or other. Sometimes the new matching methods have been passive information mediators — such as the various websites related to matching travel-related services and keen globetrotters, Booking.com and Expedia perhaps best-known among them. Other times – as with AirBnB and our original success story, Uber – the method has been based on the sharing economy. And in certain cases, the new matching method has ballooned into an entire new marketplace of its own. Thus, for example, some pundits expect Jeff Bezos's Amazon to overtake traditional bricks-and-mortar retailers in the United States in the near future.[30] Meanwhile, the abracadabra magic of Jack Ma's Internet giant Alibaba has already done so in China.

However, sometimes you can build a wider matching method relying on the bricks-and-mortar channels. Witness the insurance sector, specifically life insurances. Traditionally, life insurance has relied on buyer-finds-seller matching. The failure of seller-finds-buyer has been put down to psychological factors. That is, cold-calling from life insurance salespeople or even recommendations from third parties like your bank when you take out a mortgage, were unwelcome reminders of mortality to all but the cryogenically inclined.

But bucking the conventional wisdom, as market shapers often do, a couple of UK life insurance companies started experimenting with an unorthodox matching method: supermarkets. Supermarkets provided the bricks and mortar. In 1997, finance rivals Royal Bank of Scotland and Aviva (then NatWest) started joint ventures with supermarket chain rivals Sainsbury and Tesco, respectively, offering buyer-finds-seller matching for the simpler insurance products. In 2000, they expanded the offering to life insurance products, previously deemed too complex for this setting. First, Aviva (by then Norwich Union Life Insurance Company) life insurance covers were sold under the Tesco brand as a pilot. By 2005, Aviva's policies for Tesco's customers hit £4 billion, or over 5.5 USD billion. Tough competition ensued amongst the life companies for exclusive deals with supermarket chains offshore, too. US insurer MetLife launched a pilot in

2012 selling through Walmart, and the following year pilots
began in Australia and Canada.[31]

In order for a new matching method to unleash market-level
growth, it has to improve by at least one of the three criteria[32] put
forward by Alvin E. Roth, the Nobel economics laureate we met
in the previous chapter: (1) it has to be wider (or "thicker") than
the previous alternatives, that is, it must bring together more
potential customers and providers, and/or (2) it has to be safer
than the previous alternatives so that more customers and providers are willing to enter the marketplace, and/or (3) it must give
participants the means to choose when faced with alternatives.
The life insurance example above fulfills the first criterion: the
market size increased as the supermarkets were able to reach more
prospective buyers of life insurances. And for its part, the rapid
rise of the sharing economy is somewhat put down to the
enhanced safety for providers and customers alike, made possible
by mutual public reviews. AirBnB guests rate the host, and the
host rates the guests; the two sides on Uber transactions do
likewise.

Introducing a wider or safer matching method is a relatively
powerful market-shaping move; it needn't always be complemented with many other adjustments along the market-shaping Fan.
However, it is possible to detect two typical complementary
actions. First, if the new matching method is a stand-alone business (similar to Amazon, AirBnB, Uber, or our own New
Zealand Bookabach), then the sales item and pricing of this business have to be determined. Is it the customer or the provider –
or both – who pay to use the channel? And how is the price
determined? Second, almost all novel matching methods require
some adjustments in the social norms and conventions. It takes a
little culture shift, for instance, for ordering your next pair of
shoes online to become more natural than rolling up to the clos-
est department store.

Breaking Supply and Efficiency Bottlenecks

In the previous generic market-shaping play, the brake on market performance was the matching method. But other aspects, too, of market systems can become constraints. The next generic arrow in our market-shaping quiver homes in on bottlenecks in supply and system-level efficiency. This play has three distinct variations: eliminating supply bottlenecks by scaling up cottage industries, clearing out regulatory bottlenecks in supply, and shaking up outdated social norms to improve system efficiency.

Eliminate supply bottlenecks by scaling up cottage industries. Thanks historically to the industrial revolution and eventually to containerized trade, very few markets tied to manufacturing or retailing, respectively, run up against supply bottlenecks. But service-related markets are a different story altogether. Since service businesses lack any equivalent tradition of "industrializing" operations and often depend very largely on humans in service delivery, the size of service-related markets is frequently limited by insufficient delivery capability. Eager customers are out there, but providers just can't reach them all.

The opening case in this chapter, Les Mills International, neatly demonstrated plays to eliminate supply bottlenecks and to grow the entire market for group exercise to music. But there's no shortage of other examples — including the following one from New Zealand. In 2003, Leslie Preston and Julie Ferne founded Bachcare (and yes, up crops once again that fond Kiwi moniker for holiday home: "bach"). Leslie's vision for Bachcare was crystal clear from the outset.[33] She wanted to professionalize and consolidate full-service holiday home management — a market that she thought was (metaphorically if not also literally) a cottage industry. Bachcare's business model is based on a carefully proportioned triangle. First, you have the holiday home owners. They want to outsource every facet of managing their holiday property — rental bookings, cleaning, meeting and greeting guests, and so on – to a reliable party. Then you have your holiday home renters. They want to rent a pre-serviced holiday home – so no more packing and laundering your own towels – with access to hotel-grade guest services: Dinner reservation, Sir? Tips on local sights, Madam? "No worries," as our carefree friends Down Under are constantly reassuring us: all taken care of! And finally, straddling the two sides you have the holiday managers, employed by Bachcare. They of course make it all happen.

The supply bottleneck in full-service holiday home management mainly pertains to a squeeze between twin needs: to be simultaneously extremely local while having a nation-wide reach. Holiday managers need to be locals, both for value-adding local knowledge – "Mind how quickly the tide comes in when you're walking around those scenic rocks," "Tell the maître d' at Chez Daniel that I sent you – he's my cousin" – and to form lasting relationships with home owners. Renters, on the other hand, have no interest in browsing through dozens of regional rental websites – they want to find everything in one place, under a trusted national brand. Sounds simple enough, perhaps. But striking and keeping this balance while you grow your business from scratch is far more easily said than done. Indeed, it had never been done in New Zealand before Bachcare.[34] At time of writing, Bachcare has burgeoned from the initial five holiday homes under management to over 1,400 – and the growth seems to be continuing steadily. And not coincidentally, the market for full-service holiday home management has been flowing better and growing as well, in large measure due to Bachcare's business model unblocking the supply bottleneck.

Coming back to our trusty Fan diagram as a conceptual guide, this particular variation of a market-shaping play tends to focus on the network layer. In order to eliminate the supply bottlenecks, you've usually got to add actors to the supply network, or to alter their work division, or both. Bachcare did both. The Kiwi company procured more holiday managers and tasked them with a wider role than traditional facility managers.

Clear out regulatory bottlenecks in supply. Mention market shaping and a lot of minds jump straight to lobbying, as a way to alter the regulations governing the market system by appealing direct to politicians and policy-makers. So, for those of you who have been patiently waiting for more tips on regulations and lobbying, here comes our next variation of generic market-shaping plays, clearing regulatory bottlenecks to supply.

Regulations, both governmental and industry self-regulation, lay out the metes and bounds of action for all actors in the market system — what is allowed and deemed legal — in order to ensure that the market system remains functional. Thus, to a first approximation, regulations permit activities that are aligned with the market system and restrict activities that work against the market. However, because the wheels of both governmental and industry self-regulation grind slowly and only by many parties putting their shoulders to the wheel, the regulators are reluctant to revise their scripts unless absolutely necessary. Combine these two attributes — prescribing action to streamline the market but getting updates relatively infrequently — and you can easily imagine that oftentimes regulations will lag behind reality. They reflect a market system that used to be, and prescribe outdated models of action in a system that has already moved forward. Furthermore, it's very difficult to "future-proof" regulation, so even the most forward-thinking regulators are more or less condemned to describe the current states of the market system. And that description grows obsolete even while the ink is still drying on the page.

Sometimes this naturally occurring time lag creates a regulatory bottleneck that either prevents a new market system from emerging or precludes an existing market system from reaching its full potential in terms of value creation and growth.

The most typical way of changing regulations is forming a coalition of companies — all those feeling the squeeze of the regulatory bottleneck, usually companies competing against each other — then working collaboratively with the regulators. Stora Enso and the other Finnish forestry products companies did precisely that when they wanted to change the restrictive building codes and zoning regulations to accommodate taller wooden-framed buildings. Less typically, a single company will strike out alone to woo regulators with an eye to clearing regulatory bottlenecks. Just note, though, that in such a case, the win-win-win value proposition has to be overwhelming, since policy-makers have a horror of being seen to yield to special pleading. And should collaboration with the regulators be a dead end, you just might get away with resorting to a corporate version of civil disobedience à la Uber: deliberately breaking the obsolete regulations and hoping that the public outcry in your favor and the loud voice of market forces thus speaking will motivate the regulators to rewrite the rules.

Depending how radical a change in regulations is needed, the complementary adjustments across the Fan diagram vary from minimal intervention to total revision of everything from sales item to matching methods and actor network composition. Despite this variance, one commonality emerges. Almost all market-shaping plays based on clearing regulatory bottlenecks require changes in representations. If you want to convince the regulators that the current regulatory settings are actually harming the actors in the market system, then you'd better arm yourself with facts to support your case — cue information representations such as market research and statistics. Media attention is a reliable way of motivating politicians, since an election is never too far away. And sometimes you need to rustle up new concepts or terms to inform (read: guide) public discussion around the proposed regulatory change. Just think how effectively concepts such as "carbon footprint" or "world-wide-web" have lubricated dialogue and thinking about climate change and digital connectivity.

Shake up outdated social norms to improve system efficiency. Our final variation of generic market-shaping plays takes us to the outermost layer of the Fan framework: social norms. Similarly to regulations, social norms or mores prescribe which activities are socially acceptable in the market system and which are frowned on or taboo. Since social norms are not handed down periodically by a central authority and prescribed in some great big book, they usually evolve gradually or even imperceptibly over time — sometimes leading and sometimes lagging other development steps in the market system. Therefore, like regulatory bottlenecks, social norms become springboards for market shaping only when they are clearly harming the market system and causing system-level inefficiencies.

Fittingly for this third and final variation of the market-shaping play under the rubric of unblocking bottlenecks, we turn to the wine industry and its seals. The transition from natural cork to screwcaps as a wine bottle closure (covered in detail in Chapter 3) exemplifies altering social norms to lift system efficiency. In this case, the New Zealand wineries faced two layers of intertwined, but equally harmful, social norms. First, consumers preferred cork over screwcap, based partly on romantic ideals about the "right" way of opening a bottle of wine and partly on flawed information (the popular misconception that cork allows wine to breathe; good cork is a hermetic seal and "breathing" would lead to wine oxidization, making it undrinkable). Second, the industry conventions guiding the professionals who work with wine — winemakers, merchants, and retailers — all reflected a hallowed history of working with cork. As so often, cork was just "the way we do things around here."

Similar to unblocking regulatory bottlenecks, the key to altering outdated social norms is changing representations. Think: supplying factual information, fashioning suitable language and concepts, harnessing media coverage, and sometimes even motivating industry associations to change the interests and companies they represent. The specially formed Screwcap Wine Seal Initiative was fortunate enough to be able to draw on academic research on wine-maturing processes and the performance of screwcaps, yielding decades of evidence to support their case. They also shared their insights about the practical details of using screwcaps in a self-published manual. From its own title downwards, the initiative actively promoted the term "screwcap" when the terminology related to this technology was yet in its infancy, or at best still wearing the proverbial short pants. The global wine media really took the screwcap initiative under their wings, actively explaining why this change made sense and constituted a win-win-win for everyone. In fact, the only representation that the initiative couldn't budge was the local wine industry associations – the associations refused to take a stand publicly, even though many individuals privately wished the initiative all the luck in the world.

This final variation of generic market-shaping plays differs slightly from the rest in its outcomes. All the other generic market-shaping plays increase the size of the market system – total turnover to be generated from that market, that is. Altering outdated social norms seems to be a slightly different beast, however. This move typically leaves market size unchanged and instead eliminates system-level inefficiencies. Think: saving wine from being ruined by substandard corks, promotion of preventative health measures rather than costly medical treatment (International SOS and its "Duty of Care" concept), or improvement of patient outcomes (via a health insurer's own hospital chain). Despite the different causal pathways, altering outdated social norms can make fantastically good business sense. Weeding out inefficiencies usually raises profitability, so even if the market size remains the same, the profitability of the companies operating in that market is likely to increase. Additionally, proposing smarter and more efficient solution tends to position the company very favorably in the minds of customers – thus enabling market share gains. And finally, as environmental and social sustainability become ever more important both in global competition and in obtaining, or retaining, a license to operate from regulators, you can also view adapting outmoded social norms as a preventative strategic move.

TAKEAWAYS FROM CHAPTER 4

- Chapter 4 overlays the 13 ad hoc moves pertaining to the designable elements of the Fan with a new level of cohesive strategy. It adds *two unifying principles and highlights five generic multi-move plays* which should feature prominently in any shaper's repertoire.

- The first principle is to *time your market-shaping efforts to periods of relative shapeability* or "malleability." Although a process of educated trial-and-error, three phenomena typically signal malleability: any *shock or sudden change*, whether natural, regulatory, or technological; *dissonance and debate*; and/or a *recent history of deliberate shaping* by a firm or government.

- *First mover advantage is surprisingly rare* in market shaping. Prerequisites of such first-mover advantage are: major *network effects*, *customer lock-in*, and *flexible enough core technology and business model* to adapt when the market inevitably changes further.

- *While markets are less shapeable, "wait actively"*: perfect your readiness, build a war chest, and reserve the right to play by lowest-cost, least-committing investments.

- Market shaping *takes time*: typically years.

- The second principle is *win-win-win*. You must *demonstrate credible, specific, quantifiable wins* to all players in the minimum viable system needed to achieve your market vision. Hold your nose and *collaborate with rivals to shape the market*, but compete to share it afterwards in order to avoid improper collusion. Even giants often lack sufficient market-shaping power acting alone. Not collaborating risks painting yourself into a corner as dominant players in mere niche. And markets with few providers and much regulation simply cannot be shaped alone.

- *Five generic multi-move market shaping plays* and variations on them should feature in every shaper's repertoire: (1) *relocating the exchange interface*, either by monetizing a non-monetized activity and insourcing it from the customer, or by bundling and unbundling; (2) *delivering a step-change in use value*, either by commercializing a new, markedly netter widget (or indeed simply a better mousetrap as long as it is massively better), or by enhancing the users' know-how or improving their infrastructure, (3) *widening the market* to more frequent consumption by more customers *via pricing*, either through as-a-service pricing that lowers capital expenditure or aligns incentives, or by disruptively slashing prices and costs; (4) *widening customer catchment area* — either by turning non-payers or non-customers into paying customers, or by wider or safer matching methods; and (5) *breaking supply and efficiency bottlenecks* by scaling up cottage industries, clearing our regulatory bottlenecks to supply, or modernizing social norms to improve system efficiency.

5

LEADERSHIP FOR MARKET SHAPERS

What does leadership mean when you're trying to shape — and share — a complex market?

In strategy, leadership consists of both leading your firm and your firm leading the market.

In market-shaping strategy, actors collaborate to unleash the value potential of complex systems then share in the extra value. But market shaping requires, and rewards, the art of leadership more than ever. Only, leadership now means influencing by ideas, not dictating and dominating. Within the firm, hierarchy is flattened. Within the market, the shaping firm initiates change, but as often leads from behind as from ahead, either moving first then standing back or starting as fast follower then stepping into the lead. The market lead is shared and rotated, almost like the supported, switching solos of a jazz band.

KONE: LIFTED UP BY A NEW TYPE OF LEADERSHIP

Over the last 10 years, KONE, one of the planet's largest manufacturers of elevators and escalators, has systematically reinvented itself from a commonwealth of regionally managed organizations into one globally integrated organization able to shape markets around the world. Spurring this change was the CEO from 2005 to 2014, Matti Alahuhta.[1] The earnest, hardworking engineer, who had done his doctoral thesis on global growth strategies for high technology challengers, joined KONE from Nokia. He had been an integral member of Nokia's executive team during the golden years of Nokia from 1993 to 2004, and left on a high at the end of 2004 to join KONE.

The new CEO did what many new CEOs do: he initiated a strategy process. But this one was different. For starters, Alahuhta insisted on a high level of involvement within the organization. He also prioritized exploring changes in the market and opportunities to influence its development as a whole. A thorough competitor analysis was conducted, customer segmentation started, scenario planning results systematically used, external analyzes of various geographies scrutinized. During the strategy-formation process, participants were sensitized to present and future market conditions by using competitive gaming exercises. The result was a focus on maximizing the accessible market. The company looked around the market and set special sights on China, where urbanization was pushing up high-rises as fast as bamboo – and their occupants would hardly be happy to take 40 flights of stairs. In keeping with Alahuhta's science and tech background, KONE experimented with various plays to support the shaping of this market, including the formation of a joint-venture firm, Giant KONE. In parallel, it was emerging that modernization of existing elevator stock globally would be a growth area where resources could be configured – shaped – in a totally new way.

Next, KONE's leadership performed a classic zoom out from a product-based business definition to reframe its market view free from current product and services and targeted at customer benefits. Customers are not collectors: they don't buy or maintain elevators for elevators' sake; their object is moving people around effectively and safely in their building. KONE's R&D engineers – engineers being practical people who call a spade a spade – had formed the habit of referring to and measuring this movement as "People Flow." Through good internal communications, this catchy encapsulation filtered its way up to win Alahuhta's approval as KONE's new business definition in a 2008 repositioning.[2]

Although the market expression People Flow immediately explains what escalators and elevators enable, it is also fruitfully ambiguous and raises questions. People Flow means different things to different actors depending on their answer to the question of where they're going and how — escalator versus elevator right there, for instance, and wherever the rest of your day's personal flow will take you for business or pleasure. KONE has exploited this to turn a broadcast into a dialogue. The People Flow dialogue has been a fertile ground for engaging leadership events, both internal and external. The specific fruits of those events include new products such as destination control — those discreet little consoles in the foyer of swanky tower blocks where you program your destination and the system intelligently allocates an elevator factoring in building-wide traffic and other passengers' intentions. They also include innovation processes such as the yearly People Flow days, when employees of KONE engage with customers to better understand their people flow problems.

KONE has been very systematic in communicating their People Flow story. All KONE's internal communications invoke it, and it's also central to all customer-facing communications, from brochures to websites to sales pitches.[3] The investor community has received its fair share of the People Flow message — in fact, the People Flow strategy was launched in a Capital Markets Day in 2008.

It's hard to overstate the impact of those two little words of strategy (although you may think we're making a good fist of it). Reframing as a People Flow company revolutionized KONE's approach to customers and other stakeholders. In order to mobilize and engage people and align resources, KONE redefined their "must-win battles"[4] — development programs across functions and regions to define and test the viability of People Flow. Their goal has been to engage staff and stakeholders and mobilize resources toward realizing their strategy. The programs are reviewed and redefined at regular intervals in response to both achievements and failures and to changes in the ecosystem.

The People Flow strategy necessitated engaging new participants in what was fast becoming a mini-movement. For instance, a People Flow market needs providers of access control equipment and smart building software. KONE had to squeeze itself into numerous very different pairs of shoes to understand what People Flow meant for various actors — an architect, for instance, or a facility manager. What would be the benefits and drawbacks — one might say the ups and downs — for an architect or a facility manager of People Flow compared with the existing elevator market? Would the change be net positive? And how about construction companies, technical consultants, software developers, manufacturers of said access control equipment — and all other players needed to constitute a functioning People Flow market.[5]

You can discern the commitment to more open architecture and deeper engagement and collaboration in KONE's multiyear agreement with IBM, initiated by Alahuhta's successor as CEO, Henrik Ehrnrooth. The role of the agreement is to supply cloud-based Internet of Things (IoT) technologies and services to drive innovation in smart buildings.[6] Using IBM's open standards-based Watson platform, KONE has also tapped into a vast developer ecosystem via their API (Application Programming Interface) Challenge competitions — API being a means by which systems talk to each other. These competitions contract highly skilled volunteer labor into ad hoc think tanks for effectively peanuts and still get thank-yous from all the participants for the fun challenge. In KONE's case, the API Challenges typify a movement toward new applications delivering building users a smoother, safer, more personalized people flow experience.

REDEFINING LEADERSHIP

"Lead," "leader," and "leadership" take on radically new meanings in strategy as soon as you realize your market is a complex adaptive system, let alone once you try to shape it. To lead no longer means to stabilize uncertainty – formulate precise, closely held, long-term plans – and execute those plans using central command and control. As we've seen, the rich reality of complex systems defies such reduction into linear cause and effect and confounds prediction and control. Yet nor are market systems chaotic. And the very phenomenon of *emergence* that defies determinism is a tappable wellspring of vitality and dynamism.

Thus, the increasingly complex reality of modern markets both requires and repays astute leadership now more than ever. Only, this is an altogether subtler, more participatory, and even "distributed" sense of leadership. In fact, it may be helpful to decouple leadership from the individual altogether, to distinguish between "leadership" and "leaders." Successful market leadership can be seen as a distributed process of learning, involving a number of individuals from various organizations – sometimes "leading" and sometimes "following." Yes, the original idea might be yours, but if some other individual or organization is better equipped to promote market change in a particular instance, you should encourage them to do just that – even if they do it differently than you would.

We have grouped the leadership traits of successful market shapers into four sets of Es – Explore, Experiment, Express, and Engage – arranged as two pairs: Informing and Performing (see Figure 5.1). As usual, intuitive market shapers happen to do a number of these things well simply by instinct, but we have systematized the process so that anyone can learn to do it methodically. Each E is a trait that market shapers need to foster both inside their own firm and extend to their market partners.

Figure 5.1. Leadership for Market Shaping.

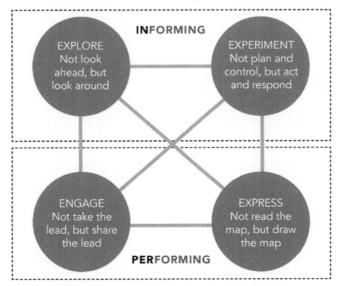

The grouping into the four Es is loose. As you read the chapter, therefore, expect overlaps. This four-point leadership rubric grapples with the difficulty of rendering into linear, page order the dizzying organic complexity of adaptive systems. That complexity transcends deterministic, mechanical models – and stretches the bounds of a linear book! The membranes between each E are porous. Indeed, we have constructed it as much for convenience and mnemonic purposes as anything.

Inform Yourself about Resource Potentiality

Through exploring and experimenting, market shapers *inform* themselves about resource potentiality: spotting resource re-configurations that could enhance value creation for themselves and partners in the market system.

Informing is about reimagining resource potential; experimenting to capitalize on whatever works and learn from what doesn't and cultivating the vitality of emergence. Market shapers informs themselves with extreme curiosity, eclecticism, open-mindedness, and an appetite for honest self-challenge, from as many angles, agents, and probes as possible, and even from seemingly catastrophic business events.

This type of informing is not the traditional learning *about* the market for the purpose of adapting *to* it. Rather, it is learning *with* the ever-evolving market, with individuals and organizations in the market system, for the purpose of developing and adapting new visions for the whole market.

Explore: not look ahead, but look around. Traditional leaders *look ahead* using decidedly slender market intel to extrapolate forecasts about the poor, external "product" market. By contrast, market-shaping leaders, knowing complex systems are profoundly dynamic, *look around* the dynamic, unpredictable system of which they're part and in the mirror at their own business definition for inspiration.

Experiment: not plan and control, but probe and respond. Traditional leaders, after analyzing markets from stock-standard models, devise intricate firm-centric *plans* for the resources and structures over which they had formal *control* or power. The emphasis is on stabilizing the firm and locking down the future. By contrast, market-shaping leaders systematically and rigorously *probe* the market to observe how it actually responds. They encourage emergence of fertile new system properties by pushing their firm to the edge of chaos to provoke dynamic new trends which may benefit them. And then they *respond* by doing more of what works.

Perform the New Market

Through expressing and engaging, market shapers enact or *perform*[7] the envisaged market system in order to make it a reality. Here performing[8] means a distributed process of bringing change into being. Distributed, because, while the market shaper by definition initiates that process, they will succeed only if fellow actors take up that vision, act in accordance with it, and in turn relay it to others who do likewise. If enough actors do so, the new market will tend to come about through a kind of self-fulfilling prophesy as the market shaper finds the market's resonant frequency and all parts of the system start to resonate in unison.

Express: not read the map, but draw the map. Traditional leaders use the above-mentioned slender and often commonly available intel about product markets or industries to metaphorically *read the map* (such as it was). They plant pins in the areas into which they want to lead their firm. By contrast, market-shaping leaders know they must co-author their whole market's future and in this sense have to *draw the map*. They then share that map widely within and outside their firm to give to collaborators in the minimum viable system and further market participants the sense that they as shaper have made of the market's potential new state.

Engage: not take the lead, but share the lead. Traditional leaders seek to dominate and *take the lead*. Even when acting as fast follower rather than first mover, their style of leadership is essentially one-way and top-down, inherently guarded, antagonistic, and competitive. By contrast, market-shapers leaders fully understand the need to engage gears by securing commitments, mobilizing resources, making investments, and making their move with the whole coalition. But they do so by strategically rotating and *sharing the lead* with other actors, like improvising fellow players in a jazz band rather than the baton-wielding conductor of an orchestra who "enforces" a set score from high on her podium.

EXPLORE – NOT LOOK AHEAD, BUT LOOK AROUND

In the – increasingly – rich reality of markets as complex adaptive systems, the future is often not only unknown but unknowable. It becomes futile or counterproductive to respond by doing more, harder and faster, of what you used to do back when you believed markets were deterministic or just plain given. Cranking up traditional forecasting will yield confusion and "paralysis by analysis" rather than clarity. Hence, market shapers should spend less time *looking ahead* and more time *looking around* to enhance learning with the system.

Explore the Potentiality and Density of Resources

When exploring, leaders inform themselves about the resources available for shaping the market and the potential of those resources to unleash value given new configurations, particularly configurations which intensify "resource density."

Understanding resource potentiality. Market-shaping firms spot and make sense of the potential value of resources or resource combinations before other firms do. Here "value" normally means to customers. Increasingly, though, we're witnessing successful market shapers originating a wider approach to value, such as microcredit banks and social entrepreneurs.

To spot value opportunities before others do, you needn't always be a first mover or a totally original thinker ("Who is?" one may ask). Often the trick is to imagine in your mind's eye combinations of ideas that are already out there, some perhaps put out by a firm that has moved before yours. So stand on the shoulders of contemporary giants, or more prosaically, just piggyback on the firm down the road!

Note that resource potentiality includes timing, or in other words the current shapeability − or not − of your market. If the market is not currently shapeable then the firm's leaders will need to lead the process of "active waiting." That process can include both further exploring and low-level experimenting.

Intensify resource density. To measure value, we use the concept of resource density.[9] The denser the resources available in a given time and space to a given actor, the higher the value. When wearing their explorer's hat, leaders look for ways to increase resource density for their own firm and potential market partners.

In the twenty-teens, opportunities for multiplying resource density abound. Digitalization is the main driver − so far, but watch this space. Digitalizing renders resources more liquid and thus mobile in time and space. Moreover, digitalized resources can be shared without being depleted and provided at next to zero marginal cost. As change accelerates exponentially and history seems to telescope (the beginning of the GFC was now almost seven iPhones ago), customers have access to far more resources via far more platforms than even five or 10 years back. And access, rather than ownership, is an operative word, by the way. In the 24/7, hyperconnected, virtual economy, digital resources are available for almost unlimited customers, any time, any place.

You may recall that famous line we quoted from Jim Barksdale: "Gentlemen, there's only two ways I know of to make money: bundling and unbundling."[10] Bundling and unbundling also made it into our list of market-shaping plays in Chapter 4. And they're relevant here because one prime way to intensify resource density for customers is to unbundle and re-bundle into new sales items resources previously held together in time and place by a single actor. A neat example is the evolution of the music business. The content, in other words the music, has been unbundled from previous carriers such as LP records, CDs, and now even from the MP3 players. This development has spawned new offerings the likes of Spotify that let you access music with a multitude of different devices, once again any time, any place, without ownership.

Sense Value by Triangulation and Peripheral Vision

Leaders exploring resource potentiality need to exercise a faculty we call value sensing: a heightened state of awareness, curiosity, and open-mindedness with a predilection for self-challenge.

The actions of value sensing are divergent, like a brainstorm, and akin to the gaming exercises that Alahuhta initiated at KONE. In them, the leader-as-explorer uses peripheral vision to perceive weak signals which can be combined to create new opportunities and they relentlessly question and challenge existing framings of the market. These weak signals can be found on all layers of the market Fan from the core outwards.

To understand value sensing, it's instructive to compare the human eye and how it naturally looks both around and ahead. Remember the last time you witnessed a stunning spectacle – the jaw-dropping majesty of the Grand Canyon, say, or the cotton-wool delicacy of a flotilla of multicolored hot air balloons taking off in a misty dawn – and reached for your nearest photographic device to capture it? Do you also remember how flatteningly trivial and circumscribed the end result looked later on your screen or in print? Two differences between the human eye and all but the fanciest camera explain what you lost in photographic translation. First, humans have two eyes, which enables stereopsis, or depth perception. Technically, this is a form of what's commonly called triangulation, albeit the corners on the base of the triangle – your eyes – are only a few centimeters apart. And second, humans enjoy peripheral vision, from the peripheries of both eyes. Each eye takes in objects outside the bull's-eye center of its gaze. Now let's apply this metaphor to your market shaping.

Use triangulation to add depth. By building capabilities for metaphorical stereopsis in the firm, leaders foster triangulation. Triangulation saves you from a "one-eyed" view of the truth about the current and potential market. Appropriately, there are three possible ways to triangulate. Either you can get persons scattered through the firm and the market system, and tasked with different roles, to analyze the same signals and report back to you. And/or you can employ different methods of collection and analysis from a single standpoint. And/or you can conduct analyses from the same place but at different times, since your interpretation of a phenomenon may change over time. Just remember, though, that the purpose of triangulation is divergence and diversity, not reinforcing unity — an overvalued ethos which we believe ended up straitjacketing traditional leadership. Triangulation should deepen and widen the organization's understanding of the market system and its potential. It needs to test and challenge your existing views; if it ends up validating them, that's pure cream. Of course, the actors outside your organization can most easily be counted on not to be Yes men, and to provide a challenging and exciting fresh perspective, since they owe you no loyalty.

Break out of tunnel vision into peripheral vision. Besides one-eyed views from being wedded to a single perspective and prioritizing unity, many leaders suffer from loss of peripheral vision — in other words, strategic tunnel vision. Managers used to interpreting only the data that are set before them tend to focus on what the former US Secretary of Defense Donald Rumsfeld popularized as the known knowns and known unknowns but to clean miss out on the unknown knowns and the unknown unknowns.

Interestingly for our metaphor, peripheral vision in the literal sense is like a lazy eye: It can be strengthened by exercise. For example, with practice jugglers learn to locate and catch objects in their peripheral vision while focusing straight ahead on a defined point in midair. By analogy, leaders of firms can improve peripheral vision[11] by a couple of simple techniques. (As it happens, triangulation itself also increases peripheral vision, because each fresh viewpoint alerts you to opportunities beyond your direct line of sight.)

Maybe the most powerful tool for improving peripheral vision is to deliberately focus on outliers, as Malcolm Gladwell famously did in his bestselling book of that name.[12] A tangible numerical way to do so is to let go of averages since these submerge outliers.[13] So forget the usual advice. Instead of large samples you should focus on so-called samples of one — each outlier — to deepen your understanding.

Fostered as a kind of deliberate serendipity, the study of outliers can provide just the kind of inspiration needed for insights in your value sensing. So, for instance, instead of profiling your average customer, find one who is using your product differently from the intention – what pharmaceutical companies call "off-label" use. Then figure out why, and what they get out of it. This also encourages firms to invest in anthropological research methods such as ethnography, wherein researchers study culture from the point of view of the subject, instead of statistical analysis with its associated quantitative predilection. Anthropological and sociological methods make a lot of sense when you remember that market systems are socially constructed.

We recently watched the outlier process in action. One day, a flooring machinery entrepreneur we know got wind that a certain customer was using his machinery against instructions. Given that this could expose the company to increased maintenance costs and bad word of mouth, a traditional leader's following the "doing my thing" or "managing my business to the best of my abilities" paradigms might have reacted by biting the head off of the incompetent sales representative. Instead, our man hurried to the company's testing ground and started operating one of the test machines in a similarly incorrect way. This willful heterodoxy from the leader of the faith uncovered a completely new way of finishing floors which these days is the cornerstone of this thriving business.

Focus on the IFAQs. Here's another rule of thumb for leaders wishing to improve their organization's peripheral vision. Dwell less on answers and more on questions. Especially worthwhile are the *in*frequently asked questions – call them IFAQs if you will. And since we've been citing notable quotes from quotable notables, when approaching market shaping, leaders should take Voltaire's advice. The French philosopher and wit tells us to "judge a man [sic] by his questions rather than by his answers." Questioning orthodoxies makes your firm more inquisitive, intelligent, and vital. Finding a single pertinent new question can generate more insight into your market system's resource potentiality than studying all the existing answers. After all, those answers share the bias of being framed by the old questions. Yet, while management consultants and incoming CEOs as new brooms sweeping clean are in the habit of asking tough, fundamental questions, it's far rarer to find a leader who will build and maintain a culture of continuing to ask the hard questions. This segues nicely into our next section on deliberately cultivating – and keeping – diverse perspectives.

Cultivate Diverse Perspectives on Your Own Firm

In addition to looking around in the market, we argue that you need to shimmy up to a mirror and look at your own firm. In doing so, we'll extend the ideas on redefining – really, truly, devotedly, even radically redefining – your business in order to reframe your current and potential market as profitably as possible.

Now, markets mirror life. How you view the world, and the market, depends on how you see yourself, and your business. To be complete, the defining process works the other way around too: Your self-concept and business definition in turn depend on your worldview and market view. A healthy company will regularly engage in a kind of recursive identity dialogue, examining its business definition, testing this and its market view against each other, and recalibrating its business definition to optimize. It defines its own role by feeling its way among other market roles, exploring boundaries, testing niches, looking for best fit. Sometimes the frame will be clear already, and pointing in a well-chosen, profitable, high-growth direction. Other times, mild corrections will be in order. And occasionally the firm might need to redefine itself entirely.

Challenge existing beliefs and business models. On the subject of redefining oneself, successful market shapers devotedly challenge the foundations of their business – and it is their leaders who will instigate the challenge or instill the culture of challenging. Seeking instead to confirm your existing beliefs will likely blind you to both important warning signs and great opportunities. Good leaders ask IFAQs, questioning even the most basic assumptions. They actively and overtly search for, and welcome from their fellow executives, evidence that their strategy is not relevant anymore. Consider how Uber is doing that right now: A company whose entire supply side, as it were, is car drivers (and their cars), is planning to go driverless by 2030! UPS made similar redefinitions of its business over a century, starting with a switch from a message business (information delivery) to a courier company (parcel delivery). Thus, true innovators turn the paradoxical capitalist engine of creative destruction on themselves in order to survive and thrive.

We've talked to market shapers whose ambition is explicitly to shake up their own organization − as it were, to disrupt themselves. In this vein, one discussion was particularly instructive. The founder of a large Asian hospitality chain told us: "We raised the bar in our industry from two to eight or nine [out of ten]. Now we have to think that this nine is actually two, so that we can find the next big thing."

Encourage constructive paranoia. Andrew "Andy" Grove would have agreed with our hospitality chain founder. The former CEO of Intel is famously allergic to complacency. His provocatively titled book *Only the Paranoid Survive* warns starkly that "Success breeds complacency. Complacency breeds failure."[14] Grove is not alone. We've also seen that a century ago Jim Casey, the founder of UPS, turned the phrase "constructively dissatisfied" to describe his own and the business's relentless questing for improvement.

Grove's advice is well heeded by any market-shaping leader. A market shaper needs to get comfortable with discomfort. And, to brow another phrase from Grove's book, one of the "uses of discomfort" is to move you to innovate pre-emptively, *before* your business model faces a known threat − because by then it's too late. The moment to move is before your business model becomes too stable.[15] Long-term success requires that we innovate even at the risk of making our current products/services or business model obsolete, because it is better to be disrupted by your in-house creations than by a threat you never saw coming.

The leaders of successful market shapers don't let themselves or their firm rest on the laurels of their initial innovation. Thus, Uber isn't content to sit on its app, for instance. Another example is the flooring system company discussed above. These folks are contemplating expanding their application area from floors to roads. That move would disrupt not only their own business model but also those of many infrastructure companies.

But let's get back to Intel's Andy Grove. How can paranoia be constructive? Following our own advice about socially constructed systems, we borrow from a − positively rock star − cultural anthropologist. A good decade and a half after Grove's book, author Jared Diamond penned a pertinent essay about paranoia for the *New York Times*.[16] Diamond defined constructive paranoia as a hyper-vigilant attitude toward repeated low risks. His point is that, whilst we obsess about risks that carry a high body count, a spectacular mental image, or intense emotional charge − like nuclear meltdown or a bomb on an airplane − we dangerously underestimate the risks of certain frequently repeated, banal events that we can control. One such event is slipping when you step out of the shower. A fall risk of one in a thousand may sound trivial, but if your personal hygiene habits are such that you shower every day, that's enough to land a reckless stepper in the emergency room several times before the age of 70 − if they make 70 at all.

Constructive paranoia means that we identify these high-frequency, low-risk commercial events and find ways to overcome them. The added blessing is the fact they are often within our control, the same way buying a 10-dollar shower mat is.

Diagnose failures in advance by pre-mortems.[17] An explorer's technique to defuse threats posed by business as usual − and to break out of group think and tunnel vision – is the pre-mortem. You instruct an assembled group to imagine that some project or the whole company has failed. Then each attendee independently jots down all possible reasons for the failure. Moreover, they must specifically brainstorm reasons which they would ordinarily tiptoe past due to office politics. Thus, forcibly liberated from loyalty to colleagues and bosses, people prove surprisingly adept and even downright competitive at diagnosing an imaginary failure and thus preventing it becoming a real one. Going around the room, each participant states one reason for failure until every reason is on a list. And based on this list, you can then analyze the magnitude and likelihood of each reason and take preventive actions. The technique demonstrably flushes out real low-risk threats.

Pre-mortems and the phenomenon of "prospective hindsight" that drives them seem to work because of a cognitive quirk: Our buggy brains can more readily imagine the detailed causes of a single specific outcome by working backwards than conjure up out of nowhere causes which may lead to multiple unspecified outcomes. Imagining that the event has already occurred improves people's ability to predict the reasons for future outcomes by 30%.

EXPERIMENT – NOT PLAN AND CONTROL, BUT PROBE AND RESPOND

The pioneer of modern social and organizational psychology, Kurt Lewin, is credited with saying: "If you want truly to understand something, try to change it." Lewin's aphorism applies to market systems: You learn most about their dynamics when you attempt to change them, or at least probe them. The experiments are small-scale, low-risk interventions to probe and thus slightly change the market system in order to observe how it responds to the stimulus.

The lesson for leaders is to do *less planning and controlling* and *more probing, observing, and responding.* Probing implies touch and involvement — more learning *with* the market rather than remotely planning to do something *to* it. Probing firms systematically invest in small-scale experiments to generate insights. Interpreting the market's reactions to your tests, the so-called emergence, deepens your market understanding.

Experimentation epitomizes another role of our multitasking modern leader: the leader as scientist and inventor, formulating hypotheses and prototypes and testing them using a safe corner of the market as their lab. Experimentation is rigorous. It learns from and feeds back into exploring.

Experiment at the Boundaries

Being non-deterministic, markets as complex adaptive systems have rendered obsolete the standardized logic of notions like product life cycle, and those resource-hungry, almost Sovietstyle five-year-plans. As complex systems have no repeating relationships between cause and effect and are sensitive to small interventions, experimentation is a far smarter approach. The more complex and elusive our environment, the more effective trial and error becomes.

Experimentation as a method for learning. Continuing our theme of cultivating diversity, leaders should use experiments to approach the market from different perspectives to bring out emergent possibilities and push market boundaries. Experiments yielding positive results should be adopted and amplified when the market system has developed further and the timing makes it shapeable. The negatives, you chalk up to a learning experience and write down as data for future reference.

Experimentation still demands rigor! If you think experimentation sounds easier than rigorous processes of formal strategic planning and product launch, think again! As every scientist worth their sodium chloride knows, experimentation is not a synonym for reflex action or a license to be sloppy.

Effective experimentation requires a systematic, three-step structure. In step one, the leader or their delegate formulates mutually exclusive hypotheses based on assumptions about how the market system works. The aim is to weed out empty "leap-of-faith" assumptions – skepticism and devotion to the truth being higher virtues than faith in the scientific arena. It is disturbingly easy and common to fashion a superficially implementable business strategy without articulating the assumptions about your organization and the operating environment. Articulation is nevertheless crucial, because those assumptions are the guiding stars for clever experimentation. Let no assumption seem too obvious, too trivial, or too embarrassing to state and grant no special privilege to your (or your one-up's) personal pets or brainchildren. You're experimenting in order to validate – or invalidate – these assumptions, so all cards belong face-up on the table, as equals. As the last part of this step, though, you now rank your assumptions based on the evidence you can muster for them simply *from existing knowledge*. The ones with little or no data to support them must be tested first.

In step two, you develop a prototype to test the assumption *in the harsher environment of real life*. Key here is understanding what constitutes the minimum viable prototype that makes testing possible. If, for instance, you're testing a new service and its market impact, it must be developed enough for customers to actually buy it and experience it – but, for efficiency, no more. Additionally, you should prefer A/B testing. A and B are two versions of the prototype, and the test determines which performs better. Say you want to test your assumptions about farmers' willingness to embrace an app to optimize water usage. You build two prototypes: one app and one "non-app" alternative such as desktop software. Then you present them to farmers and compare results. By making variations and comparing again, you speed up learning and perfect the prototype. Additionally, you can run multiple experiments in parallel, provided they can be isolated and their results can be independently evaluated.

Step three is the actual testing. The trick is making results interpretable. You can then plan your next round of experiments in promising areas and wind up the negative ones, while also recording what they taught you. We encourage you to share your results with other market actors and learn from theirs. Just don't assume that results will be replicable in different parts of the system. Context matters.

Kill your darlings? Like writers, leaders and experimenters must learn to kill their darlings — recognizing and ending failed experiments even if you were in love with them. Should the data invalidate your assumption, formulate another one and subject it, too, to A/B testing. The risk of leaders allowing large-scale experimentation is that more people fall blindly in love with their pet project.

In this regard, take a leaf out of Google's[18] book. As part of doing the right — or at last the strategic — thing, by mid-2014, they'd axed a good 40 services. And while a Google Wave or a Google Buzz may be here today, gone tomorrow, euthanizing the likes of the long-lived and highly popular Google Reader must have elicited many tears. Another project killer with shark-like efficiency is Finnish mobile and video game company Supercell. Best known for the game Clash of Clans, they report killing off 14 games to now run four successfully.

Invest in Experiments according to Affordable Loss and Simple Rules

To shape a market or simply to prosper in any complex market system (which is all of them!), leaders have to make investments.

Trouble is, our investment thinking arrested in the 19th century. So we'll start by redefining investment.

Investments are increasingly resource re-allocations. Traditional investments were purchases of goods or equipment that created wealth over a given period. Accordingly, they got recorded in the balance sheet and were duly depreciated over time using the old straight line or diminishing value methods. But nowadays most investments are intangible. When we "invest" more time and effort in some facet of our business it shows up only in the profit and loss statement, effectively as a cost reallocation. So we wear the cost of the investment in one financial year, although the benefits may be longer term. Investments in market shaping are of this latter type.

Consequently, market-shaping investments sit uneasily with the dominant way of assessing investment opportunities: the business case. Business cases tend to crumble in those increasingly frequent cases when you are investing in something more intangible, like design, customer relationships, or participation in collaborative efforts to change regulation, or where your operating environment is highly unpredictable.

Apply affordable loss as a guiding principle. So, what to do when you know your initiative is crucial for the future of your firm but the business case lacks luster? Leaders of successful market shapers share the dubious honor of creatively bypassing the official investment processes to keep such vital initiatives alive. Their bag of tricks includes skunk works, office politics, bootstrapping, and sometimes plain deceit. Usually these stories end well. But they beg a question: What is the point of investment processes that both stymie winning ideas and force good people into such dubious behaviors?

Among more honorable alternatives is the affordable loss principle[19]: Invest only what you're prepared to lose. It's elementary, yet surprisingly often ignored. Expert entrepreneurs limit risk by calculating their affordable loss at each step, instead of seeking large all-or-nothing opportunities. They choose goals and actions where even the downside comes with some upside. And they prefer small consecutive investments, just enough to keep the initiative afloat. This approach guards against premature and over-sized commitments to uncertain ventures.

The affordable loss principle epitomizes market-shaping experimentation. Each experiment becomes a small step toward some new market shape, and failure can be brushed off, or at least borne easily.

Apply simple rules to guide decisions. Retired US General Stanley McChrystal, veteran of the Afghanistan theater and now a Yale University fellow, holds certain views in common with us on leadership in complex environments. In particular, McChrystal[20] writes: "Any complex task is best approached by flattening hierarchies. It gets everybody feeling like they're in the inner circle, so that they develop a sense of ownership."

The strategy implication here, as throughout market shaping, is distributed leadership. Let as many individuals as possible lead investment decisions and other market development. This minimizes the circle time between your stimulus (or probe) and the market's response, and so accelerates learning. Now, in complex market systems, total control is impossible; you need another leadership mechanism. One attractive option for managing complexity is so-called simple rules.[21] Simple rules are some often quite specific guidelines which help individuals deal with mission-critical processes and situations and enable fast decisions and rapid adaptations to volatile circumstances, while abiding by the overall strategy of the firm. Essentially, simple rules bridge the gap between strategy and execution.

There cannot be too many simple rules and they need to be tailored to the individuals using them and the procedures where they are applied. You should not copy simple rules as they also should differentiate the firm from other actors. They must also give people latitude to exercise discretion.[22]

Specifically, decision rules set boundaries ("we do not acquire firms that have more than 75 employees"), prioritize alternatives ("our manufacturing capacity will be allocated based on a product's gross margin"), and establish stopping points for when you exit a project ("any project that loses its key member will be stopped").

By contrast, process rules tell people how to execute tasks or coordinate action ("our R&D staff must rotate through customer service") and establish the proper timing of tasks ("product development must not take longer than 18 months").

The appeal of simple rules is manifold. They can be used when recruiting (new people need to agree to the rules). They speed up execution (less haggling about how to prioritize). And they function as sense makers for individuals ("when business becomes complicated, strategy needs to be simple").

Create a Safe-to-Fail Environment

So far we've considered a specific protocol, A/B experiments. In this section, we turn to the kind of environment that fosters smart-risk experiments in general. Now, the traditional managerial wisdom of plan and control idealized a stable, mistake-free, fail-safe environment. But, with the growing complexity and unpredictability of market systems, most strategies – and certainly market-shaping strategies – will entail some false starts and dead ends and more than a few stumbles in between. A fail-safe environment is now unrealistic. Worse, the attempt to contrive one stifles the extra creativity needed when dealing with evolving systems. And "fail-safe" itself fails to exploit and safeguard the new value attainable if we try things out and learn from our mistakes.

By contrast, a *safe-to-fail* environment encourages vitality through abundant, diverse, easily survivable experiments from which you harvest information. It then enables you (as usual) to adopt and amplify those experiments where the market system has shown a favorable response to your stimulus. The now-familiar Silicon Valley motto therefore applies: Fail early and often. And to generalize from the A/B protocol, you'll need to kill your darlings, preferably while still young before they grow into monsters or an albatross around your neck (that's the "fail early" bit). A couple of further pointers are useful.

Choose your experiments with care. First, let's just stress again that experimentation demands rigor. Safe-to-fail is not "blind-hope-as-a-strategy." It builds on tried and true approaches of entrepreneurial firms, based on the lean start-up philosophy. Insofar as possible without becoming counterproductively risk-averse in one's second guessing, the leader and their culture need to encourage choosing experimental lines with small downsides and bigger learning upsides. They should also range over diverse areas. Start with ones where the expected cost of failure is lowest and its overall impact on the organization (and the market) likely most manageable. Partly this is just a matter of counting the dollars and the hours that each experiment puts at stake. Beyond that, and more systematically, you should put a structural safeguard in place – what the "undercover economist" Tim Harford[23] calls "firebreaks." These separations contain each experiment's failure and stop it spreading like wildfire. Firebreaks preserve *existing* value while you experiment to find new value.

Show the value of failure. Second, your response to failure as a leader and a firm will be determinative. Begin by appreciating just how deep-seated is aversion to failure in your executives' minds and probably your own. Surely none of us alpha business types got to where we are today by failing! While rarely fatal, failure bruises both the ego and career prospects.

A telling incident occurred recently when we were discussing experimentation with a large organization. We asked their top executives to show us some examples of failures and explain their learnings. An awkward silence fell on the room, but the nervous glances exchanged cried out: "Who's going to say it?" At last, the silently delegated spokesman admitted: "All the guys who've failed have been asked to leave the organization – we don't fail in this organization."

To overcome such deep natural and organizational aversion to failure, leaders need to celebrate the learning from failed experiments and from the successful ones which might never have been attempted in a risk-avoiding environment. They – you – have to re-define failure itself as more long-term and including calcification, or a lack of vitality, and as excluding mere negative experimental results. Think like a scientist. A negative result in the lab is not a failure. It still answers your question, and it informs you that an apparently promising avenue is in fact a dead end. A negative result in the market also helps you form better insights about the market system. A quip about experiments from Nobel prizewinning physicist and spare-time wit Enrico Fermi is apt here: "There are two possible outcomes: if the result confirms the hypothesis, then you've made a measurement. If the result is contrary to the hypothesis, then you've made a discovery."[24] Putting your money where your mouth is, you'll need to change both the culture you express and your firm's tangible career and reward structure in order to instill this wise approach to safe-to-fail experimentation.

Foster and Exploit Emergence

Meanwhile, another feature of complex systems is essential to the leader as experimenter or scientist: emergence. You'll recall emergence as the mysterious, almost magical process by which complex adaptive systems evolve properties and shapes distinct from the properties of their constituent parts. Now, new properties – and new overall system shape – can emerge either from a designed start or from non-designed forces, whether observable or un-observable. Emergence is a common pathway channeling from both starting points to a new end point.

Well-led market-shaping firms detect, read, and exploit emergence. They capitalize on any advantages an emergent trend offers — say, by amplifying a favorable ripple into a favorable wave. Or, if the emergence is unfavorable, they can take measures at least to weather the change and hopefully dampen down or divert off-course its worst implications. This process resembles the stimulus, response, amplification, and dampening of outright experiments, so belongs aside that process.

Finally, let's just note another beauty of emergence. Emergence favors shapeability, just as a body of water in motion, even if only trembling with the featheriest emergent ripple, is that much more prone to be shapeable than a millpond with a surface as still as a mirror.

Leader: live with the market and encourage emergence. A safe-to-fail and experimentation-friendly organization requires leaders who live in and with the market, not alone in the rarefied atmosphere of a top-floor office. You have to be embedded and immersed in the everyday life of the both your own firm and, through its many members and interfaces, the market system, in order to help make sense of the opportunities for value creation. So in practice you should be out there with your team meeting customers, suppliers, partners, and other actors in the market. And you should be actively involved in designing the experiments that aid organizational learning and in explaining their rationale.

A key challenge of leadership in the rich reality of complex systems involves masterly letting go. Remember that market development is only partly designed. Because it is also partly emergent you cannot entirely lead it — this part just happens. What you can do, though, apart from directly designing, is create the conditions for emergence and, as noted, foster it where you detect it and see it moving in a favorable direction. This approach includes destabilizing the organization where necessary, even pushing it to the "edge of chaos" and intensifying certain actions to create non-linear, positive change. The mastery, of course, lies in continually studying the system's responses, collaboratively and collectively making sense of the information, limiting the downside risk and knowing when to stop. All of which is a far cry from the "command and control" paradigm aimed at driving only the direction of change you worked out in the boardroom and otherwise at stabilizing the organization almost as an end in itself.

EXPRESS – NOT READ THE MAP, BUT DRAW THE MAP

By definition, market shaping leads everyone into new territory and across old functional, organizational, and mental boundaries. Because the market is a complex adaptive system, the shaping firm cannot simply read off a desired destination in this new territory from some neat market map and command the other actors to move there. For, first, no such neat, pre-printed map exists; second, the shaper enjoys no such command or control over the other components of the market, only control over its business definition and lessening influence over the next four market layers; and third, cause and effect do not proceed in such a deterministic, linear fashion. Rather, the shaper has to draw their own map of the current and desired market shapes and propose it to the other players with purpose and clarity. The aim is to persuade, inspire, and guide those other actors to adopt and relay the map, enter the unfamiliar territories it opens up, and take on any new roles it requires.

The voice with which the shaper speaks needs to give out the sense they have made of the market and encourage other actors inside the firm, around the minimum viable market system, and more widely across the market, to adopt, relay and act on it. This sharing/showing supports individuals in their collective identity formation, helping them to better frame how the market system works, how it will develop, and how they can be part of this development. The map you are sharing needs to frame the market so that all actors can understand its boundaries and its growth trajectories.

Put the "Art" into "Cartography": Market Expressions as Art

In its expressing role, market-shaping leadership is akin to art. A work of art does not simply impose meanings, and its audience does not simply receive them. While the work possesses an aura of authenticity and uniqueness, it engages the audience in a process of meaning co-creation. Substituting "customer" for "audience," the market-shaping firms should aspire to create authentic meanings that will be shared and accepted within the firm, to express these meanings consistently in all interactions with the market to become embedded in the customer's practices, and to allow the customer to co-author meanings. The customer/audience interprets the art in their own way, add their own take on it, and then enact the art by sharing it with others (or if they don't like the art, by not engaging at all with the artist or art). Note, though, that creating a shared-market view is not like painting a picture on a blank canvas. Because market actors start out with their own mental picture. What's more, different individuals and departments within one firm can start with very different mental pictures. For example, purchasing departments may value purchasing prices above everything else in the market place. By contrast, operational departments may place greater weight on the total cost of ownership. Finally, market views tend to be unstable. A sudden downturn of the economy may change the market views of multiple actors overnight.

In some cases, especially with the other members of your own firm and with actors in the rest of the minimum viable system, the circle of artistic communication closes, as the customer's response and co-authorship reach all the way back to the market shaper. In such cases, the market shaper directly receives the customer's input and may well, out of necessity or sheer recognition of its valuable insights, modify the work of art in response. The co-authoring is a dialogue.

Picking up on the word "dialogue," the art form that perhaps best resembles this process (and in its broadest definitions argu-ably subsumes other arts) is language. Like artistic language, mar-ket expressions should appeal to the heart as well as the head, invite involvement, and crystallize images of the future market.[25] The language should be expressive and inspirational, with the concentration and power of a poem.

Do you propose creating the wave or catching and curating the wave? Before you launch into expression, you need to have decided whether you are trying to create a wave − in other words, be a first mover − or to catch and curate (amplify and sculpt) one started by another market shaper − as a fast follower. Starting, or creating, the wave requires a couple of things: a wave with a promise of substantial value potential for the whole market and market-shaping power. Here, market-shaping power depends both on relative size and financial muscle and on occupying a cen-tral position in the market with many strong ties to other central actors. A reputation as a trustworthy and credible organization don't go astray either. Nor do inspirational individual leaders, even though market shaping moves away from the leader-as-hero culture of conventional strategy.

Catching the wave requires asking yourself: Is the ongoing development a game-changer or an incremental step in some sort of "normal" market evolution? Check out comparable industries to see whether similar changes are happening or have happened.

Two ingredients are key to successful curation. First, the ongo-ing change may need further development to clarify the content and direction of change. You're trying to fashion a coherent enough vision for the future so that others will understand why they would follow your lead. Second, amplifying a wave is a col-lective act. Inclusiveness in your vision is even more important in successfully expressing a curated wave to other actors and winning them over than it is when creating the wave, where at least the initial oomph comes from your own firm. Incidentally, these other actors might include governmental agencies.

Foster dialogue for collaborative sense-making. We've noted that you can't turn your new market views into shared ones by monologue, preaching, and broadcasting. Market shapers are skilled in creating opportunities for dialogue so that further collaborative sense-making can occur. Even when your context offers little room for immediate dialogue, such as giving a key note presentation in an industry seminar, you can beneficially turn that speech into a platform onto which others can latch their ideas later on. Marc Benioff could give a master class in turning monologues into platforms for dialogue. Benioff is the 50-year-old founder, CEO and chair of American cloud computing and customer relationship management (CRM) pioneer Salesforce.com. When Benioff launched the company in 1999, he frequently addressed events and industry conferences. Tellingly though, he didn't use these tempting occasions to promote his business idea of CRM software as a service. He used them as a platform to discuss fundamental forces he saw transforming the entire enterprise application arena. This broad-brush and visionary, market-level subject appealed to a wide audience in a way that CRM software would likely have been too boutique to facilitate. The concept of cloud computing was a big enough tent to start an industry-wide pow-wow.[26]

Choose Language that Moves Market Actors

You'll recall we described the leader as an orator as well as an artist. To give a sense of the market vision which will inform and move others, leaders of market-shaping firms need to use accessible, persuasive language. A handy oratorical or more generally linguistic devices is the metaphor.

Metaphors render complexity graspable and novelty familiar.
Metaphors are among the very most fundamental and powerful
figures of speech in a leader's repertoire — and, to paraphrase
Ogden Nash, you don't have to be a poet to know it. We have
already touched on the power of metaphor to carry the audience
from the familiar to the unfamiliar and from the simple to the
complex. A further example is IBM's staple branding metaphor
"Smarter Planet." The tech giant's leadership deployed this metaphor to convince other leaders in business, government, and civil
society around the world that information technology would
enhance economic growth, efficiency, and sustainable development. Instead of detailing the input technology that would be necessary, this summative metaphor crystallized the outcome, and in
just two words.

However, not every metaphor, or even every common business
metaphor, will win hearts and minds in the market place.
Specifically, you've got to jettison the spiky military metaphors
with which the language of strategy bristles. Indeed, deriving from
the Greek *strategos* for general, strategy was long synonymous
with warfare long before it even entered the lexicon of business in
the 1950s. While we could reach back even further — as far as
Lao-Tzu and *The Art of War* circa 400 BCE — the more specific
origins lie in Prussian general Carl von Clausewitz's multi-volume
tome *On War* published in 1832.[27] Von Clausewitz categorized
the three levels of activity in organizing groups: strategic, tactical,
and operational. Ever since CvC, strategy has been laden with bel-
ligerent images: not only competing and winning but attacking
and defending, dominating, penetrating, targeting, out-flanking,
and of course the constant, unsubtle aspiration to make a killing
in the process. These figures have spread from the battle field to
the boardroom, often via the sports field. Sport is war by other
means, one might say, and business itself is a game carried out on
a playing field, and for which we're writing the new "playbook"!
Yet, the confrontational language of war and even of its more

sporting civilian cousin often handicaps us and it is antithetical to the requirements in market shaping for collaboration.

Switch from zero sum to positive-sum game metaphors. The most severe handicap of both military and sporting frames is that they are zero sum. And in each, to win you have to beat the competition at their own game. There is only one way to compete.

Whereas war yields only one winner (vanquished armies rarely celebrate coming second), in most business contexts, nothing could be further from the truth. The rich reality is that markets are usually flexible — at least when the timing is ripe — and positive sum. And market-shaping strategy specifically requires win-win-win. In business, many firms can win by applying different strategies and offering different types of value to their customers. Think, for instance, of the gamut of successfully co-existing retail concepts. Likewise, there are rules of military engagement, however much more honored in the breach than the observance, and the governing bodies of each sports code also decree and enforce a single set of rules. For a player, to question the rules midplay and dare to offer a superior vision in which he just happens to do better is simply out of bounds. (The heretical — and probably apocryphal — exception that proves the rule is tearaway English schoolboy William Webb Ellis. Legend has it that, in 1823, "with fine disregard for the rules of football as played in his time at Rugby school, [Ellis] first took the ball in his arms and ran with it, thus originating the distinctive feature of the Rugby game."[28]) By contrast, we've seen that in market shaping, the Rules of the Game are up for redesigning by canny players themselves.

Finding new metaphors from the arts. To supplant bellicose metaphors, leaders are increasingly looking to creative human activities. In keeping with our own motif of the leader as artist, in this section one such activity is the arts.

In a game-theoretic frame, arts are positive-sum games: The more moving, surprising, or technically virtuosic artists there are — the bigger audiences they draw. And, since art is made and shared, the language of arts is, respectively, naturally constructive (design, paint, compose, weave) and collaborative (with the audience co-authoring meanings, and, especially in the performing arts, multiple artists). Moreover, the language is often long-term, because (excepting those performance arts perhaps) the artist aspires to an enduring creation. In the same way, leaders of market-shaping firms would do well to view customers as audiences and aim to create expressions that excite, engage, and hold them. By contrast, warring metaphors would leave audiences shaken but not stirred.

The range of the arts affords metaphors to suit a broad spectrum of organizations and situations. Within music, for instance, a symphony orchestra is very different from a jazz band. At times leadership of a market will be akin to orchestration — an original but prescriptive score conducted under a centralized baton and with set roles to showcase wind, brass and strings at different points. At other times — and, we recommend, more often — your vision for leadership will resemble jazz. In jazz, the gestalt of a basic tune and common purpose (the overall market direction) is complemented by unpredictable improvisation as one player after another takes the lead and the rest support her solo. Management scholar Frank Barrett, himself an accomplished jazz pianist, has even written a catchily titled book, *Yes to the Mess,*[29] on what jazz leadership can teach executives confronted with complexity and endless change. In our own terminology, a jazzy improvisation could also capture and express the second E of leadership, experimentation. Because, if the riff works well with the backing players, it will amplify or lengthen and may point the band into a new direction, even become a new tune in its own right. If it doesn't catch on or clashes with the other players, the "experiment" can safely "fail" as the riff fades out into the background.

Claim Markets with Labeling and Symbolic Actions

New or reshaped market are usefully ambiguous. Roles are not yet set in concrete, product/service attributes remain undefined, and so far no value chain has firmly established itself.[30] And market shapers and their leaders can use such ambiguity in their expression strategies to mold those still-plastic dimensions to fit with and favor their own market vision. In so doing, they "claim" the market. Two typical expressive strategies are labeling and using symbolic actions.

Claim markets by labeling. Claiming a new market means making one's firm the market's cognitive referent — in other words, the go-to place when you need to understand how the new market works.

Language often confers a first-mover advantage in this respect. Labeling the new market by coining a catchy or sticky terminology for something new helps you to claim a market, because you literally define it. A good example, once again, is our favorite Finnish law firm, Fondia. As you'll recall, they pioneered the "Legal-Department-As-A-Service" billing model, with fixed fees. We celebrated their as-a-service billing as a market-widening pricing play. Moreover, there is no pyramid structure at Fondia, no partners and no dress code. (In some Anglo-American law firms, at least, it seems anything less than a three-piece suit is underdressing and senior partners seem to think casual Friday means wearing a colored bow-tie instead.) Staff at Fondia "bank" hours worked and "withdraw" free time. Fondia recruiters consciously apply the "'no-assholes' rule," though maybe via some legal euphemism; they have deliberately created an inspiring office design and they invest heavily in knowledge management and document sharing.[31] The firm has so identified itself with its distinctive work environment and culture that it has entered the language as a label for them. Competitors can't beat the label, so they join it, boasting through gritted teeth of their "Fondia-like" services. Well-claimed, Fondia!

Deploy symbolic actions to secure resources. Another way to claim markets is to use symbolic actions as signals of strength or expertise. Research has shown[32] that market shapers secure more resources for new ideas if they perform symbolic actions – actions to draw attention to meanings beyond a thing's intrinsic content or functional use. The research placed these symbolic actions into four categories. The first conveyed the entrepreneur's personal credibility, capability, and commitment, for instance, in one case by emphasizing their MBA degree. The second, around professional organizing, conveyed professional structure and processes. For example, one venture showed it provided exceptionally fast and responsive customer service. The third, around organizational achievement, adduced prototypes or partially working products as non-verbal artifacts or cited the team's size and collective age and experience. Thus, one venture opened up the trophy cabinet and displayed an industry award it had won. The fourth and final symbolic action conveyed the quality of the ventures' stakeholder relationships, either showing the firm kept company with prestigious stakeholders or making themselves memorable by personal touches like sending customized email greetings or even flowers for a birthday or a career milestone.

Ironically, in this research, the maneuvers that took a more technical or analytical approach and concentrated on developing an actual product or perfecting technological capabilities garnered less interest and resources than those which invested in the skillful presentation of products, organizations, and individuals. Presentation, and in our terms representation and expression, won out over pure substance; essentially social skills carried the day, not pure technical virtuosity.

New ideas are easier to sell if they build on familiar elements. When leaders of market shapers claim markets and create labels, they have a useful habit of adopting templates from more familiar areas. These templates can be cognitive models, values, practices, or vocabulary. For instance, online retailers adopted the template of offline shopping with terms like "shopping cart" and "check-out." Such templates work as a form of sense giving by analogy to educate both your own firm and outside actors about the new or shaped market. And as a principle, they extend beyond simply labels and symbols. For instance, they are the root of metaphor and simile.

No one cultivated that useful habit more assiduously than Thomas Alva Edison, whose most remembered credit, the "perma-nent" electric light bulb, is synonymous with bright ideas. The marketer in Edison disciplined the inventor. For, even though he already envisioned a world of lighting and household appliances, Edison knew not to frighten the horses. To an extraordinary extent, his approach deliberately mirrored the familiar gas system so that customers would recognize the purpose of electricity and understand how to use it.[33] Thus, Edison chose to generate elec-tricity centrally, like gas companies, and distribute it to individual customers. He used customers' existing gas burners and chande-liers. He even hid part of his invention's light under a bushel by promoting an unnecessarily dim bulb having the "mildness of gas" (though the glow was steadier and clearer) and then decided to bury his electric cable underground, like gas pipes, despite this being manifestly unsuitable. When New York statutes barred the Edison Electric Company from doing so, his workaround was to register the Edison Illuminating Company as a gas company. And finally, to mimic gas industry billing, Edison insisted on using meters. He had first to invent one – which he did.

Without going to Edison's lengths, you can take a leaf out of the books of designers of novel products, services, or software who deliberately use "skeuomorphism." Literally "tool shape," skeuomorphism incorporates design elements that serve no func-tional purpose but help people to understand the relationship to the object being displaced. Thus, Apple users will have experienced digital skeuomorphs much favored by Steve Jobs: calendars with leather-stitching, bookshelves with wood veneers, and a shutter-click sound to imitate a mechanical shutter in the iPhone. The Apple desktop calendar, trash bin, and green tabletop were considered instrumental in acclimating users to their devices. Time will tell whether reports of the death of skeuomorphism under Apple's current designer, Jonathan Ive, are exaggerated.

ENGAGE – NOT TAKE THE LEAD, BUT SHARE THE LEAD

Performing a market requires the engagement of a multitude of different market actors, both individuals and organizations. With engagement we mean not only more interactions between individuals and organizations but also commitment to carry out activities necessary for market shaping to be successful. Within the organization aiming for a market-shaping strategy, engaging means alignment of processes across functions and regions. Intra-organizational alignment will require investments in the continuous and synchronous development of capabilities within various functions in order to support the scaling-up required by market growth.

Creating engagement in complex environments requires that leaders *not take the lead, but rather share the lead*. The shift from a firm-centric view toward a systems view changes the way leadership is exercised, and in fact what leadership means. Embracing a systems view implies an acceptance of complexity and uncertainty – and a corresponding loss of control. Leadership becomes less command and control and more enabling and sense making and sense giving. A leader encourages novelty and innovation not by directing but by allowing, not by stabilizing but by disrupting stifling patterns.

In fact, market shapers have to decouple leadership from the individual and distinguish between "leadership" and "leaders." Leadership should be seen as an emergent, interactive, and distributed process of learning, influenced and enabled by leaders. Hence, there will be a number of individuals on all levels of several organizations engaging in leadership acts.

Leaders have an important role. They can become the architects of market innovations – the artists that inspire networks of actors to partake in new value creation, by changing the form and function of the market ecosystem.

From resource potentiality to resource mobilization. A nicely concrete way to understand and distinguish Engagement is in terms of resources. The leadership acts of Exploration and Experimentation both served to *identify resource potentiality*, including apt timing. Indeed, resource potential and opportunities for new value are what the market shaper was informing itself about in the first place. Once the leadership had made sense of a new vision that would reconfigure resources for higher value, their next role was to Express that vision to the rest of the market. Finally, we come to engaging. Engaging means finding focus and aiming at closure. Focus and closure are needed in order to *mobilize resources* inside the organization and in the larger market system needed for scaling up the opportunity and performing the market.

Mobilizing resources requires investment decisions – or decisions on resource allocations or changed priorities – inside various organizations. This is particularly hard, because you may enjoy only partial information. At the same time, to ensure scalability, the market shapers need deep understanding about which assets are bottlenecks jamming market development, and for this you may refer to the fifth of our plays in Chapter 4. The idea is to control, or at least influence, the parts of the ecosystem crucial for rapid scaling.

Meanwhile all markets are dependent on complementary infrastructures or platforms, so these resources, too, must be mobilized. A car cannot be used without roads and petrol stations. Credit cards do not make a lot of sense if no one accepts them as a payment method – an iPhone is only a phone without access to complementary assets on the AppStore or iTunes platforms. And so on. Supporting other actors to specialize in building supporting assets may, therefore, be important for a market to evolve and grow.

Build Credibility for the Market-shaping Initiative

Whereas conventional visions describe the aspirational future state for your company, market-shaping visions must describe the aspirational future state for your entire market system. This sounds obvious, but we nevertheless repeat the point here because most market-shaping strategies fall at this first hurdle.

What is needed is a consistent set of activities aimed at involving all relevant actors in the envisioned market. Thus, you can engage your own firm, the members of the minimum viable system, and also more outlying market actors by three further techniques: deliberate agenda construction, working with opinion leaders and lead users, and smart usage of platforms and events for collaborative purposes.

Walk the line. We pause to make an observation. More than in the disciplining and somewhat authoritarian plan-and-control model of leadership, one of the motifs and hallmarks of leadership in market shaping is balance, along with discretion and fine judgment. Time and again market shapers have to walk a line: between order and chaos, unity and diversity, certainty and ambiguity, divergence and convergence, openness and closure, breadth of vision and focus. Explorers cultivate a diversity of perspectives, and experimenters fostering emergence push the firm to the brink of chaos (but not beyond), yet ultimately the firm needs coherence. A little bit of tension is a good thing and sometimes performs the market better that a zen-like consensus. Change takes some tensions and a degree of conflict – otherwise no one does anything; but in making your actual market-shaping move your coalition needs to … coalesce, and move in harmony, if not in lock step.

Agenda construction for shared purpose. Along similar lines, agenda construction[34] manages the uncertainty inherent in market emergence and change and creates a clear, common purpose. For, when it comes to technological alternatives, investment levels, growth and profitability potential, and viable business models, the ambiguity that was fruitful in boundary concepts may, if unchecked, put off not only firms and their management but other necessary actors in the minimum viable system: research and financing institutions, governmental agencies, and political agents.

Agenda construction affects the premises that market participants use when diagnosing such a potential future market, and hence those participants' sense-making and actions. Three factors will help you to become a successful agenda constructor: the perceived attractiveness of the agenda, its credibility, and the effective communication of the agenda. Depending on their interest and cognitive pictures of the emerging new market, different actors – say, university researchers, financial institutions, or regulatory and standardization institutions – should be targeted with different versions of the agenda through different communication forums and media.

A good example of agenda construction is the Bluetooth Coalition[35] – a cooperative technological solution offered by partly competing, partly complementary wireless technology, and service firms which became a dominant design for future commercial applications and services.

Working with opinion leaders and lead users. Assembling, engaging, and activating opinion leaders and lead users is key to building credibility. Opinion leaders can be experts: people with credibility in a specific area, who others look to for direction and advice. You'll find opinion leaders in most lines of business, including fashion, food, and wine — like the opinion leaders in the wine industry who helped facilitate screwcap bottles. Getting endorsements from these third-party gurus, including via social media can be key to success. Think of the extra boost on bestseller charts that used to come with recommendation by Oprah Winfrey's Book Club.

Lead users often play a significant role in both perfecting disruptive technologies and quickening their diffusion. Some consumers engage proactively in the perfecting as early users. Firms can leverage this active and engaged base of eager early users — really volunteer labor — by, for instance, releasing software in beta versions to enable larger scale real-life testing.

These lead users sometimes act as so-called market rebels.[36] Although we're not talking Che Guevara-style guerrillas, these civilian renegades enable disruption in markets and form social conventions and norms around new technologies. This is especially prevalent in computing. The Homebrew Computing Club of computer hobbyists in Silicon Valley helped launch the personal computer revolution through the open exchange of ideas in the biweekly meetings held from 1975 to 1986 and in the club newsletter. (The Club has been called "the crucible for an entire industry",[37] and members included the young Steve Wozniak.) Another example is the open-source software community, consisting mainly of software enthusiasts. Open Sourcers developed the Linux operating system, with users offering continual, incremental improvements. Linux has also had widespread business applications: the bulk of Internet servers use Linux, and Google's Android operating system is a variant of it. But the digital revolution is just the latest of many, albeit the fastest. A century ago the gasoline-driven automobile won acceptance against the odds through rebellious automobile clubs staging races against steam or electricity-powered rivals. Henry Ford can't take all the credit!

Build platforms for enhanced collaboration. You can support learning and knowledge transfer within the organization by staging regular meetings dedicated to understanding market development. Naturally, it is not enough simply to secure engagement inside the market-shaping firm's organization. In order for market shaping to work, it will also require engagement from other organizations in the market system. This is particularly difficult as the shaping organization does not have any formal authority over other organizations in the market system. To mobilize actors in the extended market system, leaders must aim for win-win outcomes and use power substitutes such as vision, storytelling, networking, and collaboration to wield influence.

To achieve "impact without authority," market shapers need to enable collaborative efforts by providing platforms or events that allow for emergence, by creating room for interactions, and building interdependence among individuals in the system. These platforms and events can be seen as spaces where ideas can mingle, swap, and create new forms[38] – all classic stimulators of emergence.

The shaping organization can lower the barriers for engagement by creating virtual or physical engagement platforms. Digital applications including your common or garden website can broaden and accelerate interaction beyond the restrictions of the physical world, connecting multiple and diverse actors. Many organizational processes can be designed in order to invite extensive collaboration. One example of this is open innovation processes involving a multitude of actors across functional and corporate boundaries. A leader of a market-shaping firm needs to focus primarily on the *platform* that enables collaboration, because in our information-saturated age, individuals in various organizations already have all the data. Rather as we recommended keeping some bricks-and-mortar matching methods in the Exchange layer, physical places, and conferences, such as trade shows or user meetings, where collaborators come together occasionally to share and enhance knowledge, offer a fruitful setting for these sharing events. Until that stage of our virtual e-volution when holograms might suffice, human beings are proving rather attached to communing in person and pressing the flesh.

A couple of characteristics of platforms favor success. First, you'll want minimal barriers to entry and sufficient rewards to motivate participation. Second, you'll also need mechanisms in place to foster trust among participants. A good example of this is a practice common in many sharing economy platforms, namely the ability for the customer to rate the provider and vice versa. If you use Uber, you are asked to rate the driver, but the driver is also rating you. The same principle is applied in AirBnB, eBay, and many other platforms that involve actual monetary exchange.

Orchestrate to Activate

As noted earlier in the book, the traditional strategy playbook is based on the idea of power and domination. Either you find a dominant position in your (product-based and -defined) industry[39] or you possess "rare, imperfectly imitable or non-substitutable" resources[40] that gives you a sustainable advantage against competitors. Both of these approaches by their nature pertain to the power of the individual firm.

From domination to orchestration. The new strategy playbook that we develop in this volume does not predicate domination or the wielding of power to win advantages. Because value is created in a system consisting of a number of players, leaders have to take a broader view. Rather like how access is replacing ownership at the Exchange layer of the market Fan, market-shaping success depends less on the resources a firm controls than on the ones it can connect to. Key is the ability to orchestrate actors and resources in the larger system, to allow the firm to assemble and flexibly re-configure resources so that value can be created for the system. This turns traditional strategy on its head. Rather than start with what you control and look for ways to leverage it, leaders need to begin with the opportunity and then find the resources.

Exchange self-centric for allocentric innovation. Orchestration[41] of resources and activities in the market system requires leaders to switch from a self-centric, firm-based view to an allocentric ("other-centered") view in which value is created for the whole market system by integrating resource from a network of organizations. The allocentric view allows leaders to recognize and seize opportunities to innovate that can only be created jointly by a network of organizations rather than by an individual firm, no matter how powerful.

To seize opportunities outside your own firm's grasp, you have to assemble partners, create alliances, and enter into joint development efforts. But don't look for companies you can boss around. This is not a power game. And avoid paying partners to play. Paying them induces a short-term, transactional attitude, and the risk of over-paying for the value return. Market-shaping needs is a long-term, relational, and systemic view, combined with a genuine understanding that more value can be generated by collaborating.

Learn from jazz: rotating leadership. We've mentioned the lessons jazz offers market-shaping leaders. Part of orchestration relates to improvisation and allowing others to play their solos. Even if a jazz band has a leader (a "Buddy," a "Duke," a "Sweets," or a "King," say), he or she is a far cry from the traditional orchestral conductor. The latter stands alone, high on the podium and controls the performance with their baton, based on a score. By contrast, in jazz the leader is one of the players, not a separate role. And leadership rotates during solos, as everybody else builds a platform enabling the soloist to shine.

Rather than command language, market-shaping leaders can apply a jazz band leader's "provocative competence." Thus, refuse simple answers from various organizations' past successes and challenge participants beyond their habitual behaviors and perceived limits of competence. Likewise, both the market vision and its expression should evoke higher values and ideals (for the system, not just your firm) and thereby provoke passionate engagement. This may encourage individuals to improvise and collaborate.

There is evidence behind these heuristics. Research has shown[42] that rotating leadership, where organizations take turns leading the inter-organizational collaboration in distinct phases, is associated with higher innovation outcomes than collaborations dominated by a single actor, and also than consensus leadership process where organizations work together, agree to common objectives, and follow shared decision making.

Pivot Yourself to Greatness — Repeatedly

Pivoting to a new direction is a useful play for start-ups, which often reorient their business model to find a place in the competitive market that supports their growth.[43] But pivoting also generalizes well to market shaping and not just early on in the process. In this context, a pivot is a substantive change to one or more of your business model facets, be it your product, your customer segment, your channel, pricing logic, resources, activities, or partners. But note that pivoting market shapers should keep one foot on the ground, true to the origins of the metaphor in basketball. In other words, apply your learnings from past success and failure to the new area. Note, too, that pivoting does not imply desperation. It can be a clever leadership tool to discover growth opportunities.

At its best, pivoting is a systematic, hypothesis-driven process of experimentation (hence overlap with another of our Es), to drive and evaluate market opportunities. You translate your market vision into falsifiable business model hypotheses, test the hypotheses using minimum viable set-ups, then decide whether to persevere with the existing model, or pivot by changing some elements.

Pivots continue after the start-up phase. Many a[44] successful company have pivoted both in their start-up phase and over longer periods. You may be familiar with a couple of latter-day examples. YouTube began in 2005 as a video dating site which failed to gain traction. The founders pivoted toward simply sharing videos online. And PayPal began life as a cryptography company designed for exchanging money over Palm Pilots. After a number of pivots, of course, it is now an online payments business.

Reaching back in time, though, did you know that Nintendo was formed in 1889, did business in everything from playing cards to vacuum cleaners to instant rice, operated as taxi company, and even ran a chain of short-stay love hotels? Only in 1966 did this still-household name enter the business of consoles and electronic games, such as Super Mario and Donkey Kong. And how about Sony? The Japanese electronics multinational started by producing home goods such as rice cookers and heating blankets. Meanwhile, back in the US of A, Starbucks launched in 1971 selling espresso makers and coffee beans, before being transformed into the chain of coffee shops which now inhabits every street corner. And Hewlett-Packard made electrical testing products from 1947, over 20 years before it introduced its first personal computer. The further move into consumer-friendly computers and printing/scanning accessories did not happen until the 1990s, when HP separated the production of their testing equipment into a separate company.

These pivot sagas bring us full circle to the cautionary tale which opened this book: Nokia Mobile Phones. The original incarnation of Nokia was as a paper mill in 1865, operating on the eponymous Nokianvirta river. Over the 20th century, Nokia diversified into industries including rubber goods (such as car tires and rubber boots), electronics and telecommunications devices (such as pulse analyzers for nuclear power plants and industrial robots). They never made a phone until 1992. This led to the glory days of the simple old 2G market, where Nokia Mobile Phones enjoyed more than 40% share. Our telling of the story ended when the company had disastrously crossed the threshold of complexity into the 3G market and found the old playbook no longer even approximated the rich reality of market systems. But in reality, there was another chapter. Today Nokia (no longer Nokia Mobile Phones) have embraced the rich reality of complex markets and pivoted again. Having offloaded the mobile device business to Microsoft, they kept one foot on the ground but reoriented to their telecommunications infrastructure business. And with the acquisition of French telecommunications company Alcatel-Lucent, the new Nokia has become one of the global market leaders in this market. The cautionary tale has a happy ending after all, thanks to embracing the richness of complexity and market shaping.

TAKEAWAYS FROM CHAPTER 5

- In complex adaptive market systems, leadership takes on a new, distributed meaning. One has to *decouple leadership from the individual altogether, to distinguish between "leadership" and "leaders."* Successful market leadership can be seen as a distributed process of learning, involving a number of individuals from various organizations.

- Two broad leadership tasks are *Informing and Performing.* Leaders inform themselves and their firm of the potential market in order to envisage a new shape (sense-making). They perform the new market by giving that sense to other actors and, negotiating it until they strike a resonant frequency and the system resonates with the new vision, and by then mobilizing resources and securing commitments.

- Informing and Performing each consist of two "Es": Exploring and Experimenting; and Expressing and Engaging, respectively. These represent traits market shapers must foster in themselves and in collaborating organizations' leadership. The four Es overlap and iterate, and their borders are porous.

- In *Exploring*, firms move from looking ahead (analyzing, forecasting) to looking around the market and at their own business definition. Market shapers seek opportunities to *increase resource density* by sensing value from multiple points, using triangulation and peripheral vision. They cultivate constructive paranoia, diagnosing problems by pre-mortem dissections of imagined failure.

- In *Experimenting*, market shapers move from traditional planning and controlling to *probing the system, observing responses, and provoking emergence.* Experimentation demands rigor. Failsafe environments are stifling; you should craft safe-to-fail environments. Prefer experiments with low downside and high upside, and cut firebreaks to limit loss, but educate your team that *negative results are learning opportunities.* Successes can be amplified next round, while failures must be wound up even if it means *"killing your darlings."*

- In *Expressing* a win-win-win market vision, market shapers move from traditional reading of a map to drawing their own map across the market and negotiating it within the minimum viable system. They *inspire and provoke like artists and persuade like orators.* Linguistic skills include the *use of metaphors* (but avoid zero-sum sporting and martial metaphors); claiming markets by *labeling and signaling* and by making the new, familiar, and inviting.

- In *Engaging*, leaders move from taking the lead to sharing the lead. Basic options are creating the wave as a first mover or catching and curating it as a fast follower. The aim is securing *commitments to the agenda, mobilizing resources*, and *building platforms* for collaboration. Engaging requires a move from domination to *orchestration* and from self-centric to allocentric innovation and to *rotate the lead* as in a jazz band.

NOTES

CHAPTER 1: YOUR STRATEGY PLAYBOOK HAS EXPIRED

1. Noon, C. (2007). Nokia's Kallasvuo puts brave face on iPhone. *Forbes*, February, 12. Retrieved from http://www.forbes.com/2007/02/12/nokia-kallasvuo-iphone-faces-cx_cn_0212autofacescan01.html#

2. Linden, C. G. (2016). *Nokian valtakunta. Raportti hulluilta vuosilta [Nokia's kingdom. A report from the crazy years].* Helsinki, Finland: Gaudeamus.

3. Because we see the story very much as a tale of two markets, we have superimposed this structure on the timeline below: a rise through the 2G market, decelerating climb through the transition period when 2G and 3G coexisted, and eventual nosedive in the 3G market. But the account remains faithful to the chronology.

4. Troianovski, A. (2012). Nokia had jump on Apple with tablet, smartphone prototypes. *Wall Street Journal*, July 19. Retrieved from http://www.theaustralian.com.au/business/wall-street-journal/nokia-had-jump-on-apple-with-tablet-smartphone-prototypes/story-fnay3ubk-1226430228129#

5. According to the Gartner's full-year statistics (http://www.gartner.com/newsroom/id/612207). However, in Q4/2007, Nokia global market share, also according to Gartner, was 40.4%, and some sources even report higher market share figures (upper 40s) for 2007.

6. A recent study published in *Administrative Science Quarterly* claims that one of the issue that led to Nokia's demise was fear. Top managers were afraid of external competitors and shareholders, while middle managers were mainly afraid of internal groups, including superiors and peers. Vuori, T. O., & Huy, Q. N. (2016). Distributed attention and shared emotions in the innovation process: How nokia lost the smartphone battle. *Administrative Science Quarterly*, 61(1), 9–51.

7. Professor Yvez Doz has been following the Nokia saga for many years, and recently published a book on the subject, called Ringtone: Exploring the rise and fall of Nokia in Mobile Phones. The book identifies a number of reasons for the fall. Some examples: the dominant market share led to arrogance and less risk-taking, Nokia created too many products, an organizational matrix put in place in 2004 left no strong arbitration to determine where resources should have been prioritized. See also Bedhall, R. (2017). The rise and fall of Nokia Mobile Phones. *Finland Today*. Retrieved from http://finlandtoday.fi/the-rise-andfall-of-nokia-mobile-phones/. Accessed on December 5.

8. Gartner quantity market shares.

9. It seems that the famous "Burning platform" memo wasn't technically a memo but a speech given by Stephen Elop which was later turned into an internal blog post. Arthur, C. (2011). Nokia's chief executive to staff: 'We are standing on a burning platform'. *The Guardian*. Retrieved from https://www.theguardian.com/technology/blog/2011/feb/09/nokia-burning-platform-memo-elop. Accessed on February 9.

10. This playbook is called "classical" by Reeves, M., Haanaes, K., & Sinha, J. (2015). *Your strategy needs a strategy*. Boston, MA: Harvard Business Review Press.

11. Hawkins, A. J. (2016). Uber is trying to make you forget that surge pricing exists. *The Verge*, June 23. Retrieved from

http://www.theverge.com/2016/6/23/12017002/uber-surge-pricing-upfront-fare-app-update-announcement

12. Knight, S. (2016). How Uber conquered London. *The Guardian*, April 27. Retrieved from https://www.theguardian.com/technology/2016/apr/27/how-uber-conquered-london.

13. Zhang, S., & Shih, G. (2015). Uber seen reaching $10.8 billion in bookings in 2015: Fundraising presentation. *Reuters*, August 21. Retrieved from http://www.reuters.com/article/us-uber-tech-fundraising-idUSKCN0QQ0G320150821.

14. Newcomer, E. (2015). Uber draws fresh comparison with Amazon as growth trumps profit. *Live Mint*, July 1. Retrieved from http://www.livemint.com/Companies/Lw0nxWkxbt8Bv9UPEyG1BP/Uber-draws-fresh-comparison-with-Amazon-as-growth-trumps-pro.html.

15. Bershidsky, L. (2016). Uber needs an $11 Billion war chest. *Bloomberg View*, June 2. Retrieved from http://www.bloomberg.com/view/articles/2016-06-02/uber-needs-an-11-billion-war-chest.

16. Goddin, P. (2015). Uber's plan for self-driving cars bigger than its taxi disruption. *Mobility Lab*, August 18. Retrieved from http://mobilitylab.org/2015/08/18/ubers-plan-for-self-driving-cars-bigger-than-its-taxi-disruption/.

17. Liberatore, S. (2016). Uber drivers, beware: Taxi app tests self-driving car in Pittsburgh that could put all of its 'contractors' out of work. *Daily Mail*, May 19. Retrieved from http://www.dailymail.co.uk/sciencetech/article-3599338/Uber-s-self-driving-car-revealed-pictures-autonomous-Ford-Fusion-cars-tested-Pittsburgh.html#ixzz4pGOHJbCw.

18. Fairchild, C. (2015). Uber needs a crash course in crisis management. *Linkedin*, March 18. Retrieved from https://www.linkedin.com/pulse/uber-needs-crash-course-crisis-management-caroline-fairchild.

19. Chrisafis, A. (2016). France hit by day of protest as security forces fire teargas at taxi strike. *The Guardian*, January 26. Retrieved from https://www.theguardian.com/world/2016/jan/26/french-taxi-drivers-block-paris-roads-in-uber-protest.

20. Knight, S. (2016). How Uber conquered London. *The Guardian*, April 27. Retrieved from https://www.theguardian.com/technology/2016/apr/27/how-uber-conquered-london.

21. North, D. C. (1977). Markets and other allocation systems in history: The challenge of Karl Polanyi. *Journal of European Economic History*, 6(3), 703.

22. Mele, C., Pels, J., & Storbacka, K. (2015). A holistic market conceptualization. *Journal of the Academy of Marketing Science*, 43(1), 100–114.

23. Baghai, M., Smit, S., & Viguerie, S. P. (2007). The granularity of growth. *The McKinsey Quarterly*, 2, 41–51.

24. In Lady Windermere's *Fan*, Oscar Wilde had Lord Darlington quip that a cynic was "a man who knows the price of everything and the value of nothing."

25. Political economy and especially Marxian economics propose also other aspects of value such as "labour value" to complement exchange value and use value.

26. Zenger, T. (2013). Strategy: The uniqueness challenge. *Harvard Business Review*, 91(11), 52–58.

27. See, for example, Lambkin, M., & Day, G. S. (1989). Evolutionary processes in competitive markets: Beyond the product life cycle. *Journal of Marketing*, 4–20.

28. Burgelman, R. A. (2003). *Intel beyond 2003: Looking for its third act*. Teaching Note No. SM-106. Stanford Graduate School of Business.

29. See Slater, S. F., & Narver, J. C. (1995). Market orientation and the learning organization. *Journal of Marketing*, 63–74; and Narver, J. C., Slater, S. F., & MacLachlan, D. L. (2004). Responsive and proactive market orientation and new-product success. *Journal of Product Innovation Management*, 21(5), 334–347.

30. As Daniel Kahneman points out, we humans are susceptible to WYSIATI: what You See It All There Is. If you focus on the product, your entire reality becomes the product — it is just how brain is configured. See Kahneman, D. (2011). *Thinking, fast and slow*. New York, NY: Farrar, Straus and Giroux.

31. Why would anyone think markets were not at least partly social? Clearly, markets involve human beings — even though increasingly computers are taking over a human role such as in making automatic trades when the stock hits a certain level. To posit that markets are not socially constructed seems to entail saying that the human agents are merely vehicles for market forces and drives, notably self-interest; and for laws like the canonical but under-specified law of supply and demand, which are supposedly universal and immutable like the laws of nature. So people in markets do not act "socially," that is, in concert in any way beyond working out these forces, nor are they distracted from them by other agendas.

It is easy to slip into this depersonalized view because our modern economic idiom has embedded it as an article of faith, an almost mystical metanarrative supported by the mathematical abstractions about *homo economicus*: the very terms "The Market" and "market forces" and expressions like "The market has spoken." Yet this leaves much unexplained. Consider differences across time and space in tastes, or in what is valued (the Spanish lust for gold left the Incas mystified, the modern fetish for phone paraphernalia would have looked as odd to the nineteenth century

English as their craze for Dutch tulips), or whether commerce itself is exalted or looked on as base. And the law of supply and demand is so pitted with exceptions that it is arguably as close to human legislation as to natural physical laws. If the nature of markets looks inevitable, it is only ever in hindsight – as with the market for gasoline-powered autos in our worked example below, which in fact nearly missed out on winning the social acceptance and legitimacy that we have taken as natural for the last 75 years. Were markets truly inevitable, we should have less difficulty predicting them and face fewer surprises. Besides, if the objection is that a social explanation is not scientific enough, the science and mathematics behind complex systems theory rebuts that.

While certain forces do pretty consistently drive human behavior, and thwarting them can be like trying to turn back the tide, nonetheless to totally deny a socially constructed element to markets greatly overstates the case. It reminds us of Margaret Thatcher's dictum that there is no such thing as society itself. It also entails saying that social activities themselves cannot be driven by forces either; yet try taking the drive for self-interest out of that most social of activities, politics, for example.

32. For more on the transient nature of competitive advantage, please see McGrath, R. G. (2013). *The end of competitive advantage: How to keep your strategy moving as fast as your business.* Boston, MA: Harvard Business Review Press.

33. As barrier-building competitive strategies are no longer the key to success, the traditional metaphors from war and sports should be avoided. This means less of competing, dominating, penetrating, targeting, attacking, frontlines, winning, and other confrontational words. The analogy to look for is art. Consider, for instance, performing arts. In her HBR blog in 2011, Joan Magretta crystallizes this idea: "There can be many good singers or actors — each outstanding and successful in a distinctive way.

Each finds and creates an audience. The more good performers there are, the more audiences grow and the arts flourish. This approach produces positive sum competition. Companies that do a good job can earn sustainable returns because they create more value. At the same time, customers benefit by getting real choice in how their needs are met." Magretta, J. (2011). Stop competing to be the best. *Harvard Business Review*, Blog Network. Retrieved from http://blogs.hbr.org/cs/2011/11/stop_competing_to_be_the_best.html.

34. Reeves, M., Haanaes, K., & Sinha, J. (2015). *Your strategy needs a strategy*. Boston, MA: Harvard Business Review Press.

35. Urry, J. (2004). The 'system' of automobility. *Theory, Culture & Society*, 21(4–5), 25–39.

36. We have been informed by the work of our good friend and colleague, Dr. Hans Kjellberg, who has been focusing on creating a better understanding of how markets work. Together with Dr. Claes-Fredrik Helgesson, they have proposed a framework based on practice theory that conceives markets as constituted by market practices, defined as all activities that contribute to constitute markets. They identify three categories of market practice: "(1) exchange practice, the concrete activities involved in consummating individual economic exchanges of goods; (2) normalizing practice, activities that contribute to establish normative objectives for actors, i.e., how a market and/or its actors should be (re)shaped according to some (group of) actor(s); and (3) representational practice, activities that re-present economic exchanges as markets, i.e. that depict markets and/or how they work". Kjellberg, H., & Helgesson, C. F. (2006). Multiple versions of markets: Multiplicity and performativity in market practice. *Industrial Marketing Management*, 35(7), 839–855.

37. Baron, D. P. (1995). The nonmarket strategy system. *Sloan Management Review*, 37(1), 73.

38. Agarwal, R., & Bayus, B. L. (2002). The market evolution and sales takeoff of product innovations. *Management Science*, *48*(8), 1024–1041.

39. Cochoy, F. (2009). Driving a shopping cart from STS to business, and the other way round: On the introduction of shopping carts in American grocery stores (1936–1959). *Organization*, *16*(1), 31–55.

CHAPTER 2: FRAME YOUR MARKET

1. Hess, E. D. (2014). *Learn or die: Using science to build a leading-edge learning organization*. New York, NY: Columbia University Press.

2. UPS (n.d.). *History timeline: Explore 100+ years of UPS innovation and growth using our interactive timeline*. Retrieved from https://www.pressroom.ups.com/pressroom/about/HistoryStackList.page?countrylang=US-English.

3. Laurie, D. L., Doz, Y. L., & Sheer, C. P. (2006). Creating new growth platforms. *Harvard Business Review*, *84*(5), 80–90.

4. KONE Corporation (n.d.). http://www.kone.com/en/company/

5. Morgan, J. (2017). Kone on the benefits of People FlowIntelligence. *ConstructionWeekOnline.com*, February 18. Retrieved from http://www.constructionweekonline.com/article-43100-kone-on-the-benefits-of-people-flow-intelligence/.

6. Storbacka, K., & Nenonen, S. (2011). Scripting markets: From value propositions to market propositions. *Industrial Marketing Management*, *40*(2), 255–266.

7. There is an irony in the fact that Nokia's slogan was "Connecting People."

8. Vectia Ltd, the consulting company in which we both were partners, conducted an exploratory research on market-shaping

strategies in 2011. In this research, we studied the business definitions of the 100 largest Finnish commercial organizations. The
data was collected through phone and F2F interviews, the respondents were CEOs or other relevant members of the executive management team, and we got answers from 59 organizations. In this
sample, most respondents defined their business according to one
(56%) or two (31%) criteria. The most commonly used criteria
are the product/service sold (85%) and geographical area (81%).

9. Levitt, T. (1960). Marketing myopia. *Harvard Business
Review*, 38(4), 45–56.

10. Ansoff, I. (1957). Strategies for diversification. *Harvard
Business Review*, 35(5), 113–124.

11. The late Richard Normann called products and services "frozen knowledge." He claimed that particularly tangible products
are an efficient media to make providers' knowledge and resources
available to customers because of their reproductability and
predictability. For more on "frozen knowledge" and Richard
Normann's other ideas about reconfiguring business systems,
please see Normann, R. (2001). *Reframing business: When the
map changes the landscape*. Chichester: Wiley.

12. The late Paul Geroski has researched the nature of markets in
detail, and especially the more creative market definitions. See,
for example, Geroski, P. A. (1998). Thinking creatively about
markets. *International Journal of Industrial Organization*, 16(6),
677–695; Christensen, C. M., Cook, S., & Hall, T. (2005).
Marketing malpractice. *Harvard Business Review*, 83(12),
74–83; Levitt, T. (1960). Marketing myopia. *Harvard Business
Review*, 38(4), 24–47.

13. When you progress to market shaping in Chapter 3, you'll
spot some of these terms repeating, notably "network" and "system." This is not surprising, since the business definition is negoti-
ated in that recursive dialogue with the market view and acts as a

microcosm of it. The network we examine here shares one of the same elements as the network layer of the Fan examined in Chapter 3: actors.

14. *Source*: Business Week (2006). July 17.

15. Garrett, M. (Ed.). (2014). *Encyclopedia of transportation: Social science and policy.* Thousand Oaks, CA: SAGE Publications.

16. www.jcdecaux.com and Normann, R. (2001). *Reframing business: When the map changes the landscape.* Chichester: Wiley.

17. Skanska, IKEA, BoKlok, speech by Susanna Sucksdorff, Business Development Manager in Skanska RDN Finland in 2013.

18. Bower, J. L. (2012). Sam Palmisano's transformation of IBM. *Harvard Business Review*, January 20. Retrieved from https://hbr.org/2012/01/sam-palmisanos-transformation.html; IBM (2008). *Annual Report 2007*. Retrieved from ftp://public.dhe.ibm.com/annualreport/2007/2007_ibm_annual.pdf; and van Kralingen, B. (2010). IBM's transformation – From survival to success. *Forbes*, July 7. Retrieved from https://www.forbes.com/2010/07/07/ibm-transformation-lessons-leadership-managing-change.html.

19. Singleton, M. (2016). Tidal now has 3 million subscribers. *The Verge*, March 29. Retrieved from http://www.theverge.com/2016/3/29/11325608/tidal-now-has-3-million-subscribers.

20. Singer, N. (2014). Intel's sharp-eyed social scientist. *The New York Times*, February 16. Retrieved from https://www.nytimes.com/2014/02/16/technology/intels-sharp-eyed-social-scientist.html.

21. Bright Horizons (n.d.). https://www.brighthorizons.com/about-us.

22. Cyriac, J., Koller, T., & Thomsen, J. (2012). Testing the limits of diversification. *The McKinsey Quarterly*, 2–5.

23. Favaro, K. (2014a). The dangers of adjacencies strategy. *Strategy+Business*, January 30. Retrieved from https://www.strategy-business.com/blog/The-Dangers-of-Adjacencies-Strategy?gko= 04eeb, Favaro, K. (2014b). How IKEA, Disney, and Berkshire Hathaway succeed with adjacencies. *Strategy+Business*, March 11. Retrieved from https://www.strategy-business.com/blog/How-IKEA-Disney-and-Berkshire-Hathaway-Succeed-with-Adjacencies? gko=fa07c.

24. Storbacka, K., & Nenonen, S. (2012). Competitive arena mapping: Market innovation using morphological analysis in business markets. *Journal of Business-to-Business Marketing*, *19*(3), 183–215.

25. Scientifically we are talking about multidimensional inquiry, i.e., morphological analysis (see Ritchey, T. (2006). Problem structuring using computer-aided morphological analysis. *Journal of the Operational Research Society*, *57*(7), 792–801.). Morphological analysis (MA) is a method for structuring socio-technical systems pioneered by Fritz Zwicky. He used MA as a method for investigating the totality of relationships contained in multidimensional, usually non-quantifiable complex problems (Zwicky, F. (1969). *Discovery, invention, research through the morphological analysis*. New York, NY: McMillan.)

26. Zook and Allen have been doing systematic work in helping companies to use growth opportunities provided by adjacency moves; see for example: Zook, C., & Allen, J. (2003). Growth outside the core. *Harvard Business Review*, *81*(12), 66–73.

27. http://en.wikipedia.org/wiki/The_Fox_and_the_Cat_(fable)

28. Based on the speech by Martin Cole, then COO of Starbucks, at the Strategic Management Society's annual conference in San Diego in 2007.

CHAPTER 3: SHAPE YOUR MARKET

1. Gittleson, K. (2012). Can a company live forever? *BBC News*, January 19. Retrieved from http://www.bbc.com/news/business-16611040.

2. Case description partly based on speeches by Matti Mikkola, CEO, Federation of the Finnish Woodworking Industries: "Shaping the market for wooden multistorey buildings – Case Stora Enso" (June 13, 2017) and Mikko Viljakainen, CEO, Puuinfo: "Three market shaping tools" (June 15, 2017). (Finnish Forest Industries. (2010a). *Modernisation of fire safety regulations supports the development of Finland's wood construction industry*. Press release, December 2. Retrieved from https://www.forest-industries.fi/releases/modernisation-of-fire-safety-regulations-supports-the-development-of-finlands-wood-construction-industry/. Finnish Forest Industries (2010b). *Common dimensioning system to strengthen the competitiveness of wood construction*. Press release, October 6. Retrieved from https://www.forestindustries.fi/news/common-dimensioning-system-to-strengthen-the-competitiveness-of-wood-construction/ Ministry of Employment and the Economy, Finland. (2011). *Status and possibilities of wood construction in Finland*. Retrieved from https://tem.fi/documents/1410877/2937056/Status+and+possibilities+of+wood+construction+in+Finland; Stora Enso. (2014). *SRV and Stora Enso partner up to build multi-storey wooden residential housing for City of Helsinki*. Press release, May 6. Retrieved from http://buildingandliving.storaenso.com/news/news-and-press-releases/srv-and-stora-enso-partner-up-to-build-multi-storey-wooden-residential-housing-for-city-of-helsinki).

3. Kafafi, Z. H., Martín-Palma, R. J., Nogueira, A. F., O'Carroll, D. M., Pietron, J. J., Samuel, I. D., … Tsakalakos, L. (2015). The role of photonics in energy. *Journal of Photonics for Energy*, 5(1),

050997-050997. Retrieved from http://photonicsforenergy.spiedigitallibrary.org/article.aspx?articleid=2463108.

See also: https://commons.wikimedia.org/wiki/File:PV_cume_semi_log_chart_2014_estimate.svg.

4. Vazquez Sampere, J. P. (2016). Apple's shrinking impact in the smartphone industry. *Harvard Business Review*, February 2. Retrieved from https://hbr.org/2016/02/apples-shrinking-impact-in-the-smartphone-industry.

5. Benner, K. (2016). Apple says sales of iPhones have slowed. *The New York Times*, January 26. Retrieved from http://www.nytimes.com/2016/01/27/technology/apple-earnings-iphone-sales.html?_r=0.

6. Fox, J. (2014). How to succeed in business by bundling – and unbundling. *Harvard Business Review*, June 24. Retrieved from https://hbr.org/2014/06/how-to-succeed-in-business-by-bundling-and-unbundling.

7. Air Transport Action Group. (2014). *Aviation benefits beyond borders. Powering global economic growth, employment, trade links, tourism and support for sustainable development through air transport*. Retrieved from http://aviationbenefits.org/media/26786/ATAG__AviationBenefits2014_FULL_LowRes.pdf.

8. BreadTalk (n.d.). Retrieved from http://www.breadtalk.com.sg/; Asia, R. (2016). The evolution of BreadTalk Singapore through the years. *Retail News Asia*, September 22. Retrieved from https://www.retailnews.asia/evolution-breadtalk-singapore-years/. http://www.breadtalk.com.sg/

9. Fondia (n.d.). http://www.fondia.com/services/ldaas

10. Roth, A. E. (2007). The art of designing markets. *Harvard Business Review*, 85(10), 118.

11. Statistics New Zealand. (2013). *Census QuickStats about housing*. Retrieved from http://www.stats.govt.nz/Census/2013-census/profile-and-summary-reports/quickstats-about-housing.

12. Gary, L. (2005). Dow Corning's big pricing gamble. *Harvard Business School Working Knowledge*, July 3. Retrieved from http://hbswk.hbs.edu/archive/4677.html.

13. FRANK by OCBC (n.d.). https://www.frankbyocbc.com/

14. Pilcher, J. (2011). Meet FRANK, maybe the coolest bank Gen-Y has ever seen. *The Financial Brand*, May 31. Retrieved from https://thefinancialbrand.com/18642/ocbc-frank-gen-y-banking-brand/.

15. Yeo, R. (2016). *FRANK by OCBC – The future of consumer banking to millennials*. Case S/N 88-16-010. The Nanyang Technopreneurship Case Centre (NTCC) at the Nanyang Technological University. Retrieved from http://www.ntc.ntu.edu.sg/ntcc/Documents/Full%20Version/10.%20FRANK%20BY%20OCBC%20-%20THE%20FUTURE%20OF%20CONSUMER%20BANKING%20TO%20MILLENNIALS.pdf.

16. *A word about terminology.* As we note elsewhere, the Fan is not something you can walk out onto the street and see, but rather a conceptual representation of a complex system, the market. We therefore stipulate certain terms of art to mean somewhat specialized things, and both the terms and the real-world things they reference may actually or apparently overlap between and within layers.

Thus, the word "network" is loosely synonymous with "system" in general parlance, and the description we've given of the network layer might at first sound as though it is co-extensive with the whole market system. But, like a color filter in photography, the Network layer picks out only elements of a certain hue: actors (with their roles and resources) and infrastructure. In the process, it abstracts from the other vital components of the market system, which have their own, different colors: language (dealt with in the Representations layer); the rules of the game (dealt with under Rules of the Game); and what items and rights are exchanged, how and with what pricing logic (Exchange).

Also, note that our use of "infrastructure" is not synonymous with "network" (or for that matter "system"): infrastructure excludes people. Meanwhile, note that the actors listed in the Network influence other layers. For instance, media clearly engage in Representations, while regulators impose Rules of the Game. But the Network layer collects those actors here for conceptual convenience.

17. This method of picturing one's wider business network is heavily influenced by the work done in the IMP (Industrial Marketing & Purchasing) Group, and particularly by the ARA (Actors-Resources-Activities) model by Håkan Håkansson and Ivan Snehota. For an overview of the ARA model and other things related to business-to-business relationships, please see Snehota, I., & Hakansson, H. (Eds.). (1995). *Developing relationships in business networks*. London: Routledge.

18. Ferdows, K., Lewis, M. A., & Machuca, J. A. (2004). Rapid-fire fulfillment. *Harvard Business Review*, *82*(11), 104–117; Smith, K. (2014). Zara vs H&M – Who's in the global lead? *Edited*, April 15. Retrieved from https://edited.com/blog/2014/04/zara-vs-hm-whos-in-the-global-lead/; and Verma, M. (2007). *H&M vs Zara: Competitive growth strategies*. Case study COM0196P. Retrieved from http://www.ibscdc.org/Case_Studies/Strategy/Competitive%20Strategies/COM0196P.htm.

19. International SOS (n.d.). https://www.internationalsos.com/; https://www.internationalsos.com/about-us/philosophy-and-values; https://en.wikipedia.org/wiki/International_SOS

20. Agarwal, R., & Bayus, B. L. (2002). The market evolution and sales takeoff of product innovations. *Management Science*, *48*(8), 1024–1041.

21. Press, G. (2016). From IBM mainframe users group to Apple 'Welcome IBM. Seriously': This week In tech history. *Forbes*. Retrieved from https://www.forbes.com/sites/gilpress/2016/08/21/from-ibm-ainframe-users-group-to-apple-welcome-ibm-seriously-this-week-in-tech-history/#7290b873beb4. Accessed on August 9.

22. Aspers, P. (2009). *How are markets made?* MPIfG Working Paper No. 09/2.

23. Fair Dinkum (n.d.). http://www.fairdinkumsheds.com.au/; http://www.fairdinkumsheds.com.au/about-us-0

24. Fonterra Food Services (n.d.). http://www.fonterrafoodser-vices.net/en/cn/home; http://www.fonterrafoodservices.net/en/cn/news/10; http://www.fonterrafoodservices.net/en/cn/news/15

25. Hubject (n.d.). https://www.hubject.com/en/

26. Wärtsilä (n.d.). https://www.wartsila.com/twentyfour7/gas/small-carriers-diversify-the-lng-fleet

27. Hindustan Unilever Limited (n.d.). *Enhancing livelihoods through Project Shakti*. Retrieved from https://www.hul.co.in/sus-tainable-living/case-studies/enhancing-livelihoods-through-project-shakti.html and Bhasin, K. (2012). Unilever now has an army of 50,000 'Shakti Women' selling its products in India. *Business Insider*, July 3. Retrieved from http://www.businessinsider.com/unilevers-shakti-women-fight-pg-in-india-2012-7?r=US&IR=T&IR=T.

28. Sealed Air Corporation (1960).

29. Dempster Brothers (1936).

30. Universal Fastener Company (1917).

31. Otis (1900).

32. Arnott, S. (2010). International SOS: How to avoid turning a crisis into a drama. *Independent*. Retrieved from http://www.independent.co.uk/news/business/analysis-and-features/international-sos-how-to-avoid-turning-a-crisis-into-a-drama-1957327.html. Accessed on April 28.

33. Wise, T. A. (1960). The auditors have arrived. *Fortune Magazine, 62(5)*.

34. Water Footprint Network (n.d.). http://waterfootprint.org/en/

35. NORD National Organization for Rare Disorders (n.d.). https://rarediseases.org/

36. Chesire, T. (2012). Europe's 100 hottest startups 2012: Stockholm. *Wired*, August 15. Retrieved from http://www.wired.co.uk/article/stockholm-3.

37. Forrester. (2008). *Electronic invoice presentment and payment market in the Forrester Wave: Accounts payable EIPP. Q2* 2008 Report, published June 18 and Basware Plc. (2008). *Interim report January 1—June 30*. Retrieved from https://www.basware.com/fr-fr/actualites/basware-interim-report-january-1-june-30—2008.

38. KONE Corporation (2015). What's a people flow day? *YouTube*, October 27. Retrieved from https://www.youtube.com/watch?v=FsfCjGskJVE.

39. Martin, J. (2012). Keith Tantlinger — The man behind the container. *Sea Breezes*, January 18. Retrieved from http://www.seabreezes.co.im/index.php?option=com_content&view=article&id=812:keith-tantlinger-the-man-behind-the-container&catid=34:ships&Itemid=56, Wikipedia (n.d.). *Malcom McLean*. Retrieved from http://en.wikipedia.org/wiki/Malcom_McLean; http://www.telegraph.co.uk/news/obituaries/finance-obituaries/8766380/Keith-Tantlinger.html, http://www.telegraph.co.uk/news/obituaries/

finance-obituaries/8766380/Keith-Tantlinger.html, and Hagel, J., Brown, J. S., & Davison, L. (2008). Shaping strategy in a world of constant disruption. *Harvard Business Review*, 86(10), 80–89.

40. Robinson, J. (2011). Our man in Washington. *Stuff*, February 5. Retrieved from http://www.stuff.co.nz/sunday-star-times/features/4619280/Our-man-in-Washington.

41. Storbacka, K., & Nenonen, S. (2015). Learning with the market: Facilitating market innovation. *Industrial Marketing Management*, 44, 73–82.

42. Wikipedia (n.d.). *Uber protests and legal actions*. Retrieved from https://en.wikipedia.org/wiki/Legal_status_of_Uber%27s_service.

43. Munford, M. (2016). Estonia embraces Uber and Taxify as first European country to legalize and regulate ride-sharing. *Forbes*, February 28. Retrieved from http://www.forbes.com/sites/montymunford/2016/02/28/estonia-embraces-uber-and-taxify-as-first-european-country-to-legalize-and-regulate-ride-sharing/#757ed1b56968.

44. Gunningham, N., & Rees, J. (1997). Industry self-regulation: An institutional perspective. *Law & Policy*, 19(4), 363–414.

45. Everett Rogers demonstrated his diffusion theory in the 1962 published book *Diffusion of Innovations,* which later gained classic status. Rogers studied the penetration of new agricultural tools in the Midwest and figured out that the spreading of new ideas among a population always follows the same principles. These include among other things the revelation that the time measured from innovation launch to implementation follows the normal distribution curve, also known as the Gauss bell curve. This indicates that all populations have five adopting categories: innovators, early adopters, early majority, late majority, and delayed adopters

Rogers, E. (2003). *Diffusion of innovations* (5th ed.). New York, NY: Simon and Schuster.

46. Woodard, R. (2011). Screwcap now 'the norm': New study. *Decanter*, November 14. Retrieved from http://www.decanter. com/news/wine-news/529514/screwcap-now-the-norm-new-study.

47. Stelzer, T., Grosset, J., Brajkovich, M., Forrest, J., & Rankine, B. (2005). *Taming the SCREW: A manual for winemaking with screw caps*. Tarragindi: Wine Press.

CHAPTER 4: LEARN SHAPING PRINCIPLES AND PLAYS

1. Gow, P. (2012). History of Les Mills – Documentary 2013. *YouTube*, April 16. Retrieved from https://www.youtube.com/ watch?v=X1GD-NZaVJs.

2. Sanchez, J. T. (2011). The history of BODYPUMP™ with Phillip Mills. *YouTube*, November 7. Retrieved from https://www. youtube.com/watch?v=p1CqX_M7lmM.

3. Wikipedia (n.d.). *Performativity*. Retrieved from https://en.wiki-pedia.org/wiki/Performativity and Crossley, J. (2012). Les Mills an international success. *Stuff*, January 27. Retrieved from http:// www.stuff.co.nz/business/industries/6327563/Les-Mills-an-international-success.

4. Mills, P. (2014). Secrets of success. *LesMills*, July 3. Retrieved from https://www.lesmills.com/clubs-and-facilities/industry-insights/ secrets-of-success/.

5. Greco, C. C., Oliveira, A. S., Pereira, M. P., Figueira, T. R., Ruas, V. D., Goncalves, M., & Denadai, B. S. (2011). Improvements in metabolic and neuromuscular fitness after 12-week Bodypump® training. *The Journal of Strength & Conditioning Research,* 25(12), 3422–3431, Petersen, B. A., Hastings, B., & Gottschall, J. S. (2017). Low load, high repetition

resistance training program increases bone mineral density in untrained adults. *The Journal of Sports Medicine and Physical Fitness, 57*(1−2), 70−76.

6. Les Mills International (n.d.). Retrieved from https://www.les-mills.com/ondemand/. Retrieved from https://www.lesmills.com/ondemand/

7. Reeves, M., Love, C., & Tillmanns, P. (2012). Your strategy needs a strategy. *Harvard Business Review*, 90(9), 76−83.

8. See Aspers, P. (2009). *How are markets made?* MPIfG Working Paper No. 09/2.

9. This adds another sense of "network" to those discussed in the terminology box under the Network layer in Chapter 3.

10. The comparison of Sony Walkman and Apple iPod is explained in more detail in Adner, R. (2012). *The wide lens: A new strategy for innovation.* UK: Penguin.

11. For those familiar with McKinsey's Three Horizons framework, market shaping can be seen as a second-horizon activity ("Build emerging businesses") or even a third-horizon activity ("Create viable options").

12. For more about active waiting, please see Sull, D. N. (2005). Strategy as active waiting. *Harvard Business Review, 83*(9), 120.

13. Bershidsky, L. (2016). Uber needs an $11 Billion war chest. *Bloomberg View*, June 2. Retrieved from http://www.bloomberg.com/view/articles/2016-06-02/uber-needs-an-11-billion-war-chest.

14. For more information about the moral and ethical problems related to markets and market shaping, please see for example: Sandel, M. J. (2012). *What money can't buy: The moral limits of markets.* New York, NY: Macmillan; Roscoe, P. (2014). *I spend, therefore I am: The true cost of economics.* New York, NY:

Viking.; and Kuttner, R. (1999). *Everything for sale: The virtues and limits of markets.* Chicago, IL: University of Chicago Press.

15. For more about minimum viable systems, please refer to the viable systems approach, e.g., Golinelli, G. M. (2010). *Viable systems approach (VSA): Governing business dynamics.* Padova: Cedam.

16. Even though not invented by Stephen Covey, the abundance mentality is explained in great detail in his 1990's classic Covey, S. R. (1991). *The 7 habits of highly effective people.* New York, NY: Simon & Schuster.

17. This value quantification is provided to us by Bo Harald and the Real-Time Economy Community. There are also other value quantification examples about e-invoicing in Europe, such as http://ec.europa.eu/internal_market/payments/einvoicing/index_en.htm

18. Cramo Plc (2013). Cramo's and Ramirent's joint venture company for the operations in Russia and Ukraine, Fortrent, launches its logo and corporate identity. *Nasdaq GlobeNewsWire*, April 12. Retrieved from https://globenewswire.com/news-release/2013/04/12/537882/0/en/Cramo-s-and-Ramirent-s-joint-venture-company-for-the-operations-in-Russia-and-Ukraine-Fortrent-launches-its-logo-and-corporate-identity.html.

19. Air New Zealand. (2013). *Air New Zealand Investor Day 2013.* Retrieved from https://p-airnz.com/cms/assets/NZ/PDFs/investor-day-2013.pdf.

20. CAPA Centre for Aviation. (2013). *New Zealand negotiating open skies agreements to attract air services, even without reciprocity.* Retrieved from https://centreforaviation.com/insights/analysis/new-zealand-negotiating-open-skies-agreements-to-attract-air-services-even-without-reciprocity-125072. Accessed on August 27.

21. Kirk, S. (2013). Air New Zealand and Virgin alliance extended. *Stuff*, September 20. Retrieved from http://www.stuff. co.nz/business/9190040/Air-New-Zealand-and-Virgin-alliance-extended.

22. Ministry of Transport, New Zealand. (2017). Alliance and codeshare agreements, April 19. Retrieved from http://www.transport.govt.nz/air/internationalairservices/internationalaircarriage-competition/.

23. Bridgman, B., Dugan, A., Lal, M., Osborne, M., & Villones, S. (2012). Accounting for household production in the national accounts, 1965–2010. *Survey of Current Business*, 92(5), 23–36.

24. Coor Service Management (n.d.). Retrieved from http://www. coor.com/about-coor/history/.

25. Linas Matkasse (n.d.). Retrieved from https://www.linasmat-kasse.se/hur-det-borjade/.

26. Chin Leong, K. (2013). Google reveals its 9 principles of innovation. *Fast Company*, November 20. Retrieved from http://www. fastcompany.com/3021956/how-to-be-a-success-at-everything/googles-nine-principles-of-innovation.

27. Newitz, A. (2012). Medieval monks complained about their jobs in the margins of ancient manuscripts. Retrieved from http:// io9.gizmodo.com/5896008/medieval-monks-complained-about-their-jobs-in-the-margins-of-ancient-manuscripts.

28. For an overview of Clayton Christensen's theory of disruptive innovations, please see: Christensen, C. M. (1997). *The innovator's dilemma: When new technologies cause great firms to fail.* Boston, MA: Harvard Business School Press and Christensen, C. M., & Raynor, M. E. (2003). *The innovator's solution: Creating and sustaining successful growth.* Boston, MA: Harvard Business School Press.

29. Yong, N. (2014). The secret recipe that sold over 100 Million BreadTalk Flosss Buns. *TheSmartLocalSingapore*, October 3. Retrieved from http://thesmartlocal.com/read/breadtalk-flosss-buns.

30. Garcia, T. (2016). Amazon is about to overtake Macy's as biggest seller of clothing in U.S. *MarketWatch*, May 14. Retrieved from http://www.marketwatch.com/story/traditional-retailers-stumble-in-their-efforts-to-compete-with-amazon-2016-05-12.

31. Aughney, J. (2002). Tesco now offering life assurance. *Independent*, November 2. Retrieved from http://www.independent.ie/business/irish/tesco-now-offering-life-assurance-26025947.html; Cumbo, J. (2009). Check out supermarkets' life cover. *Financial Times*, May 8. Retrieved from https://www.ft.com/content/adcb18d6-3be0-11de-acbc-00144feabdc0; Elsworth, S. (2013). Push to have life insurance sold by supermarket chains. *News.com.au*, March 24. Retrieved from http://www.news.com.au/finance/money/push-to-have-life-insurance-sold-by-supermarket-chains/news-story/739ea3478f03da941f18dc1c16b2d0ef, and Shannon, L. (2012). Life insurance trap at the checkout: Supermarkets use aggressive tactics to push cover that may not fit. *ThisIsMoney.co.uk*, August 16. Retrieved from http://www.thisismoney.co.uk/money/article-2124630/Supermarkets-use-aggressive-tactics-sell-customers-life-insurance.html.

32. Roth, A. E. (2007). The art of designing markets. *Harvard Business Review*, *85*(10), 118.

33. Bachcare (n.d.). Retrieved from https://www.bachcare.co.nz/about-us.

34. Wood, A. (2015). Bachcare shows the how an SME proposition can take off. *Stuff*, October 3. Retireved from http://www.stuff.co.nz/business/72610441/bachcare-shows-the-how-an-sme-proposition-can-take-off and New Zealand Herald (2015). The

death of the Kiwi bach. *The Big Read*, October 25. Retrieved from http://www.nzherald.co.nz/business/news/article.cfm?c_id=3&objectid=11534648.

CHAPTER 5: LEADERSHIP FOR MARKET SHAPERS

1. Dr. Alahuhta has written a book about his leadership philosophy – the book is, however, only available in Finnish: Alahuhta, M. (2015). *Johtajuus. Kirkas suunta ja ihmisten voima. Kokemuksia ja näkemyksiä johtamisesta KONEen ja Nokian vuosilta [Leadership. Clear direction and people power. Experiences and insights from my years at KONE and Nokia].* Jyväskylä, Finland: Docendo Oy.

2. Egon Zender (n.d.). *The continuity coming from the family ownership history is an asset for us in developing a strong performance culture.* Interview with Matti Alahuhta, CEO KONE Corporation. Retrieved from http://www.egonzehnder.com/the-focus-magazine/topics/the-focus-on-family/expertise/interview-with-matti-alahuhta-ceo-kone-corporation.html.

3. 358.fi. (n.d.). Retireved from http://358.fi/work/people-flow/.

4. Killing, P., Malnight, T., & Keys, T. (2006). *Must-win battles: How to win them, again and again.* New York, NY: Pearson Education.

5. Virtanen, A. (2015). Digitalization enables user-centric people flow planning in smart buildings. In A. Wood & D. Malott (Eds.), *Global interchanges: Resurgence of the Skyscraper City* (pp. 603–608). Chicago, IL: Council on Tall Buildings and Urban Habitat. Retrieved from http://global.ctbuh.org/resources/papers/download/2514-digitalization-enables-user-centric-people-flow-planning-in-smart-buildings.pdf.

6. Murison, M. (2016). Kone partners with IBM IoT for smarter buildings. *Internet of Business*, March 4. Retrieved from https://internetofbusiness.com/kone-partners-with-ibm-iot-for-smarter-buildings/.

7. The alternative wording here would be "transform." However, "transform" would be both too generic and suggest too much power in the shaper: a simple command; the whole move in market shaping is from power to influence.

8. Performativity is the property of expressed views and ideas impacting on reality per se and helping bring about the state of affairs they express. In the market-shaping context this means that any actor's expressed market view can potentially shape the market toward itself as the actor repeatedly and consistently proposes that view to other market actors and they relay the signal. So, preaching the gospel to the parish may make the gospel real – or at least it will persuade everyone to act as if it were! See Wikipedia (n.d.f). *Andrew Grove*. Retrieved from https://en.wikipedia.org/wiki/Andrew_Grove.

9. Normann, R. (2001). *Reframing business: When the map changes the landscape*. Chichester: Wiley.

10. Fox, J. (2014). How to succeed in business by bundling – and unbundling. *Harvard Business Review*, June 24. Retrieved from https://hbr.org/2014/06/how-to-succeed-in-business-by-bundling-and-unbundling.

11. The best managerial book about this subject is by Day, G. S., & Schoemaker, P. J. H. (2006). *Peripheral vision. Detecting the weak signals that will make or break your company*. Boston, MA: Harvard Business School Press.

12. The classic go-to-book in this context is by Gladwell, M. (2008). *Outliers: The story of success*. London: Hachette.

13. In statistical terms, an outlier is an observation that is distant and different from other observations. Strictly, averages — or means — only partially submerge outliers. Medians submerge them entirely, so should be avoided like the plague!

14. Grove, A. S. (1996). *Only the paranoid survive*. New York, NY: Doubleday urged senior executives to allow people to test new techniques, new products, new sales channels, and new customers, to be ready for unexpected shifts in business or technology. Grove explains his reasoning as follows: "A corporation is a living organism; it has to continue to shed its skin. Methods have to change. Focus has to change. Values have to change. The sum total of those changes is transformation" (see Wikipedia (n.d.). *Andrew Grove*. Retrieved from https://en.wikipedia.org/wiki/Andrew_Grove).

15. Thompson, M. (2011). The uses of discomfort. *The Radical Ear*, May 21. Retrieved from https://theradicalear.wordpress.com/2011/05/12/the-uses-of-discomfort/.

16. Diamond, J. (2013). That daily shower can be a killer. *New York Times*, January 28. Retrieved from http://www.nytimes.com/2013/01/29/science/jared-diamonds-guide-to-reducing-lifes-risks.html.

17. Klein, G. (2007). Performing a project premortem. *Harvard Business Review*, 85(9), 18–19.

18. Kirk, C., & Brady, H. (2014). The Google graveyard. *Slate*, June 30. Retrieved from http://www.slate.com/articles/technology/map_of_the_week/2013/03/google_reader_joins_graveyard_of_dead_google_products.html.

This is a virtual space for grieving, in which followers of various services can leave a flower and the gravestone, and "let the healing process begin." There were 42 headstones by June 30, 2014.

19. The affordable loss principles is one of the principles in the so-called Effectuation approach to business development, originally developed by Saras Sarasvathy (see Sarasvathy, S. D. (2009). *Effectuation: Elements of entrepreneurial expertise.* Northampton, MA: Edward Elgar Publishing). She did long-term research with successful serial entrepreneurs and noted that the way that they approach business development is radically different from the "traditional" business school approach. Based on this, she identified five core principles (https://en.wikipedia.org/wiki/Effectuation) that define Effectual Logic: (1) The Bird in Hand Principle. Entrepreneurs start with what they have. They will look at who they are, what they know, and who they know. Their education, tastes, and experience are examples of factors which are important in this stage. Besides these examples, this is also the stage where entrepreneurs look at their 3Fs, better known as friends, family, and fools. From this point, they will look at their abilities. So an entrepreneur does not start with a given goal, but with the tools he or she has. (2) The Affordable Loss Principle. An entrepreneur does not focus on possible profits, but on the possible losses and how they can minimize those losses. (3) The Crazy Quilt Principle. Entrepreneurs cooperate with parties they can trust. These parties can limit the affordable loss by giving pre-commitment. (4) The Lemonade Principle. Entrepreneurs will look at how to leverage contingencies. Surprises are not necessarily seen as something bad, but as opportunities to find new markets. (5) The Pilot-in-the-Plane. In this stage, all the previous principles are put together. The future cannot be predicted, but entrepreneurs can control some of the factors which determine the future.

20. The quote can be found here: Kaplan, R. D. (2010). Man versus Afghanistan. *The Atlantic*, April. Retrieved from http://www.theatlantic.com/magazine/archive/2010/04/man-versus-afghanistan/307983/. He has also written a book that is relevant in this

context: McChrystal, S., & Fussell, C. (2015). *Team of teams: The power of small groups in a fragmented world*. New York, NY: Portfolio Hardcover.

21. See Eisenhardt, K. M., & Sull, D. N. (2001). Strategy as simple rules. *Harvard Business Review*, 79(1), 106–119; Sull, D., & Eisenhardt, K. M. (2015). *Simple rules: How to thrive in a complex world*. Boston, MA: Houghton Mifflin Harcourt; Sull, D., & Eisenhardt, K. M. (2012). Simple rules for a complex world. *Harvard Business Review*, 90(9), 68.

22. Kinni, T. (2015). Conquering complexity with simple rules. *Insights by Stanford Business*, April 14. Retrieved from https://www.gsb.stanford.edu/insights/conquering-complexity-simple-rules.

23. *Economist* and *Financial Times* columnist Tim Harford writes in his new book: *Adapt: Why Success Always Starts with Failure* (Harford, T. (2011). *Adapt: Why success always starts with failure*. London: Little, Brown).

24. https://en.wikiquote.org/wiki/Enrico_Fermi

25. The key tool in this is language development and the ability to create expressions of the envisioned market. In his seminal work from 2001, Richard Normann illustrates how firms can influence their landscape by reframing their role and creating a language to convey this to other players in the network.

26. Hagel, J., Brown, J. S., & Davison, L. (2008). Shaping strategy in a world of constant disruption. *Harvard Business Review*, 86(10), 80–89.

27. The book can nowadays be found free on the Internet: http://www.gutenberg.org/files/1946/1946-h/1946-h.htm

28. http://www.rugbyfootballhistory.com/originsofrugby.htm

29. Barrett, F. (2012). *Yes to the mess: Surprising leadership lessons from jazz*. Boston, MA: Harvard Business Review Press.

30. See Santos, F. M., & Eisenhardt, K. M. (2009). Constructing markets and shaping boundaries: Entrepreneurial power in nascent fields. *Academy of Management Journal*, 52(4), 643–671.

31. Turula, T. (2017). This Finnish law firm has transformed an age-old industry – By going digital and taking 'no a-holes'. *Business Insider Nordic*, March 16. Retrieved from http://nordic.businessinsider.com/40-hour-weeks-playrooms-and-no-assholes-this-finnish-pioneer-has-brought-law-to-the-21st-century-2017-3/

32. Zott, C., & Huy, Q. N. (2007). How entrepreneurs use symbolic management to acquire resources. *Administrative Science Quarterly*, 52(1), 70–105.

33. Hargadon, A. B., & Douglas, Y. (2001). When innovations meet institutions: Edison and the design of the electric light. *Administrative Science Quarterly*, 46(3), 476–501.

34. See Möller, K. (2010). Sense-making and agenda construction in emerging business networks –How to direct radical innovation. *Industrial Marketing Management*, 39(3), 361–371.

35. Bluetooth SIG (n.d.). Retrieved from http://www.bluetooth.com.

36. Rao, H. (2009). Market rebels and radical innovation. *McKinsey Quarterly*, January.

37. McCracken, H. (2013). For one night only, Silicon Valley's Homebrew computer club reconvenes. *TIME Magazine*, November 12. Retrieved from http://techland.time.com/2013/11/12/for-one-night-only-silicon-valleys-homebrew-computer-club-reconvenes/.

38. Johnson, S. (2010). Where good ideas come from. *YouTube*, September 17. Retrieved from https://www.youtube.com/watch?v=NugRZGDbPFU.

39. Porter, M. E. (2008). *Competitive strategy: Techniques for analyzing industries and competitors*. New York, NY: Simon and Schuster.

40. RBV – resource-based view of the firm (Barney, J. (1991). Firm resources and sustained competitive advantage. *Journal of Management*, 17(1), 99–120). VRIN stands for "Valuable, Rare, Imperfectly Imitable and Non-substitutable." It covers identification of all the potential key resources. It helps to analyze whether these resources can fulfill VRIN criteria: (1) *Valuable* – It involves value-creating strategies which can help one outperform its competitors or reduce its weakness by improving its effectiveness and increase in efficiencies; (2) *Rare* – includes all resources which are rare and not available to the competitor; (3) *Imperfectly Imitable* – value of a particular resource governed by only one firm and others can't duplicate the resource for its use; and (4) *Non-substitutable* – the resources can't be substituted by any other available resources.

41. Sull, D. L., & Ruelas-Gossi, A. (2010). Strategic orchestration. *Business Strategy Review*, 21(4), 58–63.

42. Davis, J. P., & Eisenhardt, K. M. (2011). Rotating leadership and collaborative innovation recombination processes in symbiotic relationships. *Administrative Science Quarterly*, 56(2), 159–201.

43. Ries, E. (2011). *The lean startup: How today's entrepreneurs use continuous innovation to create radically successful businesses*. New York, NY: Crown Business; Blank, S. (2013). Why the lean start-up changes everything. *Harvard Business Review*, 91(5), 63–72.

44. See, for instance: Nazar, J. (2013). 14 famous business pivots. *Forbes*, October 8. Retrieved from http://www.forbes.com/sites/jasonnazar/2013/10/08/14-famous-business-pivots/#2aa9617f1fb9;

Thomas, N. (2011). 11 startups that found success by changing direction. *Mashable*, July 8. Retrieved from http://mashable.com/2011/07/08/startups-change-direction/#XP_r8qAnksq7; O'Hear, S., & Lomas, N. (2014). Five super successful tech pivots. *TechCrunch*, May 28. Retrieved from https://techcrunch.com/gallery/five-super-successful-tech-pivots/; and Engel, K. (2015). Startup pivots that changed the world. *WhoIsHostingThis?* February 5. Retrieved from http://www.whoishostingthis.com/blog/2015/02/05/startup-pivots/.

REFERENCES

Adner, R. (2012). *The wide lens: A new strategy for innovation.* UK: Penguin.

Agarwal, R., & Bayus, B. L. (2002). The market evolution and sales takeoff of product innovations. *Management Science, 48*(8), 1024–1041.

Air New Zealand. (2013). *Air New Zealand Investor Day 2013.* Retrieved from https://p-airnz.com/cms/assets/NZ/PDFs/investor-day-2013.pdf

Air Transport Action Group. (2014). *Aviation benefits beyond borders. Powering global economic growth, employment, trade links, tourism and support for sustainable development through air transport.* Retrieved from http://aviationbenefits.org/media/26786/ATAG_AviationBenefits2014_FULL_LowRes.pdf

Alahuhta, M. (2015). *Johtajuus. Kirkas suunta ja ihmisten voima. Kokemuksia ja näkemyksiä johtamisesta KONEen ja Nokian vuosilta [Leadership. Clear direction and people power. Experiences and insights from my years at KONE and Nokia].* Jyväskylä, Finland: Docendo Oy.

Ansoff, I. (1957). Strategies for diversification. *Harvard Business Review, 35*(5), 113–124.

Arnott, S. (2010). International SOS: How to avoid turning a crisis into a drama. *Independent.* Retrieved from http://www.independent.co.uk/news/business/analysis-and-features/internationalsos-how-to-avoid-turning-a-crisis-into-a-drama-1957327.html. Accessed on April 28.

Arthur, C. (2011). Nokia's chief executive to staff: 'We are standing on a burning platform'. *The Guardian*. Retrieved from https://www.theguardian.com/technology/blog/2011/feb/09/nokia-burning-platform-memo-elop. Accessed on February 9.

Asia, R. (2016). The evolution of BreadTalk Singapore through the years. *Retail News Asia*, September 22. Retrieved from https://www.retailnews.asia/evolution-breadtalk-singapore-years/

Aspers, P. (2009). *How are markets made?* MPIfG Working Paper No. 09/2.

Aughney, J. (2002). Tesco now offering life assurance. *Independent*, November 2. Retrieved from http://www.independent.ie/business/irish/tesco-now-offering-life-assurance-26025947.html

Baghai, M., Smit, S., & Viguerie, S. P. (2007). The granularity of growth. *The McKinsey Quarterly*, 2, 41–51.

Barney, J. (1991). Firm resources and sustained competitive advantage. *Journal of Management*, 17(1), 99–120.

Baron, D. P. (1995). The nonmarket strategy system. *Sloan Management Review*, 37(1), 73–86.

Barrett, F. (2012). *Yes to the mess: Surprising leadership lessons from jazz*. Boston, MA: Harvard Business Review Press.

Basware Plc. (2008). *Interim report January 1–June 30*. Retrieved from https://www.basware.com/fr-fr/actualites/basware-interim-report-january-1-june-30–2008

Bedhall, R. (2017). The rise and fall of Nokia Mobile Phones. *Finland Today*. Retrieved from http://finlandtoday.fi/the-rise-and-fall-of-nokia-mobile-phones/. Accessed on December 5.

Benner, K. (2016). Apple says sales of iPhones have slowed. *The New York Times*, January 26. Retrieved from http://www. nytimes.com/2016/01/27/technology/apple-earnings-iphone-sales. html?_r=0

Bershidsky, L. (2016). Uber needs an $11 Billion war chest. *Bloomberg View*, June 2. Retrieved from http://www.bloomberg. com/view/articles/2016-06-02/uber-needs-an-11-billion-war-chest

Bhasin, K. (2012). Unilever now has an army of 50,000 'Shakti Women' selling its products in India. *Business Insider*, July 3. Retrieved from http://www.businessinsider.com/unilevers-shakti-women-fight-pg-in-india-2012-7?r=US&IR=T&IR=T

Blank, S. (2013). Why the lean start-up changes everything. *Harvard Business Review*, 91(5), 63–72.

Bower, J. L. (2012). Sam Palmisano's transformation of IBM. *Harvard Business Review*, January 20. Retrieved from https://hbr. org/2012/01/sam-palmisanos-transformation.html

BreadTalk. (n.d.). Retrieved from http://www.breadtalk.com.sg/

Bridgman, B., Dugan, A., Lal, M., Osborne, M., & Villones, S. (2012). Accounting for household production in the national accounts, 1965–2010. *Survey of Current Business*, 92(5), 23–36.

Burgelman, R. A. (2003). *Intel beyond 2003: Looking for its third act*. Teaching Note No. SM-106. Stanford Graduate School of Business.

CAPA Centre for Aviation. (2013). *New Zealand negotiating open skies agreements to attract air services, even without reciprocity*. Retrieved from https://centreforaviation.com/insights/ analysis/new-zealand-negotiating-open-skies-agreements-to-attract-air-services-even-without-reciprocity-125072. Accessed on August 27.

Census QuickStats About Housing. (2013). Retrieved from http://www.stats.govt.nz/Census/2013-census/profile-and-summary-reports/quickstats-about-housing.aspx

Chesire, T. (2012). Europe's 100 hottest startups 2012: Stockholm. *Wired*, August 15. Retrieved from http://www.wired.co.uk/article/stockholm-3

Chin Leong, K. (2013). Google reveals its 9 principles of innovation. *Fast Company*, November 20. Retrieved from http://www.fastcompany.com/3021956/how-to-be-a-success-at-everything/googles-nine-principles-of-innovation

Chrisafis, A. (2016). France hit by day of protest as security forces fire teargas at taxi strike. *The Guardian*, January 26. Retrieved from https://www.theguardian.com/world/2016/jan/26/french-taxi-drivers-block-paris-roads-in-uber-protest

Christensen, C. M. (1997). *The innovator's dilemma: When new technologies cause great firms to fail*. Boston, MA: Harvard Business School Press.

Christensen, C. M., Cook, S., & Hall, T. (2005). Marketing malpractice. *Harvard Business Review*, *83*(12), 74–83.

Christensen, C. M., & Raynor, M. E. (2003). *The innovator's solution: Creating and sustaining successful growth*. Boston, MA: Harvard Business School Press.

Cochoy, F. (2009). Driving a shopping cart from STS to business, and the other way round: On the introduction of shopping carts in American grocery stores (1936–1959). *Organization*, *16*(1), 31–55.

Covey, S. R. (1991). *The 7 habits of highly effective people*. New York, NY: Simon & Schuster.

Cramo Plc (2013). Cramo's and Ramirent's joint venture company for the operations in Russia and Ukraine, Fortrent, launches its logo and corporate identity. *Nasdaq GlobeNewsWire*, April 12. Retrieved from https://globenewswire.com/news-release/ 2013/04/12/537882/0/en/Cramo-s-and-Ramirent-s-joint-venture-company-for-the-operations-in-Russia-and-Ukraine-Fortrent-launches-its-logo-and-corporate-identity.html

Crossley, J. (2012). Les Mills an international success. *Stuff*, January 27. Retrieved from http://www.stuff.co.nz/business/industries/6327563/Les-Mills-an-international-success

Cumbo, J. (2009). Check out supermarkets' life cover. *Financial Times*, May 8. Retrieved from https://www.ft.com/content/ adcb18d6-3be0-11de-acbc-00144feabdc0

Cyriac, J., Koller, T., & Thomsen, J. (2012). Testing the limits of diversification. *The McKinsey Quarterly*, 2–5.

Davis, J. P., & Eisenhardt, K. M. (2011). Rotating leadership and collaborative innovation recombination processes in symbiotic relationships. *Administrative Science Quarterly*, *56*(2), 159–201.

Day, G. S., & Schoemaker, P. J. H. (2006). *Peripheral vision. Detecting the weak signals that will make or break your company.* Boston, MA: Harvard Business School Press.

Diamond, J. (2013). That daily shower can be a killer. *New York Times*, January 28. Retrieved from http://www.nytimes.com/2013/ 01/29/science/jared-diamonds-guide-to-reducing-lifes-risks.html

Doz, Y., & Wilson, K. (2017). *Ringtone: Exploring the rise and fall of Nokia in Mobile Phones.* Oxford University Press.

Eisenhardt, K. M., & Sull, D. N. (2001). Strategy as simple rules. *Harvard Business Review*, *79*(1), 106–119.

Elsworth, S. (2013). Push to have life insurance sold by supermarket chains. *News.com.au*, March 24. Retrieved from http://www. news.com.au/finance/money/push-to-have-life-insurance-sold-by-

supermarket-chains/news-story/739ea3478f03da941f18dc1
c16b2d0ef

Engel, K. (2015). Startup pivots that changed the world.
WhoIsHostingThis? February 5. Retrieved from http://www.
whoishostingthis.com/blog/2015/02/05/startup-pivots/

Fairchild, C. (2015). Uber needs a crash course in crisis management. *Linkedin*, March 18. Retrieved from https://www.linkedin.
com/pulse/uber-needs-crash-course-crisis-management-caroline-
fairchild

Favaro, K. (2014a). The dangers of adjacencies strategy.
Strategy + Business, January 30. Retrieved from https://www.strat-
egy-business.com/blog/The-Dangers-of-Adjacencies-Strategy?gko=
04eeb

Favaro, K. (2014b). How IKEA, Disney, and Berkshire Hathaway
succeed with adjacencies. *Strategy + Business*, March 11.
Retrieved from https://www.strategy-business.com/blog/How-
IKEA-Disney-and-Berkshire-Hathaway-Succeed-with-Adjacencies?
gko=fa07c

Ferdows, K., Lewis, M. A., & Machuca, J. A. (2004). Rapid-fire
fulfillment. *Harvard Business Review*, 82(11), 104–117.

Finnish Forest Industries. (2010b). *Common dimensioning system
to strengthen the competitiveness of wood construction.* Press
release, October 6. Retrieved from https://www.forestindustries.fi/
news/common-dimensioning-system-to-strengthen-the-competi-
tiveness-of-wood-construction/

Finnish Forest Industries. (2010b). *Modernisation of fire safety
regulations supports the development of Finland's wood construction industry.* Press release, December 2. Retrieved from https://
www.forestindustries.fi/releases/modernisation-of-fire-safety-regu-
lations-supports-the-development-of-finlands-wood-construction-
industry/

Forrester. (2008). *Electronic invoice presentment and payment market in the Forrester Wave: Accounts payable EIPP*. Q2 2008 Report, published June 18.

Fox, J. (2014). How to succeed in business by bundling – and unbundling. *Harvard Business Review*, June 24. Retrieved from https://hbr.org/2014/06/how-to-succeed-in-business-by-bundling-and-unbundling

Garcia, T. (2016). Amazon is about to overtake Macy's as biggest seller of clothing in U.S. *MarketWatch*, May 14. Retrieved from http://www.marketwatch.com/story/traditional-retailers-stumble-in-their-efforts-to-compete-with-amazon-2016-05-12

Garrett, M. (Ed.). (2014). *Encyclopedia of transportation: Social science and policy*. Thousand Oaks, CA: SAGE Publications.

Gary, L. (2005). Dow Corning's big pricing gamble. *Harvard Business School Working Knowledge*, July 3. Retrieved from http://hbswk.hbs.edu/archive/4677.html

Geroski, P. A. (1998). Thinking creatively about markets. *International Journal of Industrial Organization, 16*(6), 677–695.

Gittleson, K. (2012). Can a company live forever? *BBC News*, January 19. Retrieved from http://www.bbc.com/news/business-16611040

Gladwell, M. (2008). *Outliers: The story of success*. London: Hachette.

Goddin, P. (2015). Uber's plan for self-driving cars bigger than its taxi disruption. *Mobility Lab*, August 18. Retrieved from http://mobilitylab.org/2015/08/18/ubers-plan-for-self-driving-cars-bigger-than-its-taxi-disruption/

Golinelli, G. M. (2010). *Viable systems approach (VSA): Governing business dynamics*. Padova: Cedam.

Gow, P. (2012). History of Les Mills — Documentary 2013. *YouTube*, April 16. Retrieved from https://www.youtube.com/watch?v=X1GD-NZaVJs

Greco, C. C., Oliveira, A. S., Pereira, M. P., Figueira, T. R., Ruas, V. D., Goncalves, M., & Denadai, B. S. (2011). Improvements in metabolic and neuromuscular fitness after 12-week Bodypump® training. *The Journal of Strength & Conditioning Research*, 25(12), 3422–3431.

Grove, A. S. (1996). *Only the paranoid survive*. New York, NY: Doubleday.

Gunningham, N., & Rees, J. (1997). Industry self-regulation: An institutional perspective. *Law & Policy*, 19(4), 363–414.

Hagel, J., Brown, J. S., & Davison, L. (2008). Shaping strategy in a world of constant disruption. *Harvard Business Review*, 86(10), 80–89.

Harford, T. (2011). *Adapt: Why success always starts with failure*. London: Little, Brown.

Hargadon, A. B., & Douglas, Y. (2001). When innovations meet institutions: Edison and the design of the electric light. *Administrative science quarterly*, 46(3), 476–501.

Hawkins, A. J. (2016). Uber is trying to make you forget that surge pricing exists. *The Verge*, June 23. Retrieved from http://www.theverge.com/2016/6/23/12017002/uber-surge-pricing-upfront-fare-app-update-announcement

Hess, E. D. (2014). *Learn or die: Using science to build a leading-edge learning organization*. New York, NY: Columbia University Press.

IBM (2008). *Annual Report 2007*. Retrieved from ftp://public.dhe.ibm.com/annualreport/2007/2007_ibm_annual.pdf

Johnson, S. (2010). Where good ideas come from. *YouTube*, September 17. Retrieved from https://www.youtube.com/watch?v=NugRZGDbPFU

Kafafi, Z. H., Martín-Palma, R. J., Nogueira, A. F., O'Carroll, D. M., Pietron, J. J., Samuel, I. D., ... Tsakalakos, L. (2015). The role of photonics in energy. *Journal of Photonics for Energy*, *5*(1), 050997-050997. Retrieved from http://photonicsforenergy.spiedigitallibrary.org/article.aspx?articleid=2463108

Kahneman, D. (2011). *Thinking, fast and slow*. New York, NY: Farrar, Straus and Giroux.

Kaplan, R. D. (2010). Man versus Afghanistan. *The Atlantic*, April. Retrieved from http://www.theatlantic.com/magazine/archive/2010/04/man-versus-afghanistan/307983/

Killing, P., Malnight, T., & Keys, T. (2006). *Must-win battles: How to win them, again and again*. New York, NY: Pearson Education.

Kinni, T. (2015). Conquering complexity with simple rules. *Insights by Stanford Business*, April 14. Retrieved from https://www.gsb.stanford.edu/insights/conquering-complexity-simple-rules

Kirk, C., & Brady, H. (2014). The Google graveyard. *Slate*, June 30. Retrieved from http://www.slate.com/articles/technology/map_of_the_week/2013/03/google_reader_joins_graveyard_of_dead_google_products.html

Kirk, S. (2013). Air New Zealand and Virgin alliance extended. *Stuff*, September 20. Retrieved from http://www.stuff.co.nz/business/9190040/Air-New-Zealand-and-Virgin-alliance-extended

Kjellberg, H., & Helgesson, C. F. (2006). Multiple versions of markets: Multiplicity and performativity in market practice. *Industrial Marketing Management*, *35*(7), 839–855.

Klein, G. (2007). Performing a project premortem. *Harvard Business Review*, *85*(9), 18–19.

Knight, S. (2016). How Uber conquered London. *The Guardian*, April 27. Retrieved from https://www.theguardian.com/technology/2016/apr/27/how-uber-conquered-london

KONE Corporation (2015). What's a people flow day? *YouTube*, October 27. Retrieved from https://www.youtube.com/watch?v=FsfCjGskJVE

Kuttner, R. (1999). *Everything for sale: The virtues and limits of markets*. Chicago, IL: University of Chicago Press.

Lambkin, M., & Day, G. S. (1989). Evolutionary processes in competitive markets: Beyond the product life cycle. *Journal of Marketing*, 4–20.

Laurie, D. L., Doz, Y. L., & Sheer, C. P. (2006). Creating new growth platforms. *Harvard Business Review*, *84*(5), 80–90.

Levitt, T. (1960). Marketing myopia. *Harvard Business Review*, *38*(4), 24–47.

Liberatore, S. (2016). Uber drivers, beware: Taxi app tests self-driving car in Pittsburgh that could put all of its 'contractors' out of work. *Daily Mail*, May 19. Retrieved from http://www.dailymail.co.uk/sciencetech/article-3599338/Uber-s-self-driving-car-revealed-pictures-autonomous-Ford-Fusion-cars-tested-Pittsburgh.html#ixzz4pGOHJbCw

Linden, C. G. (2016). *Nokian valtakunta. Raportti hulluilta vuosilta [Nokia's kingdom. A report from the crazy years]*. Helsinki, Finland: Gaudeamus.

Magretta, J. (2011). Stop competing to be the best. *Harvard Business Review*, Blog Network. Retrieved from http://blogs.hbr.org/cs/2011/11/stop_competing_to_be_the_best.html

Martin, J. (2012). Keith Tantlinger — The man behind the container. *Sea Breezes*, January 18. Retrieved from http://www.seabreezes.co.im/index.php?option=com_content&view=article&id=812:keith-tantlinger-the-man-behind-the-container&catid=34:ships&Itemid=56

McChrystal, S., & Fussell, C. (2015). *Team of teams: The power of small groups in a fragmented world.* New York, NY: Portfolio Hardcover.

McCracken, H. (2013). For one night only, Silicon Valley's Homebrew computer club reconvenes. *TIME Magazine*, November 12. Retrieved from http://techland.time.com/2013/11/12/for-one-night-only-silicon-valleys-homebrew-computer-club-reconvenes/

McGrath, R. G. (2013). *The end of competitive advantage: How to keep your strategy moving as fast as your business.* Boston, MA: Harvard Business Review Press.

Mele, C., Pels, J., & Storbacka, K. (2015). A holistic market conceptualization. *Journal of the Academy of Marketing Science*, *43*(1), 100−114.

Mills, P. (2014). Secrets of success. *LesMills*, July 3. Retrieved from https://www.lesmills.com/clubs-and-facilities/industry-insights/secrets-of-success/

Ministry of Employment and the Economy, Finland. (2011). *Status and possibilities of wood construction in Finland.* Retrieved from https://tem.fi/documents/1410877/2937056/Status+and+possibilities+of+wood+construction+in+Finland

Ministry of Transport, New Zealand. (2017). *Alliance and codeshare agreements*, April 19. Retrieved from http://www.transport.govt.nz/air/internationalairservices/internationalaircarriage competition/

Möller, K. (2010). Sense-making and agenda construction in emerging business networks —How to direct radical innovation. *Industrial Marketing Management, 39*(3), 361–371.

Morgan, J. (2017). Kone on the benefits of People FlowIntelligence. *ConstructionWeekOnline.com*, February 18. Retrieved from http://www.constructionweekonline.com/article-43100-kone-on-the-benefits-of-people-flow-intelligence/

Munford, M. (2016). Estonia embraces Uber and Taxify as first European country to legalize and regulate ride-sharing. *Forbes*, February 28. Retrieved from http://www.forbes.com/sites/monty-munford/2016/02/28/estonia-embraces-uber-and-taxify-as-first-european-country-to-legalize-and-regulate-ride-sharing/#757ed1b56968

Murison, M. (2016). Kone partners with IBM IoT for smarter buildings. *Internet of Business*, March 4. Retrieved from https://internetofbusiness.com/kone-partners-with-ibm-iot-for-smarter-buildings/

Narver, J. C., Slater, S. F., & MacLachlan, D. L. (2004). Responsive and proactive market orientation and new-product success. *Journal of Product Innovation Management, 21*(5), 334–347.

Nazar, J. (2013). 14 famous business pivots. *Forbes*, October 8. Retrieved from http://www.forbes.com/sites/jasonnazar/2013/10/08/14-famous-business-pivots/#2aa9617f1fb9

New Zealand Herald (2015). The death of the Kiwi bach. *The Big Read*, October 25. Retrieved from http://www.nzherald.co.nz/business/news/article.cfm?c_id=3&objectid=11534648

Newcomer, E. (2015). Uber draws fresh comparison with Amazon as growth trumps profit. *Live Mint*, July 1. Retrieved from http://www.livemint.com/Companies/Lw0nxWkxbt8Bv9UPEyG1BP/Uber-draws-fresh-comparison-with-Amazon-as-growth-trumps-pro.html

Newitz, A. (2012). *Medieval monks complained about their jobs in the margins of ancient manuscripts.* Retrieved from http://io9. gizmodo.com/5896008/medieval-monks-complained-about-their-jobs-in-the-margins-of-ancient-manuscripts

Noon, C. (2007). Nokia's Kallasvuo puts brave face on iPhone. *Forbes*, February, 12. Retrieved from http://www.forbes.com/2007/02/12/nokia-kallasvuo-iphone-faces-cx_cn_0212autofaces-can01.html#

Normann, R. (2001). *Reframing business: When the map changes the landscape.* Chichester: Wiley.

North, D. C. (1977). Markets and other allocation systems in history: The challenge of Karl Polanyi. *Journal of European Economic History*, 6(3), 703–716.

O'Hear, S., & Lomas, N. (2014). Five super successful tech pivots. *TechCrunch*, May 28. Retrieved from https://techcrunch.com/gallery/five-super-successful-tech-pivots/

Petersen, B. A., Hastings, B., & Gottschall, J. S. (2017). Low load, high repetition resistance training program increases bone mineral density in untrained adults. *The Journal of Sports Medicine and Physical Fitness*, 57(1–2), 70–76.

Pilcher, J. (2011). Meet FRANK, maybe the coolest bank Gen-Y has ever seen. *The Financial Brand*, May 31. Retrieved from https://thefinancialbrand.com/18642/ocbc-frank-gen-y-banking-brand/

Porter, M. E. (2008). *Competitive strategy: Techniques for analyzing industries and competitors.* New York, NY: Simon and Schuster.

Press, G. (2016). From IBM mainframe users group to Apple 'Welcome IBM. Seriously': This week In tech history. *Forbes*. Retrieved from https://www.forbes.com/sites/gilpress/2016/08/21/from-ibm-mainframe-users-group-to-apple-welcome-ibm-seriously-this-week-in-tech-history/#7290b873beb4. Accessed on August 9.

Rao, H. (2009). Market rebels and radical innovation. *McKinsey Quarterly*, January.

Reeves, M., Haanaes, K., & Sinha, J. (2015). *Your strategy needs a strategy*. Boston, MA: Harvard Business Review Press.

Reeves, M., Love, C., & Tillmanns, P. (2012). Your strategy needs a strategy. *Harvard Business Review*, 90(9), 76–83.

Ries, E. (2011). *The lean startup: How today's entrepreneurs use continuous innovation to create radically successful businesses*. New York, NY: Crown Business.

Ritchey, T. (2006). Problem structuring using computer-aided morphological analysis. *Journal of the Operational Research Society*, 57(7), 792–801.

Robinson, J. (2011). Our man in Washington. *Stuff*, February 5. Retrieved from http://www.stuff.co.nz/sunday-star-times/features/4619280/Our-man-in-Washington

Rogers, E. (2003). *Diffusion of innovations* (5th ed.). New York, NY: Simon and Schuster.

Roscoe, P. (2014). *I spend, therefore I am: The true cost of economics*. New York, NY: Viking.

Roth, A. E. (2007). The art of designing markets. *Harvard Business Review*, 85(10), 118.

Sanchez, J. T. (2011). The history of BODYPUMP™ with Phillip Mills. *YouTube*, November 7. Retrieved from https://www.youtube.com/watch?v=p1CqX_M7lmM.

Sandel, M. J. (2012). *What money can't buy: The moral limits of markets*. New York, NY: Macmillan.

Santos, F. M., & Eisenhardt, K. M. (2009). Constructing markets and shaping boundaries: Entrepreneurial power in nascent fields. *Academy of Management Journal, 52*(4), 643–671.

Sarasvathy, S. D. (2009). *Effectuation: Elements of entrepreneurial expertise.* Northampton, MA: Edward Elgar Publishing.

Shannon, L. (2012). Life insurance trap at the checkout: Supermarkets use aggressive tactics to push cover that may not fit. *ThisIsMoney.co.uk,* August 16. Retrieved from http://www.thisis-money.co.uk/money/article-2124630/Supermarkets-use-aggres-sive-tactics-sell-customers-life-insurance.html

Singer, N. (2014). Intel's sharp-eyed social scientist. *The New York Times,* February 16. Retrieved from https://www.nytimes.com/2014/02/16/technology/intels-sharp-eyed-social-scientist.html

Singleton, M. (2016). Tidal now has 3 million subscribers. *The Verge,* March 29. Retrieved from http://www.theverge.com/2016/3/29/11325608/tidal-now-has-3-million-subscribers

Slater, S. F., & Narver, J. C. (1995). Market orientation and the learning organization. *Journal of Marketing,* 63–74.

Smith, K. (2014). Zara vs H&M – Who's in the global lead? *Edited,* April 15. Retrieved from https://edited.com/blog/2014/04/zara-vs-hm-whos-in-the-global-lead/

Snehota, I., & Hakansson, H. (Eds.). (1995). *Developing relationships in business networks.* London: Routledge.

Statistics New Zealand. (2013). *Census QuickStats about housing.* Retrieved from http://www.stats.govt.nz/Census/2013-census/profile-and-summary-reports/quickstats-about-housing

Stelzer, T., Grosset, J., Brajkovich, M., Forrest, J., & Rankine, B. (2005). *Taming the SCREW: A manual for winemaking with screw caps.* Tarragindi: Wine Press.

Stora Enso. (2014). *SRV and Stora Enso partner up to build multi-storey wooden residential housing for City of Helsinki.* Press release, May 6. Retrieved from http://buildingandliving.stor-aenso.com/news/news-and-press-releases/srv-and-stora-enso-part-ner-up-to-build-multi-storey-wooden-residential-housing-for-city-of-helsinki

Storbacka, K., & Nenonen, S. (2011). Scripting markets: From value propositions to market propositions. *Industrial Marketing Management, 40*(2), 255–266.

Storbacka, K., & Nenonen, S. (2012). Competitive arena mapping: Market innovation using morphological analysis in business markets. *Journal of Business-to-Business Marketing, 19*(3), 183–215.

Storbacka, K., & Nenonen, S. (2015). Learning *with* the market: Facilitating market innovation. *Industrial Marketing Management, 44,* 73–82.

Sull, D., & Eisenhardt, K. M. (2012). Simple rules for a complex world. *Harvard Business Review, 90*(9), 68–75.

Sull, D., & Eisenhardt, K. M. (2015). *Simple rules: How to thrive in a complex world.* Boston, MA: Houghton Mifflin Harcourt.

Sull, D. L., & Ruelas-Gossi, A. (2010). Strategic orchestration. *Business Strategy Review, 21*(4), 58–63.

Sull, D. N. (2005). Strategy as active waiting. *Harvard Business Review, 83*(9), 120–129.

Thomas, N. (2011). 11 startups that found success by changing direction. *Mashable,* July 8. Retrieved from http://mashable.com/2011/07/08/startups-change-direction/#XP_r8qAnksq7

Thompson, M. (2011). The uses of discomfort. *The Radical Ear,* May 21. Retrieved from https://theradicalear.wordpress.com/2011/05/12/the-uses-of-discomfort/

Troianovski, A. (2012). Nokia had jump on Apple with tablet, smartphone prototypes. *Wall Street Journal*, July 19. Retrieved from http://www.theaustralian.com.au/business/wall-street-journal/nokia-had-jump-on-apple-with-tablet-smartphone-prototypes/story-fnay3ubk-1226430228129#

Turula, T. (2017). This Finnish law firm has transformed an age-old industry — By going digital and taking 'no a-holes'. *Business Insider Nordic*, March 16. Retrieved from http://nordic.businessinsider.com/40-hour-weeks-playrooms-and-no-assholes-this-finnish-pioneer-has-brought-law-to-the-21st-century-2017-3/

Urry, J. (2004). The 'system' of automobility. *Theory, Culture & Society*, 21(4–5), 25–39.

van Kralingen, B. (2010). IBM's transformation — From survival to success. *Forbes*, July 7. Retrieved from https://www.forbes.com/2010/07/07/ibm-transformation-lessons-leadership-managing-change.html

Vazquez Sampere, J. P. (2016). Apple's shrinking impact in the smartphone industry. *Harvard Business Review*, February 2. Retrieved from https://hbr.org/2016/02/apples-shrinking-impact-in-the-smartphone-industry

Verma, M. (2007). *H&M vs Zara: Competitive growth strategies*. Case study COM0196P. Retrieved from http://www.ibscdc.org/Case_Studies/Strategy/Competitive%20Strategies/COM0196P.htm

Virtanen, A. (2015). Digitalization enables user-centric people flow planning in smart buildings. In A. Wood & D. Malott (Eds.), *Global interchanges: Resurgence of the Skyscraper City* (pp. 603–608). Chicago, IL: Council on Tall Buildings and Urban Habitat. Retrieved from http://global.ctbuh.org/resources/papers/download/2514-digitalization-enables-user-centric-people-flow-planning-in-smart-buildings.pdf

Vuori, T. O., & Huy, Q. N. (2016). Distributed attention and shared emotions in the innovation process: How nokia lost the smartphone battle. *Administrative Science Quarterly, 61*(1), 9–51.

Wise, T. A. (1960). The auditors have arrived. *Fortune Magazine, 62*(5).

Wood, A. (2015). Bachcare shows the how an SME proposition can take off. *Stuff*, October 3. Retrieved from http://www.stuff.co.nz/business/72610441/bachcare-shows-the-how-an-sme-proposition-can-take-off

Woodard, R. (2011). Screwcap now 'the norm': New study. *Decanter*, November 14. Retrieved from http://www.decanter.com/news/wine-news/529514/screwcap-now-the-norm-new-study

Yeo, R. (2016). *FRANK by OCBC – The future of consumer banking to millennials.* Case S/N 88-16-010. The Nanyang Technopreneurship Case Centre (NTCC) at the Nanyang Technological University. Retrieved from http://www.ntc.ntu.edu.sg/ntcc/Documents/Full%20Version/10.%20FRANK%20BY%20OCBC%20-%20THE%20FUTURE%20OF%20CONSUMER%20BANKING%20TO%20MILLENNIALS.pdf

Yong, N. (2014). The secret recipe that sold over 100 Million BreadTalk Flosss Buns. *TheSmartLocalSingapore*, October 3. Retrieved from http://thesmartlocal.com/read/breadtalk-flosss-buns

Zenger, T. (2013). Strategy: The uniqueness challenge. *Harvard Business Review, 91*(11), 52–58.

Zhang, S., & Shih, G. (2015). Uber seen reaching $10.8 billion in bookings in 2015: Fundraising presentation. *Reuters*, August 21. Retrieved from http://www.reuters.com/article/us-uber-tech-fundraising-idUSKCN0QQ0G320150821

Zook, C., & Allen, J. (2003). Growth outside the core. *Harvard Business Review*, *81*(12), 66–73.

Zott, C., & Huy, Q. N. (2007). How entrepreneurs use symbolic management to acquire resources. *Administrative Science Quarterly*, *52*(1), 70–105.

Zwicky, F. (1969). *Discovery, invention, research through the morphological analysis*. New York, NY: McMillan.

ABOUT THE AUTHORS

Dr. Suvi Nenonen is Associate Professor and Director of the Graduate School of Management at the University of Auckland Business School. She has previously been an Associate Professor at Hanken School of Economics in Finland. Prior to entering academia full time, she worked for more than 10 years as a strategy consultant to major European companies in several industries such as financial services, manufacturing, healthcare, construction, utility, telecommunications, fast-moving consumer goods industries, and non-profit organizations.

Suvi is passionate about building bridges over the academia-practice gap. In addition to teaching in the MBA programs, she is also involved in several executive education programs in New Zealand and Europe and is a frequent key note speaker at conference and internal seminars. She has designed and led several large business development programs ranging from applied research consortium projects to executive education programs.

Suvi has published extensively in the top marketing and management journals. In 2013, she received a Marsden Fund grant from the Royal Society of New Zealand together with Professor Kaj Storbacka. In 2015, Suvi received the Research Excellence Award for Research Relevance at the University of Auckland.

Dr. Kaj Storbacka is Professor of Markets and Strategy at the Graduate School of Management at the University of Auckland Business School. He has previously been Professor at the Nyenrode Business Universiteit in the Netherlands and at Hanken School of Economics in Finland. Dr. Storbacka has throughout his career worked on the borderline between academic and applied research within marketing and strategic management. He has 30 years of background as a strategy consultant to European and global companies – in finance, media, travel, retail, utility, manufacturing, and telecommunications. Out of this time, he spent 18 years leading Vectia Ltd, a consultancy operating in Finland, Sweden, Germany, and the Netherlands that he founded in 1994. Since 2004, he is on the board of the Strategic Account Management Association (SAMA) in Chicago, IL.

Kaj has a long background in executive education, running MBA, executive MBA, and firm-specific executive education programs in Europe, New Zealand, Singapore, and Shanghai. He is a frequent key note speaker at internal seminars for major global corporations, and at leading management development institutions in Europe, Asia, and the United States.

Kaj has published extensively in the top academic marketing and management journals and has published 13 managerial books, some of which have been translated into several languages.

INDEX

Abundance mentality, 164
Academy Awards, 126
Actor competency, 39
Actors and their roles, 42,
        107–114
    adding/removing players,
        108–109
    drawing map of network,
        107–108
    educating customers and other
        partners, 114–115
    fostering emergence of
        competitors, 110–111
    modifying roles, 112–114
Adobe, 132
Aerobic exercise, 146
Aerobics industry, 146
Agenda construction for shared
        purpose, 238
AirBnB, 188
Alahuhta, Matti, 199–202, 209
Alcatel-Lucent, 245
Alibaba, 187
Amazon, 187
American National Standards
        Institute (ANSI), 131
Ancillary language and concepts,
        120–122
Android operating system, 239
Ansoff, Igor, 57
API (Application Programming
        Interface), 202
Apple, 2, 8, 9, 235
    fast-follower strategy,
        155–156
    iPod business, 73

Mac, 73
    minimum viable system, 162
    MP3 player market, 155
Arena generator. *See* Business
        arena generator
Arts
    metaphors from, 230–231
    as positive-sum games, 230
As-a-service contracts, 181–182
As-a-service play, 180–182
    service context, 181–182
    tangible goods context,
        180–181
Associations, 126–129
Auckland, New Zealand, 146
Aviva, 187–188
Awards, 126–129

Barrett, Frank, 231
Benioff, Marc, 228
BetaMax, 132
Better Mousetrap Syndrome, 178
Bezos, Jeff, 187
Big Oil, 116
Black box thinking, 20
Bluetooth Coalition, 238
BodyPump, 147
BoKlok, 65–66
Bookabach, 104
Booking.com, 187
Boston Consulting Group, 37
Brainstorming, business
        definitions, 57–58
    zooming in, 73–86
    zooming out, 58–73, 60f
Brand ownership, 81

BreadTalk, 185
Bricks-and-mortar matching
        methods, 105−106, 187
Bridging concepts, 123
Bright Horizons, 71−72
Burgelman, Robert, 21
Business arena generator, 75−85,
        75f
    brand ownership, 81
    customer segments, 79−80
    customized/targeted data for
        arena analysis, 82−84
    distribution channel, 80
    end use/application, 81
    geography, 79
    identifying interesting arenas,
        81−82
    price, 80−81
    prioritization, 84−85
    products/services, 79
    time, 80
    value chain position, 80
Business definitions, 41, 51−58
    brainstorming, 57−58
    casting out the worm of
        product, 56
    frames, 53−55
    polishing and pointing, 57
    zooming in, 73−86
    zooming out, 58−73, 60f
Buyer-finds-seller matching,
        187−188

Camp, Garrett, 9−10
Capabilities
    defined, 61
    network, 62−66
    resources and, 61−62
Capital expenditure
    as-a-service lowering, 180−182
Casey, Jim, 49, 50, 54−55, 213
Chateau Margaux, 140
Christensen, Clayton, 184
Collaboration
    platforms for, 239−241

as win-win-win strategy,
        166−169
Collaborative sense-making,
        dialogue for, 228
Complacency, 213
Complex adaptive system (CAS),
        25−29
    See also Markets/market system
Conceptual extensions, 122−123
Confederation of Finnish
        Construction Industries,
        128−129
Constructive paranoia, 213−215
Consumer practices, 68−69
Containerization, 133
Coor, 172−173, 186
Credibility building, 237−241
Credit cards, 237
CRM. See Customer relationship
        management (CRM)
Customer-oriented zooming out,
        66−69
    B2B, 66−67
    B2C, 68−69
Customer preferences
    industry conventions as an
        obstacle to, 141−142
    making product/service
        desirable by influencing,
        139−141
Customer processes
    to consumer practices, 68−69
    improving, 66−67
Customer relationship
        management (CRM), 228
Customers' customers, 70
Customer segments, 79−80
Customized/targeted data for
        arena analysis, 82−84

Dell Computers, 109
Dialogue for collaborative
        sense-making, 228−229
Diamond, Jared, 214
Didi Chuxing, 14

Digitalization, and matching
  methods, 103–105
Digital revolution, 239
Disruptive economics, 182–184
Disruptive innovations, 182–183,
  184
Distribution channel, 80
Dow Corning, 104–105
Durkheim, Emile, 138

Earthquake in Christchurch, New
  Zealand, 151
Economic profit, 16
Edison, Thomas Alva, 234–235
Edison Electric Company, 234
Edison Illuminating Company,
  234
E-invoicing, 165
Electricity Act of India (2003),
  135
Electronic games, 244
Ellis, William Webb, 230
Elop, Stephen, 5–6, 9, 11, 17, 26
Emergence
  encouraging, 224–225
  fostering and exploiting,
    223–225
End use/application, 81
Engagement, 206, 235–245
  building credibility, 237–241
  in complex environments, 235
  decoupling leadership, 235
  intraorganizational alignment,
    235
  meaning of, 235
  orchestration, 241–243
  pivoting, 243–245
  resource mobilization,
    236–237
Ericsson, 3, 172
ERoaming, 116
European Committee for
  Standardization, 131
Events, 126–129
Exchange, 94–106

matching methods, 103–106
  pricing, 99–102
  sales item, 95–99
Exchange interface relocation,
  170–175
  bundling and unbundling of
    sales item, 173–175
  price tag to non-monetized
    activities, 171–173
  See also Generic market-
    shaping plays
Exchange layer, 41–42
Exchange value, 18, 19
  obsession with, misses the
    opportunities of growing
    use value, 23
Expedia, 187
Experimentation, 205, 215–225
  affordable loss, 219–220
  at boundaries, 216–218
  emergence, 223–225
  investments, 219–221
  as method for learning, 216
  recognizing and ending failed
    experiments, 218
  resource re-allocations, 219
  rigorous processes, 216–217
  safe-to-fail environment,
    221–223
Exploration, 205, 207–215
  challenging existing beliefs
    and business models,
    212–213
  constructive paranoia,
    213–214
  cultivating diverse perspectives,
    212–215
  pre-mortems, 215
  triangulation and peripheral
    vision, 208–212
Expression, 206, 225–235
  as art, 226–228
  labeling, 232–233
  metaphors, 229–231
  symbolic actions, 233

Facebook, 154
Fair Dinkum Shed, 113−114
Fast-follower strategy, 153−156
Fast-food restaurants, 183−184
Fermi, Enrico, 223
Finnish Timber Council, 128
Finnish Wood Research, 128
Firebreaks, 222
First International Screw Cap
        Symposium, 142
Fonda, Jane, 146
Fondia, 181, 232−233
Fonterra Foodservice, 179
Frame-storming, 58
FRANK by OCBC, 105−106
Freestyle, 146

Game layer, rules for, 44
Gasoline-driven automobile, 239
General Motors, 61
Generic market-shaping plays,
        169−195, 170f
    breaking supply and efficiency
        bottlenecks, 189−195
    concept, 170
    delivering step-change in use
        value, 176−179
    exchange interface relocation,
        170−175
    matching methods, 186−188
    turning non-users/non-payers
        into customers,
        184−186
    using market-widening pricing,
        179−184
    widening customer catchment
        area, 184−188
Geography, business arena and,
        79
Gladwell, Malcolm, 210
Global System for Mobile
        Communications
        Standard (GSM), 2, 6
    See also 2G
Google Buzz, 218

Google Inc., 178
    search engine, 71
Google Reader, 218
Google Wave, 218
Great Recession, 13
Grosset, Jeffrey, 141
Grove, Andrew "Andy",
        213−214
GSM. See Global System for
        Mobile Communications
        Standard (GSM)
Gutenberg, Johannes, 182−183

Harford, Tim, 222
Healthcare market, 43
Hendrik, Toomas, 137
Hewlett-Packard, 244
Homebrew Computing Club, 239
Household work, 171−172

IBM
    customers' processes, 66
    Smarter Planet, 229
IETF. See Internet Engineering
        Task Force (IETF)
IKEA, 37, 184
    Skanska and, 65−66
India
    Electricity Act (2003), 135
    National Electricity Policy, 136
    Wärtsilä in, 135−136
Inditex, 109
Industrial organization, 16
Industry associations, 128−129
Industry self-regulation, 137−138
Industry view, 15−16
Information, 123−126
    media, 124−125
    research and statistics,
        125−126
    See also Representations layer
Infrastructure, 43, 115−117
    influencing others for building,
        117
    investment in, 115

separate business opportunity
from lack of, 116–117
Innovating technology, 38
Instagram, 154
Intel, 70–71
Intellectual property (IP) rights,
132–133
International Organization for
Standardization (ISO),
131
International Screw Cap Seal
Initiative, 142
International SOS, 109–110
Internet Engineering Task Force
(IETF), 131
Invoices
e-invoicing, 165
manual processing of, 164–165
IPhone, 2, 4, 5
IPod, 73
ISO. See International
Organization for
Standardization (ISO)
Ive, Jonathan, 235

Jay Z, 69
Jazz, 231–232
JCDecaux, 64, 71
Jobs, Steve, 8, 235

Kahneman, Daniel, 22, 99–100,
171
Kaizen system, 62
Kalanick, Travis, 9–10, 13
Kallasvuo, Olli-Pekka, 1–2, 4
Kamprad, Ingvar, 65
Khan, Kublai, 94
Know-how, 42, 112–115
KONE
API Challenge, 202
business definition, 52–53
events and awards, 127–128
as globally integrated
organization, 199
leadership, 199–202

People Flow, 53, 127–128,
201–202
R&D engineers, 200–201

Labeling, claiming market by,
232–233
Language, 228–231
ancillary language and
concepts, 120–122
bridging concepts, 123
conceptual extensions,
122–123
generic names, 120
trademarks, 119
See also Metaphors
Leaders, and leadership, 236
Leadership
building credibility, 237–241
challenging existing beliefs and
business models, 213
constructive paranoia,
213–214
cultivating diverse perspectives,
212–215
engagement, 206, 235–245
See also Engagement
experimentation, 205,
215–225
See also Experimentation
exploration, 205, 207–215
See also Exploration
expression, 206, 225–235
See also Expression
informing about resource
potential, 204–205
KONE, 199–202
leaders and, 236
looking around approach, 205,
207–215
market shaping traits,
203–204, 204f
orchestration, 241–243
performing/enacting new
market, 205–206
pivoting, 243–245

pre-mortems and prospective
hindsight, 215
probing and responding, 205
redefining, 203–206
resource mobilization,
236–237
Lead users, 238–239
Lee, Katherine, 185
Les Mills International, 145–149
background, 146–147
BodyPump, 147, 148, 149
instructors, 148–149
regional distribution rights, 148
Les Mills On Demand, 149
Levitt, Theodore, 57
Lewin, Kurt, 215–216
Life insurance companies,
187–188
Linux operating system, 239
London Wine Fair (2002),
141–142
Low-cost airlines, 183
Lower prices for disruptive
economics, 182–184

Ma, Jack, 187
Mac, 73
MacLean, Malcolm, 133
Market Fan, 39–45, 42f
business definition, 41
exchange layer, 41–42
network layer, 42–43
representations layer, 41,
43–44
rules of game, 41, 44
Market making, as market
shaping, 35
Market orientation, 21–22
Market rebels, 239
Market segmentation, 74–75
Market shaping, 32–39
concept, 32, 34–35
environments, 38
FAQs, 36–38
firms practicing, 37–38

main ingredients for, 36
mainstream strategic thinking
vs. strategies of, 36–37
market making as, 35
Markets/market system, 14–31
black box thinking, 20
complex adaptive system
(CAS), 25–28
exchange for value creation, 29
human agents, 30–31
industry view, 15–16
misconception, 17
poor market view, 20–24
product market view, 17–20
rich reality of, 24–31
as social system, 30
Matching methods, 103–106
bricks-and-mortar, 105–106,
187
buyer-finds-seller matching,
187
digitalization, 103–105
passive information mediators,
186
wider or safer, 186–188
McDonalds, 183
McKinsey & Company, 16, 72,
150–151
Media, 124–125
MeeGo, 4
Merchant Parcel Delivery, 50
See also UPS
Metaphors, 122, 229–231
arts and, 231
zero sum to positive-sum game,
230
MetLife, 187
Microsoft, 2
Mills, Leslie Royce, 145–149
Mills, Phillip, 146–147
Minimum viable system,
win-win-win strategies
in, 158–163
Moore, Mike, 134
Motorola, 3

MP3 player market, 155–156
Myspace, 154

Napster, 69
Nash, Ogden, 229
National Electricity Policy of India
    (2012), 136
National Organization for Rare
    Disorders (NORD), 123
Nelson, Kent "Oz", 50
Nespresso, 109
Nestlé, 109
Network-based zooming out,
    62–66
Network layer, 41, 42–43,
    106–117
    actors and their roles, 42–43,
        107–115
    infrastructure, 115–117
    know-how, 42, 112–115
New Zealand
    Fonterra Foodservice, 179
    Les Mills International,
        145–149
    wineries, 193
N-Gage (Nokia), 3
Nicholson, Jack, 53
Nintendo, 244
Nokia, 1–9, 157, 162, 244–245
    Alahuhta, 200
    demise/failure of, 2, 4–7
    diversification, 244–245
    GSM, 2
    management, 4–5
    Microsoft and, 2, 245
    old playbook and theory, 7–9
    original incarnation of, 244
    rival, 5
    smart phone, 3
    success story, 2–4
    supply chain, 2–4
    3G handset, 3, 4
    touch-screen phone, 3
    2G handsets, 4
Nokia 9000 Communicator, 2

Non-monetized activities, price tag
    to, 171–173
Non-shapeable market, 156–158
NORD. See National
    Organization for Rare
    Disorders (NORD)
North, Douglass, 15

Online ride-sharing company.
    See Uber Technologies
    Inc.
Open-source software community,
    239
OP Group, 160–161, 165
Opinion leaders, 238–239
Oprah Winfrey's Book Club, 239
Orchestration, 241–242
    allocentric innovation, 242
    from domination to, 241–242
    rotating leadership, 242–243
Orphan Drug Act of 1983, 123
Oscars. See Academy Awards
Other actors, 39
Other-benefactor perspective,
    69–72
Outliers, 210–211
Oversea-Chinese Banking
    Corporation (OCBC),
    105
    See also FRANK by OCBC

Panasonic, 154
PayPal, 244
People Flow, 201–202
People Flow (KONE), 53
Peripheral vision, 208–212
    focusing on IFAQs, 211–212
    focusing on outliers, 210–211
    metaphor, 210
    See also Triangulation
Petrini, Carlo, 123
Pivoting, 243–245
    after start-up phase, 243–245
    concept of, 243
    for start-ups, 243

Platforms for enhanced
      collaboration, 239–241
Poor market view, 20–24
Post, Emily, 138
Practices. *See* Consumer practices
Pre-mortems, 215
Price carriers, 101–102
Price/pricing, 99–102
   arena and, 81
   as-a-service, 180–182
   changing level of, 100–101
   errors relevant to, 100
   lowering of, 182–184
   non-monetized activities,
      171–173
   using market-widening,
      179–184
Printing press, 182
Product-geography matrix, 57
Product market view, 17–20
   data bias, 19–20
   stock market analysis, 20
Products, business arena and, 79
Prospective hindsight, 215
Provocative competence, 242

Quantifying win-win-win
      strategies, 163–166
Quek, George, 185

Red Bull, 122
Regulations/laws, 134–138
   breaking regulations to change,
      136–137
   cooperation with regulators to
      change, 134–136
   industry self-regulation,
      137–138
Representations layer, 41, 43–44,
      118–129
   devices, 118–119
   information, 123–126
   language, 119–123
   symbols, 126–129
Research and statistics, 125–126

Resource mobilization,
      236–237
Resource potentiality, 204–205,
      236
Resources
   capabilities and, 61–62
   defined, 61
   network, 62–66
Rey-Herme, Pascal, 110
Rotating leadership, 242–243
Roth, Alvin E., 42, 188
Royal Bank of Scotland, 187
Rules of the game, 41, 44,
      129–142
   regulations, 134–138
   social norms, 44, 138–142
   standards, 130–133
Rumsfeld, Donald, 210
Ryanair, 183

Safe-to-fail environment,
      221–223
Sainsbury, 187
Sales item, 95–99
Samsung, 5
Sanyo, 154
Savvy market shapers, 150
Schörling, Melker, 65
Screwcaps, 141–142, 193–194
Screwcap Wine Seal Initiative
      (SWSI), 141–142, 194
S-curve, 139
Sea-Land, 133
Search engine (Google), 71
SEPA. *See* Single Euro Payments
      Area (SEPA)
Services, business arena and, 79
Short Message Service (SMS), 2
Siemens, 2
Single Euro Payments Area
      (SEPA), 165
Skanska, 172
Skanska and IKEA, 65–66
Skeuomorphism, 235
Smarter Planet (IBM), 229

SMS. *See* Short Message Service
(SMS)
Social norms, 44, 138–142
Sony Walkman, 154
Spotify, 37, 69
Standards, 130–133
compatibility, 130
de jure *vs.* de facto, 131–132
intellectual property (IP) rights,
132–133
technical, 131–132
wars, 132
Starbucks, 244
zooming in success story,
85–86
Stock market analysis, 20
Stora Enso, 91–94, 128, 152
BoKlok, 65–66
Strategies, for market shaping,
32–39, 158–169
collaboration, 166–169
minimum viable system,
158–163
poor market view, 20–24
quantifying win-win-win,
163–166
Strategy&, 73
Supply bottlenecks
clearing out regulatory,
191–193
elimination by scaling up
cottage industries,
189–191
Symbian, 4
Symbolic actions, claiming market
by, 233
Systems theory, 151–152

Tantlinger, Keith, 133
Telenokia, 2
Tesco, 187
3G, 3, 4, 5, 6–7
See also Nokia
Tidal, 69
Time, 80

Timing, in market shaping,
149–158
assessing shapeability, 149–153
fast-follower strategy, 153–156
non-shapeable market, 156–158
Toyota
capabilities, 61–62
sideline businesses, 62
Trademarking, 119
Triangulation, 209–210
See also Peripheral vision
2,4,6-Trichloroanisole (TCA), 140
2G, 2, 3, 4, 5, 6, 8
See also Nokia

UberGREEN, 13
Uberification, 14
Uber Technologies Inc., 9–14,
157, 213, 214
background, 9–10
country-specific taxi regulations
and, 136–137
goodwill and trust, 12
growth, 12
matching methods, 187
private car owners, 10, 11
surge pricing, 11
UberX, 10
Unilever
hygiene products, 117
Shakti program, 117
University of California, Los
Angeles (UCLA), 146
UPS, 49–51, 213
US Department of Commerce
Bureau of Economic
Analysis, 171
User/payer split, 71–72
Use value, 19, 176–179
commercializing a new widget,
176–178
creation, 18
defined, 18
enhancing customers' use
environment, 178–179

Vaissié, Arnaud, 110
Value chain position, 80
Value quantification, 165
Value sensing, 209
VHS, 132
Voltaire, 211
Von Clausewitz, Carl, 229

Walkman (Sony), 154–155
Walmart, 188
Wärtsilä, 116–117
Water footprint, 122
Water Footprint Network, 122
Watson platform of IBM, 202
WhatsApp, 154
What You See Is All There Is
        (WYSIATI), 22, 171
Wilde, Oscar, 18
Wineries
    screwcaps, 193–194
    Screwcap Wine Seal Initiative,
        194

social norms, 193–194
Wozniak, Steve, 239

Xiameter, 104–105

YouTube, 244

Zara, 109
Zooming in, 73–86
    business arena generator, 75–85
    as market segmentation, 74–75
    Starbucks, 85–86
Zooming out, 58–73, 60f
    capabilities and resources,
        61–62
    demand perspective, 60
    diversification, 72–73
    network perspective, 63
    other-benefactor perspective,
        69–72
    supply perspective, 59–60
Zuckerberg, Mark, 154